The American Assembly, *Columbia University*

THE PROMISE
OF TAX REFORM

Prentice-Hall, Inc., *Englewood Cliffs, New Jersey*
A SPECTRUM BOOK

Library of Congress Cataloging-in-Publication Data
Main entry under title:

The Promise of Tax Reform.

 Edited by Joseph A. Pechman.
 "A Spectrum book"—Copr. p.
 Bibliography: p.
 Includes index.
 1. Taxation—United States—Addresses, essays,
lectures. I. Pechman, Joseph A.
II. American Assembly.
HJ2381.P76 1985 336.2'05'0973 85-12361
ISBN 0-13-731092-7
ISBN 0-13-731084-6 (pbk.)

This book is available at a special discount when ordered in bulk quantities. Contact Prentice-Hall, Inc., General Publishing Division, Special Sales, Englewood Cliffs, N.J. 07632.

Editorial/production supervision by Betty Neville and Eric Newman
Cover design © 1985 by Jeannette Jacobs
Manufacturing buyer: Anne Armeny

A SPECTRUM BOOK

10 9 8 7 6 5 4 3 2 1

ISBN 0-13-731092-7

ISBN 0-13-731084-6 (PBK.)

PRENTICE-HALL INTERNATIONAL (UK) LIMITED (*London*)
PRENTICE-HALL OF AUSTRALIA PTY. LIMITED (*Sydney*)
PRENTICE-HALL CANADA INC. (*Toronto*)
PRENTICE-HALL HISPANOAMERICANA, S.A. (*Mexico*)
PRENTICE-HALL OF INDIA PRIVATE LIMITED (*New Delhi*)
PRENTICE-HALL OF JAPAN, INC. (*Tokyo*)
PRENTICE-HALL OF SOUTHEAST ASIA PTE. LTD. (*Singapore*)
WHITEHALL BOOKS LIMITED (*Wellington, New Zealand*)
EDITORA PRENTICE-HALL DO BRASIL LTDA. (*Rio de Janeiro*)

Table of Contents

Preface

One of the fundamental causes of the American War for Independence was the rebellion of British colonists against taxes that were perceived as inequitable. Ever since those antecedents, citizens of the United States have been especially touchy about taxes and perceptions of tax equity.

In the twentieth century, the principal federal tax that has affected most citizens has been the income tax. Other federal taxes have been relatively obscure and specialized. Sales and real estate taxes have been largely the province of state and local governments.

In the latter half of the twentieth century, many aspects of the income tax, especially those concerned with corporations and other businesses, have been structured for purposes other than raising revenue. They have been designed to advance economic or social objectives, and they have distorted the tax bases that are subject to assessment. One major consequence has been that different sources of income are subject to widely differing tax rates. Therefore, the same amounts of income often produce greatly varying amounts of taxes. Perceptions of inequity are widespread.

Some economists have been expressing concern about this situation for years and have proposed tax reform. As the tax structure has become more complicated, these reformers have been joined in their demands by members of Congress, who have called not only for reform but also for simplification of taxes. In 1985, President Reagan made tax reform a major objective of his administration and led a public campaign in favor of that objective; a widespread public debate ensued.

In order to shed some light on the subject and to seek consensus among various interested groups and institutions, The American Assembly convened a meeting at Arden House in Harriman, New York, from April 11 through 14, 1985. Participants attended from Congress, the federal executive branch, state and local governments, businesses, universities, not-for-profit organizations, communications media, and the legal profession. In preparation for the meeting, the Assembly retained Dr. Joseph A. Pechman of The Brookings Institution as editor and director of the undertaking. Under his editorial supervision, background papers on various aspects of the federal tax system were prepared for the participants in the Arden House discussions.

This book itself is a compilation of these papers and is published as a stimulus to further thinking and discussion about this subject among informed and concerned citizens. We hope it will serve to provoke a broader national consensus for public action.

The Arden House participants, in the course of their deliberations, achieved a substantial consensus on recommendations for public policy. Their proposals are contained in a report that is reproduced at the end of this book.

Funding assistance for this project was provided by the Alfred P. Sloan Foundation and the William and Flora Hewlett Foundation. The opinions expressed in this volume are those of the individual authors and not necessarily those of the sponsors nor of The American Assembly, which does not take stands on the issues it presents for public discussion.

William H. Sullivan
President
The American Assembly

Joseph A. Pechman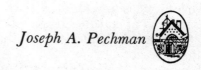

Introduction

Some of the most familiar quotations in history have been comments by famous men about taxes. Benjamin Franklin once wrote to a friend: "In this world, nothing is certain but death and taxes." And everyone remembers the expression "the power to tax involves the power to destroy," even though they may not recall that it was Chief Justice John Marshall who said it. This unpleasant side of taxes is, of course, the first thing that comes to mind when the question of taxes is raised, because, after all, taxes are used by government to deprive citizens of part of their income or wealth for which they have other uses.

But there is another, more pleasant, side of taxes that most people appreciate after giving the matter a little thought. Taxes are not levied merely because a few members of Congress or the president like the idea—taxes are needed to pay the govern-

JOSEPH A. PECHMAN *is a senior fellow in the Economics Studies Program of The Brookings Institution. He served as director of the program from 1962 to 1983 and was executive director of The Brookings Studies of Government Finance from 1960 to 1970. Previously, Dr. Pechman was at the Committee for Economic Development and earlier on the staffs of the Council of Economic Advisers, the U.S. Department of the Treasury, and the Office of Price Administration. In addition to serving as a fellow and an officer of several distinguished honorary and economic organizations, he has held appointments at six prestigious universities, has served as an advisor to presidential candidates and presidents, and been a consultant to many government agencies and congressional offices. Dr. Pechman is the author of numerous books and articles on a wide variety of subjects; his most recent book is* Who Paid the Taxes, 1966–1985?

1

ment's bills. While there may be differences of opinion about the proper size and role of government, no one denies that government is an essential part of living. In fact, government plays so vital a role in society that Justice Oliver Wendell Holmes was moved to remark that "taxes are what we pay for a civilized society."

However, the public's attitude toward taxes has become increasingly hostile as the federal tax structure has become more complicated and new preferences have been introduced to achieve various social or economic objectives. The general perception is that the tax system is unfair and favors wealthy taxpayers and large business firms, while the average taxpayer continually pays high taxes. In fact, the tax system as a whole is still progressive; on the average, wealthy taxpayers pay a higher percentage of their income in taxes than those in lower brackets. However, the actual degree of progression is mild.

Another criticism of the tax system is that it does not raise sufficient revenue. The federal budget is expected to run annual deficits amounting to 4 percent or more of the gross national product for years to come. Despite continued efforts to trim outlays, it is generally agreed that tax increases will be needed to reduce the deficit to reasonable proportions. It is difficult, however, to raise taxes when the tax system is widely regarded as unfair. Thus, the objectives of tax reform and deficit reduction are interrelated.

Under the circumstances, it is not surprising that new proposals are being advanced to improve and simplify the tax system and increase its revenue potential. Some strategists intend to reform and simplify the individual and corporation income taxes and lower the tax rates; additional revenue presumably could be obtained by a surtax or a modest increase in the rates. There are also those who would introduce a new tax on consumption into the federal revenue system as a substitute for, or supplement to, the income tax. Still others are more or less satisfied with the present tax system and would make only minor refinements to make it more palatable to the public.

The purpose of this book is to explain the major issues in federal taxation and the various alternative proposals. Beginning with an overview of the present tax system, which is intended to put recent tax developments in historical perspective, it turns to a discussion of individual and corporation income taxes, the two that have been the backbone of the federal tax system and yet are subject to severest criticism. A separate chapter is devoted to the effect of income taxes on the nation's financial markets, which are so vital to the functioning of the economy. Two chapters on major alternatives to income taxes follow, one on the graduated expenditure tax and the other on the value-added tax. The former is supported by many who believe that consumption is a better tax base than income and would replace the income tax with an expenditure tax; the latter is often proposed as a supplement to the income tax. Another chapter addresses estate and gift taxes, which are intended to reduce the concentration of wealth but actually produce little revenue. The volume ends with a summary of the various alternatives for restructuring the tax system and their potential to raise revenue to help reduce the federal deficit.

In his overview chapter, Richard Goode reviews the attitudes of American taxpayers toward the major taxes used in this country and the criticisms of the tax system by tax specialists. He points out that taxpayers take inconsistent positions on tax policy and are misinformed about major issues. Also, tax specialists have been highly critical of the federal tax system—excessively so, according to Goode. He believes that the U.S. tax system compares favorably with the systems of other countries and that its defects can be remedied by improving the taxes now being used, not by substituting other, less desirable, tax sources.

The most important tax in the federal tax system is the individual income tax, which now produces about 45 percent of federal tax revenue. The most frequent criticism of this tax contends that it is too complicated and permits many people to avoid their fair share of taxation. Unnecessary personal deductions, tax preferences, and tax credits have reduced the tax base and forced tax rates higher in order to raise needed revenue. Alvin C. Warren, Jr., explains the deficiencies of the income tax and how they might be remedied. A number of tax reform plans by liberals and conservatives alike are now being considered, including a far-reaching and constructive proposal by the U.S. Department of the Treasury. Action along these lines would reverse the long history of erosion and make the income tax more equitable and easier for the average taxpayer to understand.

In a tax system based on income, a tax on corporate profits is needed to safeguard the individual income tax. Otherwise, people could avoid the income tax by accumulating income in corporations. At one time, the corporation income tax raised more revenue than the individual income tax; today it accounts for less than 10 percent of total federal revenue. Alan J. Auerbach traces the history of the corporation income tax in this country and explains how it has become a minor source of revenue. Subsidies for investment and other tax preferences have greatly reduced the average corporate tax paid, but the more important criticism is that the tax burden is extremely uneven among different investments—in some cases this "burden" becomes a subsidy—and thereby introduces huge distortions into the economy. He reviews various tax reform options and concludes that it is possible to simplify the tax and also remove most distortions, without hurting investment incentives.

Healthy capital markets are essential to a growing economy; yet, many people believe, tax laws discourage investment and distort financial incentives. Irwin Friend examines the provisions of tax laws that affect financial markets and evaluates the impact on saving and investment. Most financial institutions—including commercial banks, savings and loan associations, and insurance companies—receive highly favorable tax treatment. In addition, income from capital is taxed at various rates that range from negative rates (i.e., outright subsidies) for tax shelters through a zero rate for interest from municipal bonds and a maximum of 20 percent for realized capital gains to regular rates for interest and dividends. Friend concludes that, on efficiency and equity grounds, the same tax rate should apply to all sources of economic return. Current tax reform proposals at least go part of the way toward this objective, but the opposition is considerable from groups they would affect.

Although the income tax is used almost universally, many economists since John Stuart Mill have been trying to persuade the public and Congress that consumption is a better basis of taxation than income. They argue that it is more appropriate to tax people on what they take out of the common pool (consumption) than on what they contribute to it (income). Progressivity is not an issue because graduated rates can be imposed under a consumption expenditure tax as well as they can under an income tax. Joseph E. Stiglitz explains that an expenditure tax in effect exempts income from capital; it is, therefore, equivalent to a wage tax. The strength of the expenditure tax is that it would not distort individual decisions to consume or to save; by contrast, the taxation of savings under the income tax makes future consumption less attractive. Since saving would not be subject to tax, the distribution of wealth would become more concentrated unless the expenditure tax were accompanied by equivalent taxes on gifts and bequests. However, as Michael J. Graetz indicates in his chapter on estate and gift taxes, recent experience suggests that effective estate and gift taxation would be difficult to achieve. Stiglitz concludes that it is more important to broaden the tax base and lower tax rates than to choose between an income tax and an expenditure tax.

Among proposals to tax consumption, the leading contender is the value-added tax. The value-added tax is paid by producers and sellers of particular items of consumption rather than by individuals and families on their total consumption. It is similar to a sales tax, except it is collected as goods move through the system of production and distribution rather than at the retail level alone. The tax is intended to be a tax on consumers, and most economists believe that consumers in fact do pay the tax. George F. Break discusses the strengths and weaknesses of this tax and concludes that it has a number of advantages in the current context, particularly its neutrality toward different kinds of business and consumer choices, its favorable treatment of saving and investment, and its manageable administrative and compliance costs. He points out that a value-added tax cannot achieve the degree of progressivity of the income tax, particularly in higher income ranges. However, he believes that a value-added tax would be a useful addition to the tax system if combined with effective reforms of other taxes.

The estate and gift taxes have not raised significant amounts of revenue in the United States since World War II, but recent increases in exemptions and reductions in the top tax rates have converted them to a mere appendage of the federal revenue system. Michael Graetz believes that strengthening these taxes would add a desirable degree of progressivity to the tax system.

The major obstacle to their increased use is the widespread belief that they are likely to hurt people of modest means, even though the statute permits substantial undervaluations of farm and business properties and generous personal exemptions. Estate and gift taxes are hardly likely to add significantly to federal revenue.

But it is clear from these discussions of the various taxes that considerable revenue could be raised to reduce the federal deficit. The basic question, according to Emil M. Sunley, is whether the existing revenue sources should continue to be used or new revenue sources adopted. Broadening the income taxes and lowering the tax rates along the lines proposed in the major tax reform plans now being considered would keep revenue at current levels; additional revenue could be raised by smaller rate reductions that are now contemplated. As an alternative, a surcharge could be levied on present income taxes, but the result would be higher taxes on people already paying them and continued exemption for those now avoiding them.

Still another approach would be to introduce a consumption tax into the federal revenue system. One possibility is to substitute a progressive expenditure tax for the present income tax. The exemption of savings in this type of tax requires higher rates than those needed to raise the same revenue from an income tax with the same degree of comprehensiveness; still higher rates would be needed to increase revenue. As another choice, a value-added tax could be added to the federal tax system. Because it would apply to most consumption items, the value-added tax is a powerful revenue producer—raising as much as $15 billion to $20 billion for each percentage point of tax. Such a tax is opposed by those who are concerned with the burden it would impose on low-income families. Others oppose it on the very ground that its great revenue potential might encourage excessive federal spending.

A final approach to raise more revenue would be to rely on a new or enhanced set of energy taxes. These possibilities include an oil import fee, an excise tax on imported and domestically produced oil, a broad excise on all forms of energy, and an increased gasoline tax. Although the revenue potential of these taxes is more limited than that of income or consumption taxes, they deserve consideration as a method to encourage energy conservation, as well as to increase federal revenue.

Tax reform and deficit reduction are high on the nation's legislative agenda. Because tax increases are unacceptable in a democracy if taxpayers believe themselves unfairly taxed, tax reform and simplification would greatly facilitate the effort to lower the federal deficit to a manageable size. The administration and Congress recognize that tax reform is essential to effective fiscal policy. The only question is whether or not the general interest will prevail over special interests that have been able in the past to forestall significant action for reform and simplification.

Richard Goode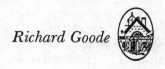

1
Overview of the U.S. Tax System

The main function of a tax system is to raise enough revenue to cover government expenditures without excessive reliance on domestic and foreign borrowing or money creation. Judged by that elementary standard, the American tax system is deficient. The deficiency occurs at the federal level, where the budget deficit for the foreseeable future is generally conceded to be excessive. State and local governments have been running a surplus that is large relative to their expenditures, but much smaller than the federal deficit.

The growing conviction that tax reform is urgently needed, however, appears to be based on criteria other than revenue adequacy. These criteria include fairness, economic efficiency, and simplicity. These broad principles are often supplemented by specific concerns about tax evasion and the influence of

RICHARD GOODE *is a guest scholar at The Brookings Institution and professorial lecturer at the School of Advanced International Studies, Johns Hopkins University. Previously, Dr. Goode was the director of the Fiscal Affairs Department at the International Monetary Fund. He also has been assistant professor of economics at the University of Chicago and served in the U.S. Department of the Treasury and the U.S. Bureau of the Budget. In addition to having written many journal articles and contributing to reports and conference volumes, he is the author of* The Corporation Tax, The Individual Income Tax, *and the recently published* Government Finance in Developing Countries.

taxation on innovation, saving, economic growth, distribution of income and wealth, and socially desirable or undesirable forms of behavior.

Owing to the complexity of the subject and the conflicting interests involved, it is easy to understand why advocates of tax reform usually try to separate issues of tax structure from questions of revenue adequacy and to propose revenue-neutral schemes. Presumably, a system superior in that context would raise more revenue with smaller undesirable effects than would otherwise occur. In the past, however, significant changes in the tax structure always have been connected with revenue increases or decreases.

Briefly describing the U.S. tax system and comparing it with systems of other industrial countries, this chapter attempts to account for taxpayers' dissatisfaction revealed by opinion polls and other evidence. It summarizes criticisms of the existing system by economists, lawyers, and accountants and includes comments on popular and expert criticism. Although the chapter concentrates on the federal tax system, it is reviewed in the setting of the overall federal, state, and local system.

General Description

Federal, state, and local taxes in 1983 amounted to $973 billion, 29.4 percent of gross national product (GNP). Sixty-five percent of the total consisted of federal taxes. In addition, all levels of government, particularly local governments, received some nontax revenue, which in the aggregate equaled only about 6 percent of total tax revenue.

At the federal level, the individual income tax was by far the largest revenue source. Social security contributions, mainly in the form of payroll taxes, were also important. The corporation income tax, excises and customs duties, and estate and gift taxes raised only a minor amount of federal tax revenue. State and local taxes were more diversified than federal taxes. Property taxes and general sales taxes were two important state and local taxes that were not used by the federal government. The amount of income taxes and social security contributions was significant at the state and local levels but relatively much less important than for the federal government. The statistics for calendar year 1983 given in Table 1 are estimates from the Bureau of Economic Analysis of the Department of Commerce and are based on national income accounts, which differ somewhat from other presentations.

TABLE 1.   TAX REVENUE BY GOVERNMENT LEVEL AND MAJOR SOURCE, 1983

(National Income Accounts Basis)		
Amount (billions of dollars)	*Percent of Total*	*Percent of GNP*
Federal, State, & Local		
Individual income taxes $347.5	35.7	10.5
Corporation income taxes 75.8	7.8	2.3
Estate & gift taxes 8.5	0.9	0.3
Social Security contributions 272.7	28.0	8.3
General sales taxes 70.1	7.2	2.1
Excises & customs duties 82.5	8.5	2.5
Property taxes 92.8	9.5	2.8
Other taxes 22.9	2.4	0.7
Total* $972.9	100.0	29.4
Federal		
Individual income tax $288.8	45.6	8.7
Corporation income tax 59.8	9.4	1.8
Estate & gift taxes 5.9	0.9	0.2
Social Security contributions 233.7	36.9	7.1
Excises & customs duties 45.2	7.1	1.4
Total* $633.5	100.0	19.2
State & Local		
Individual income taxes $ 58.7	17.3	1.7
Corporation income taxes 16.0	4.7	0.5
Estate & gift taxes 2.6	0.8	0.1
Social Security contributions 39.0	11.5	1.2
General sales taxes 70.1	20.7	2.1
Excises 37.3	11.0	1.1
Property taxes 92.8	27.3	2.8
Other taxes 22.8	6.7	0.7
Total* $339.4	100.0	10.3

Source: U.S. Department of Commerce, *Survey of Current Business*, July 1984.

*Because column entries have been rounded, their sums may not equal the totals stated.

CHANGES SINCE THE 1960s

Significant changes in the federal tax system occurred in the two decades before 1983. The most striking were the decline in the relative yield of the corporation income tax and the rise in the share of payroll taxes and other social security contributions. From the early 1960s to the early 1980s, the share of payroll taxes and other social security contributions more than doubled, while the share of the corporate tax fell to less than 50 percent of its initial level. Payroll tax rates increased sharply. The decline in the corporate tax share was due partly to a reduction in the rate—from 52 percent in the early 1960s to 46 percent after 1978—and to a greater extent, to an investment credit and accelerated write-off of the cost of equipment and structures.

The change in composition of revenue made the federal tax system distinctly less progressive. The degree of progressivity and the extent of change, however, are subject to dispute because of differences of opinion about who bears the corporate tax and the payroll taxes. The best statistical estimates are those of Joseph A. Pechman in *Who Paid the Taxes, 1966–1985?*, a sequel to the well-known 1974 study of Pechman and Benjamin A. Okner. These studies include alternative estimates based on different assumptions about the incidence of some of the main taxes.

On a set of plausible assumptions, Pechman found the federal tax system clearly progressive in 1966; the ratio of federal taxes to income rose with successively higher incomes. Even on assumptions least favorable to that conclusion, his estimates for 1966 indicate a degree of progressivity up through the high-income classes. In contrast, for provisions that were scheduled to be in effect in 1985, Pechman estimates only very mild progressivity. Between 1966 and 1985, the federal tax burden increased considerably for the lowest income tenth of the population but decreased for the highest income tenth. These estimates are summarized in Table 2. The main reason for the tax increase in the bottom income group was higher payroll taxes. The highest decile benefited especially from the diminished role of the corporation income tax and, to some extent, from changes in the individual income tax. The largest part of the change in progressivity of the federal tax system had occurred by 1975. The legislation of 1981–83 resulted in a further reduction.

TABLE 2.   EFFECTIVE RATES OF FEDERAL, STATE, AND LOCAL TAXES BY POPULATION DECILE, 1966, 1975, AND 1985*

| | *(in percent)* | | |
Population Decile	1966	1975	1985
First**	16.8	21.2	21.9
Second	18.9	19.9	21.3
Third	21.7	20.5	21.4
Fourth	22.6	22.0	22.5
Fifth	22.8	23.0	23.1
Sixth	22.7	23.3	23.5
Seventh	22.7	23.6	23.7
Eighth	23.1	24.4	24.6
Ninth	23.3	25.3	25.1
Tenth	30.1	27.1	25.3
All Deciles	25.2	25.0	24.5

Source: Joseph A. Pechman, *Who Paid the Taxes, 1966–1985?* (Brookings Institution, 1985), p. 68.

*Most progressive set of incidence assumptions: individual income tax borne by income recipients; half the corporation income tax borne by stockholders and half by owners of capital in general; social security payroll taxes borne by workers; sales taxes and excises borne by consumers; property tax on land and improvements borne by owners of capital in general.

**Includes only those in the sixth to tenth percentiles.

Comparison with Other Countries

Statistics compiled by the Organization for Economic Cooperation and Development show that the ratio of tax revenue of all government levels to gross domestic product in 1982 was lower in the United States than in most other industrial countries, as can be seen in Table 3. (The gross domestic product of the United States was slightly smaller than the more familiar gross national product used for Table 1.) Sweden, Norway, the Netherlands, Belgium, Denmark, France, Italy, the United Kingdom, and West Germany maintained tax ratios much higher than the United States. The ratio was about the same in Switzerland as in the United States; Japan's was considerably lower. Although tax ratios rose in all the leading industrial countries between 1965 and 1982, the increase was greater in several European countries and Japan than in the United States.

Although objections to high taxes have been heard in many countries, they have been especially vehement in the United States. Some features of the American culture and political system appear to cause particular reluctance to pay taxes.

The biggest difference between the revenue systems of the high-tax countries of Western Europe and that of the United States is the larger role of sales and excise taxes (including value-added taxes) in the European systems. The European countries obtain a greater fraction of their revenues from such taxes on goods and services, and, since their total tax ratios are higher than that of the United States, these taxes are much heavier in relation to national income. The European value-added taxes, the sales taxes of state and local governments in the United States, and the excise taxes of Europe and the United States fall almost entirely on consumption. The usual opinion, confirmed by Pechman's estimates for the United States, is that sales and excise taxes are regressive; that is, they take a declining fraction of income as income rises with successive classes. Some studies indicate that the value-added taxes of some of the European countries are approximately proportional or even somewhat progressive. This distribution is explained by the application of higher rates to luxuries than to basic items and lower rates to certain necessities.

Federal, state, and local governments in the United States obtain a greater fraction of their revenues from taxes on income and profits than do most European countries, but, because of their higher overall tax ratios, several European countries collect larger amounts in relation to gross domestic product. France is a notable exception since its overall tax ratio is above average for industrial countries, but taxes on income and profits are much below the average.

Social security taxes and contributions are much heavier in some European countries than in the United States. In 1982, the ratio of these taxes to gross domestic product exceeded 18 percent in France, the Netherlands, and Italy; it was also above 10 percent in Sweden, Belgium, Norway, and West Germany. But in two other high-tax countries—Denmark and the United

Kingdom—the ratio was well below the 8.4 percent of the United States. For the two European countries, the relatively low social security taxes were due to the use of general revenue to finance social security rather than to lower benefits.

TABLE 3.   TOTAL TAX REVENUE AS PERCENTAGE OF GROSS DOMESTIC PRODUCT, SELECTED INDUSTRIAL COUNTRIES, 1965 AND 1982

| | *(by percent)* | |
Country	1965	1982
Belgium	31.2	46.6
Canada	25.9	34.8
Denmark	29.9	44.0
France	35.0	43.7
West Germany	31.6	37.3
Italy	27.2	38.3
Japan	18.4	27.2
Netherlands	33.7	45.5
Norway	33.2	47.8
Sweden	35.8	50.3
Switzerland	20.7	30.9
United Kingdom	30.6	39.6
United States	26.3	30.5

Source: Organization for Economic Cooperation and Development, *Revenue Statistics of OECD Member Countries, 1965–1983* (Paris, 1984), p. 85.

Attitudes of Taxpayers

The attitudes of American taxpayers toward the benefits they receive from government and toward major taxes and possible tax revisions have been changing. A rich source of information on these changes is the public opinion polls that have been conducted annually since 1972 by the Advisory Commission on Intergovernmental Relations. The results for the whole period, summarized in its 1984 publication, deserve attention here.

OPPOSITION TO THE INDIVIDUAL INCOME TAX

The individual income tax, which is the most prominent federal tax, has become less acceptable to the public. Although a plurality of adults in 1972 considered the federal income tax the fairest of all the major taxes used by the federal, state, and local governments, in 1979–84 a plurality rated it the worst or least fair.

Public opinion polls do not explain what people disliked about the income tax or why attitudes changed, though they do offer some clues. A factor that may have contributed to its declining reputation was tax preferences that many people considered unjustified or beneficial mainly to the rich. These preferences took the form of exclusions from taxable income and deductions unrelated to the cost of earning income. They were publicized and quantified under the name "tax expenditures" in a special budget analysis, congressional reports, and newspaper articles.

There was a rapid increase in the number of tax expenditures and their revenue costs, especially after 1979. According to the Joint Committee on Taxation and the Congressional Budget Office, tax expenditures grew from the equivalent of 25 percent of federal revenue to 41 percent between 1971 and 1982. Most of the revenue cost in 1982 was due to provisions already in effect in 1971, but in intervening years those provisions became better known, were more widely used, and were joined by new provisions that attracted attention even though their immediate revenue cost was small.

When asked in May 1984 how the federal government could best raise taxes substantially, if that were necessary, almost half of those polled opted for reducing special tax treatment for capital gains and cutting deductions such as those for charitable contributions, state and local taxes, and medical expenses. The popularity of that approach was not new; in 1972 it already was preferred by sizable margins to a sales tax or an increase in individual income tax rates. However, the poll did not ask about some large tax preferences that were widely used by low- and middle-income groups, including those related to fringe benefits in the form of employer contributions to pension funds and medical insurance plans, as well as to interest paid on home mortgages and consumer debt.

Much publicity was given in the early 1980s to tax shelters that were designed to avoid taxes on large incomes. Ordinary citizens did not understand these complex schemes and appear to have formed an exaggerated impression of the prevalence and effectiveness of such shelters. Many became convinced that most persons with incomes much higher than theirs paid less tax or none at all. A poll taken in 1978 by the Survey Research Center of the University of Michigan found that 69 percent of respondents agreed with the proposition that "most people who have a higher income than I do manage to get away with paying less than their fair share of taxes." Roper surveys commissioned by H & R Block found that, in 1977 and 1978, the public believed that as many as half of the wealthy paid no income tax at all. Respondents generally underestimated the amount paid by high-income people who were taxed and overestimated the amount they themselves paid. In 1984, a national survey conducted for the Internal Revenue Service found that four out of five taxpayers believed that the tax system benefited the rich and was unfair to ordinary workers. In 1983, the poll for the Advisory Commission on Intergovernmental Relations asked what *one* change would be the single most important step to make the nation's tax system fairer. About 50 percent of the respondents chose "make the upper-income taxpayers pay more."

TAX EVASION

Another possible cause of taxpayer discontent was the belief that outright evasion was widespread. Stories about the underground economy attracted popular attention in the late 1970s and early 1980s, and the phenomenon was a subject of scholarly research. Reports of prosecution for large-scale tax fraud well may have had an ambiguous influence on public opinion, exciting a mixture of gratification that evaders were caught and suspicion that many others escaped detection.

Estimates published by the IRS in 1983 supported the belief that tax evasion was a serious problem. According to the estimates, there was a gap of $68.5 billion in 1981 between the federal income liability voluntarily reported by individuals and the amount actually due. It was attributable to failure to report income, overstatement of personal deductions and exemptions, overstatement of business expenses, and other errors. The estimated gap equaled 23 percent of total reported liabilities and had increased slightly faster than total liabilities between 1973 and 1981.

No doubt, some of the gap was due to honest mistakes, but

much of it must have been deliberate. The 1984 survey commissioned by the IRS found that almost one person in five admitted to cheating on taxes. Some of the understatements of tax would have been detected in the normal course of administration, but probably no more than a small proportion would have been found since only a very low percentage of individual returns are audited (1.3 percent in 1984).

Owing to incomplete data and methodological difficulties, the accuracy of the tax gap estimate is uncertain, but there is little doubt that failure to comply voluntarily with the income tax reduced its yield and resulted in inequities. In addition to estimates of the tax gap related to legal income, the IRS report contains an estimate for tax evasion related to illegal income from certain sources, but these figures are more speculative, and they are less relevant when considering tax reform.

INFLATION

The interaction between inflation and the income tax probably contributed to the declining popularity of the income tax after 1972. Between 1972 and 1983, the consumer price index (CPI) increased 138 percent. The buying power of personal exemptions fell. They remained unchanged from 1972 through 1978, and then increased only 33 percent. Rates and rate brackets were changed somewhat but not enough to prevent so-called "bracket creep," which caused taxpayers to move into more highly taxed brackets even though the real purchasing power of their income had not increased. As a result, total federal individual income taxes rose from 9.8 percent of personal income in 1972 to 11.7 percent in 1981.

Beyond the arithmetic of bracket creep, it can be conjectured that people feel frustrated in a period of inflation, regardless of whether or not their income keeps pace with prices, because they find that their dollars buy less than they expect. Part of this frustration may be directed at the income tax, since it visibly cuts their spending power. The income tax, a direct tax that uses an annual return showing the total amount due and the payments, including the amount withheld from salaries and wages, is also an easy target for the hostility of those who consider government expenditures excessive or wasteful and taxation too heavy.

Whatever the causes, Gallup polls showed that a majority of people felt they were paying "too much in federal income taxes" in the late 1960s and the 1970s.

SOCIAL SECURITY TAXES AND CONTRIBUTIONS

Information on the public's attitude is much less extensive for social security taxes and contributions than for income taxes. A 1978 opinion poll found that almost half of the respondents thought that their social security taxes were "excessively high" or "somewhat high," but much larger numbers had similar opinions of property taxes and the federal income tax. Labor unions at times have opposed increases in social security taxes, but usually the taxes have not been controversial. The majority of people appear to accept them as a necessary means of payment for an important program.

The relative acquiescence to the social security taxes may seem surprising. They are the second largest source of federal revenue. For many families, including most of those in lower-income classes, social security taxes are heavier than income taxes. This is especially true if, as most economists believe, workers bear both the tax deducted from their pay and the employer's contribution. Not only do the taxes lack personal exemptions and graduated rates, as provided by the income tax, they apply only to earnings below a set maximum ($37,800 in 1984).

Social security taxes apparently are looked at in a different way than other taxes. The use of the term "contributions" as another name for social security taxes suggests the difference in perception. The idea that social security is an insurance system whereby benefits are earned by contribution payments appears to be widely accepted by the public, although experts reject that interpretation. Official accounting is somewhat ambivalent. On one hand, social security taxes are paid into separate trust funds; on the other, they have been included in the unified budget since 1969. In its January 1983 report, the National Commission on Social Security Reform (the Greenspan commission) recommended that social security trust funds be removed from the unified budget, and Congress amended the law to do that, effective in fiscal year 1993. There appears to be a broad consensus that payroll taxes will be used exclusively to finance social security benefits and that they will be the only important source of finance for the benefits.

CORPORATION INCOME TAX

The corporation income tax has long been an object of criticism by business executives and the financial community. Proposals for fundamental reform of the tax, however, attracted little support from business executives in the late 1970s and early 1980s. Emphasis was placed instead on reduction of the tax rate and liberalization of depreciation allowances. The 1981 revenue act, without changing the nominal rate of the tax, reduced the effective rate greatly, but unevenly, by adoption of an accelerated capital-cost recovery system in place of depreciation allowances related to the normal useful life of machinery, equipment, and structures. It was generally supported by business executives, including those of industries that benefited little, if at all.

The general public, understandably, gives much less thought to the corporation income tax than to the individual income tax. Available evidence suggests that the public regards corporations as separate economic entities rather than mere conduits through which investment capital flows from stockholders and profits are returned. The majority seem to believe that corporations should pay their fair share of taxes, though "fair share" is vaguely defined. This idea has played a role in political campaigns. For example, in 1984 a successful congressional candidate was reported to feature in his campaign the rhetorical question, "Why should General Electric pay less taxes than you?"

EXCISES, CUSTOMS, AND SALES TAXES

Excises and customs duties are concealed taxes, and few consumers are aware of their rates, much less of the aggregate amounts they pay in the course of a year. These characteristics have commended the taxes to opportunistic governments throughout history. But the role of excises and customs in the federal revenue system steadily declined after the Korean War, and the federal government did not avail itself of the great revenue-raising capacity of a broad sales tax or value-added tax, as did all other industrial countries except Japan.

Producer groups, notably tobacco farmers and members of Congress from the producing states, have opposed increases in excise tax rates. The 1982 revenue act, however, temporarily doubled the cigarette tax and raised some other excises.

The most important traditional excises are imposed at specific rates; that is, they are fixed in money amounts per physical unit. Their real amount, therefore, declines during inflation unless frequent changes are made in their nominal rates. Over the period 1952 to 1983, for example, the federal tax on distilled spirits remained constant at $10.50 per proof gallon, and the taxes on wine and beer were also unchanged in nominal amounts. Yet during that period the rise in the CPI implied a 73 percent cut in the real value of the taxes—to the equivalent, in 1952 purchasing power, of $2.84 per proof gallon of spirits.

Opinion polls report considerable public acceptance of a federal sales tax if a substantial tax increase were necessary. In 1983, 52 percent of respondents chose a new national sales tax on all purchases other than food, while only 24 percent favored increasing individual income taxes, and 25 percent could not choose between these options. In 1984, when the question was stated differently, only 32 percent chose a sales tax, while 47 percent preferred to reduce the special treatment of certain items in the income tax.

Among the most politically conscious, however, the sales tax is viewed skeptically. Liberals oppose a sales tax because it is regressive; many conservatives are against the introduction of a federal sales tax or value-added tax because they see it as a big revenue producer that would relax constraints on government expenditures. Some state political leaders dislike a federal sales tax because it would overlap their largest revenue source.

ESTATE AND GIFT TAXES

Estate and gift taxes always have been perceived as having social significance disproportionate to their revenue yield. Some opponents of progressive income taxes have supported heavy estate or inheritance taxes (collectively called death taxes) as a check on the growth of family fortunes and as a means to prevent heirs from leading idle lives. But opposition to death taxes has grown. Probably the widely distributed inflation-caused gains in the nominal value of real estate and farms had much to do with the change of attitudes. (Canada and Australia repealed their taxes.) In the United States, the 1981 act scheduled increases in the estate that can be transferred tax free to a level of $600,000 effective in 1987. It has been estimated that fewer than 1 percent of all estates will be subject to tax.

Criticism by Economists and Tax Specialists

Economists, lawyers, and accountants have indicted the federal tax system for unfairness, economic inefficiency, and complexity. The precise standards of fairness and efficiency that the system allegedly violates are open to dispute, as is the compatibility of these standards with each other and with the objective of simplicity. Another standard sometimes applied may be called transparency, or clarity, implying that taxes should be visible rather than concealed and that, to the extent possible, the consequences of tax provisions should be generally understood and agreed.

MEANING OF FAIRNESS AND EFFICIENCY

Without delving into the abstruse aspects of the subject, it is possible to find a fair degree of agreement that the core meaning of fairness in taxation is equal treatment of similarly situated persons and reasonable differentiation, according to their ability to pay, between persons in different circumstances. Admittedly, this formulation begs many questions. What characteristics are relevant for defining similarity or differences in circumstances? First, cutting through the subtleties, it is apparent that the great majority of those who have examined the subject agree that the most relevant characteristic is the taxpayer's (and dependents') total income or total consumption. Second, they agree that the ability-to-pay principle calls for progressivity with respect to income or consumption. Differentiation in taxation on the basis of other characteristics, the consumption of gin or cigarettes, for example, is more debatable and, in the opinion of many tax specialists, must be justified by appeal to ad hoc arguments or fiscal expediency.

Arguments on Efficiency—Supply-side economists regard taxes as inherently inefficient because they weaken incentives and

reduce production. Mainstream economists are more skeptical
about the effects on total activity. They tend to distinguish between taxes and to judge a tax's efficiency or inefficiency by its
influence on methods of production and the composition of
consumption. An inefficient tax system may unnecessarily increase production cost or result in a pattern of output and
consumption that yields less satisfaction to consumers than that
obtained from another pattern producible at the same cost. For
example, taxation is held to be inefficient if it causes firms to
use either more or less capital to produce a given output than
they otherwise would use. This is so because either overuse or
underuse of capital will increase production cost per unit. On
the consumption side, many economists would assert that a tax
on beer, for example, is inefficient, if, as is likely, it causes
consumers to drink less beer and more coffee than they would
if the same amount of revenue were raised in a more neutral
way.

Several assumptions underlie these judgments about efficiency. In general, a critical assumption is that both the cost of
input and the value of output are correctly measured by prevailing market prices, wage rates, and interest rates. Of course,
correctness in this context implies social acceptability. It is
specifically implied that the government, reflecting social values, is neutral in regard to the choice of consumption goods
and services; by levying taxes the government intends to influence people to curtail their consumption but is indifferent
about how people cut back—whether, for example, on beer or
coffee, on video cassettes or theater tickets.

Qualifications to Efficiency—While all economists would recognize some qualifications or exceptions to these efficiency concepts, there are wide differences about how far the modifica-
tions should extend. It is apparent that important qualifications
are appropriate. First, real-world markets do not correspond
closely to the theoretical conditions of perfect information, ra-
tionality, competition, mobility, and full employment that
underlie the assumption that cost and output will be valued
correctly in the absence of unneutral taxation. Second, there
are respectable motives for encouraging or discouraging certain kinds of consumption.

These qualifications lead to a weak version of the efficiency argument: deliberate use of the tax system to influence behavior does not necessarily conflict with economic efficiency, but a positive case is needed to justify it. Unneutral tax provisions are likely to be inefficient—indeed, may be presumed to be inefficient—unless they effectively serve an agreed-upon social purpose or advance a social preference. Incidental or unintended discrimination of the taxation of industries or production methods, for example, is suspect. Even if tax provisions advance an agreed-upon objective, they are inefficient if the direct and indirect costs (somehow appraised) are disproportionate to the gain. An indirect cost frequently overlooked by advocates of provisions intended to encourage some desirable activity derives from the loss of revenue, which, in turn, necessitates raising other taxes, cutting expenditures, or increasing the budget deficit.

EROSION OF THE INDIVIDUAL INCOME TAX

Tax specialists, like the general public, are critical of many provisions of the individual income tax. They have long emphasized that many exclusions and deductions from taxable income cause nominal tax rates to be higher than would otherwise be required. If the exclusions and deductions were spread evenly, they would offend against the principle of transparency but would not cause unfairness or inefficiency. But, of course, they are not evenly spread. They differ greatly among sources and uses of income and, hence, among individuals.

Exclusions and Deductions—The failure to include the rental value of owner-occupied houses and apartments in taxable income, together with the deduction of mortgage interest and property taxes, unfairly favors owners, as compared to tenants, and encourages investment in both principal residences and vacation dwellings as compared with other investments that, at the margin, may be more socially productive. These provisions are more valuable to the wealthy than to low- and middle-income families.

The exemption of interest from municipal bonds favors investors subject to high marginal rates of income tax because the difference between the yields of tax-exempt bonds and taxable securities is too narrow to offset the advantage of exemption for those investors. The use of tax-exempt revenue bonds to finance municipally owned public utilities and of industrial revenue bonds for purposes that range from high-technology plants to fast-food establishments favors the beneficiaries over other firms engaged in similar activities. No doubt some of the projects merit encouragement, but they need pass no close scrutiny to qualify for tax-exempt financing.

The deduction of interest paid on consumer debt benefits spendthrifts while the thrifty are taxed on interest from their savings accounts. May not these tax provisions—not found in most other tax systems—help explain why the rate of personal saving in the United States is much lower than in several other industrial countries?

The omission from employees' taxable income of the value of employer-provided health insurance, group term life insurance, and other fringe benefits enhances the attractiveness of these perquisites and must have influenced compensation plans. As for many other tax preferences, a case can be made for the social desirability of health insurance and some other fringe benefits, but the open-ended nature of the tax advantage may stimulate overuse. A rational worker subject to a marginal tax rate of 25 percent would prefer additional health insurance worth only $76 to $100 of additional wages. Did the provisions contribute to the escalation of the cost of insurance and medical care?

Other special provisions that had a big impact on the 1984 income tax include deductions for state and local taxes, deductions for charitable contributions, exclusion from taxable income of social security benefits (except for those with incomes well above the average for recipients) and most unemployment compensation, exclusion of 60 percent of long-term capital gains and losses, exclusion of interest on life insurance savings, and deferral of tax on employers' contributions as well as interest for pension plans and contributions to individual retirement accounts (IRAs).

Effects of Special Provisions—Most of these provisions had been in effect for a long time, but over the years they came to be used more often, creating a greater impact on the income tax. After 1970, and especially after 1979, the older provisions were joined by many new ones. Initially these had less effect on revenue, but they complicated the income tax and may come to be used more widely in the future.

A long line of tax specialists have criticized exclusions and deductions. Among the first was Henry Simons, the most influential American writer on income taxation, who declared in 1938 that the time had come "for Congress to quit this ludicrous business of dipping so deeply into great incomes with a sieve." Simons's many notable successors include Joseph Pechman, who quantified the erosion of the tax base and estimated what a comprehensive income tax would yield; Stanley Surrey, who coined the term "tax expenditures" to describe special provisions; and the U.S. Department of the Treasury and congressional staff members.

The critics called for restriction or elimination of special provisions and simultaneous reduction of nominal rates that would make the income tax fairer, simpler, and less inefficient. By the mid-1980s, specific proposals to accomplish these goals were embodied in congressional bills and in a massive report on tax reform prepared by the Treasury Department at the request of President Reagan in his 1984 State of the Union Message. Although differing in content, the proposals all agreed that large reductions in nominal tax rates would be possible without sacrificing revenue.

TAXATION OF BUSINESS INCOME

The effective rate of tax on business income was greatly reduced by the introduction of an investment credit in 1962, acceleration of depreciation allowances in 1962, and adoption of an accelerated capital-cost recovery system (ACRS) in 1981. The investment credit, intended to stimulate investment, allowed investors in equipment that had a life of more than three years to deduct 10 percent of the cost against their tax. With limited exceptions, it did not apply to buildings or investment abroad. The credit continued in effect, with two short interruptions, after 1962. ACRS abandoned the effort to relate the deduction of capital cost closely to the economic life of the property, a feature of commercial accounting that had been included in the income tax from its beginning. Instead, equipment and structures were assigned to four classes, only roughly in accordance with their durability. Their cost could be written off against taxable income over periods of three, five, ten, or fifteen years, which for most items allowed quicker recovery than under normal depreciation accounting. (The fifteen-year period was extended to eighteen years by a 1983 amendment.)

Difficulties with the Investment Credit and ACRS—The resulting cut in effective tax rates was far from uniform for different assets and industries. ACRS was generous for some items, less so for others. Although the investment credit was neutral in its treatment of different kinds of equipment, it did not apply to structures. Neither the investment credit nor ACRS applied to investment in inventories. The effective tax rate in relation to economic income varied greatly across industries depending on their capital mix and the amount of capital used relative to other factors of production. "Smokestack" industries, such as metals, chemicals, and petroleum refining, benefited much more than less capital-intensive, more technological industries, including machinery and instruments and electrical equipment, and also more than services and trade. Since calculated effective rates of tax, which are sensitive to assumptions about inflation and some other variables, indicate negative rates on new investment in certain industries, not only was no tax paid on the return from the new investment but also the tax on other income was reduced.

Another characteristic of the investment credit and ACRS was that their benefits were immediately available only to established, profitable firms with enough profits from past investments to absorb the credit and capital-cost deductions. New or unprofitable firms that would have paid little or no tax in the absence of special provisions were not helped. The benefits could have been extended to such firms by giving cash rebates to those lacking sufficient income to absorb the credit and deduction, but the Department of the Treasury and Congress understandably were unwilling to go that far. Instead, a complex provision was adopted that allowed the benefits to be sold to profitable firms ("safe-harbor leasing"). Some of the companies that sold the benefits were in fact profitable concerns whose tax liabilities had been cancelled by other tax preferences; some of the buyers were well-known companies that, thus, escaped taxation. A public outcry occurred, and the provision for transfer of the benefits was first limited and then terminated at the end of 1983. However, revised rules for leasing did allow transfer of some benefits after that year.

Technical provisions lessening the taxation of returns from new investments may have helped stimulate the expansion of gross private domestic investment and gross national product in 1983 and 1984, but it is far from clear that the pattern of incentives offered conformed to any coherent set of priorities. Several critics asserted that the United States had instituted an ill-considered industrial policy through the tax system. In regard to business income, many tax specialists advanced recommendations analogous to those for the individual income tax; they argued that the investment credit should be terminated and ACRS replaced by economic depreciation and that the corporation income tax rate should be reduced simultaneously.

TAXATION OF CORPORATE PROFITS

The method of taxing corporate profits is a controversial feature of the taxation of business income that has been in effect much longer than the investment credit and ACRS. Corporations and their shareholders are legally separate and, generally, are separately taxed in the United States. Corporations are taxed on profits when earned, and shareholders are taxed on dividends when received. Critics maintain that the result is unfair and uneconomic double taxation of distributed corporate profits. Interest paid on debt, however, is deductible at the corporate level. In contrast, partnerships are not taxed as entities; the partners include in their tax returns their portion of the firm's income or loss.

Analysts have argued that the system is economically inefficient because it penalizes the corporate form and discourages investment in activities in which that form is especially advantageous as compared with investment in areas, such as real estate and agriculture, in which sole proprietorships and partnerships thrive. They also argue that debt finance is encouraged in preference to equity finance, a practice that may lead to insolvencies during bad times. Although evidence on these points, as on many others, is subject to differing interpretations, many tax specialists—probably the majority— believe that the United States should follow the lead of the European countries that, except for the Netherlands, have adopted provisions to provide tax relief for distributed profits.

TAX SHELTERS

The coexistence of different effective rates of tax on income from various sources created many opportunities to avoid taxes. While details differed greatly, the common characteristic was that part of the cost associated with tax-favored investments could be deducted against fully taxable income. Tax-favored investments comprised those that benefited from tax exemption or low tax rates, from deductions exceeding economic costs, or from deferral of tax payment. In such cases, the tax saving from the deduction exceeded the tax, if any, on the additional income reported from the tax-favored investment.

Simple Shelters—A simple arrangement for an individual investor, perfectly legal and not at all uncommon, was to borrow to acquire and carry stocks that were expected to throw off their return in the form of capital gains. Interest payments could be deducted from fully taxable income, providing a tax saving of up to 50 percent of the amount paid, while capital gains were taxable at a maximum rate of 20 percent, provided the shares were held longer than six months. Still greater advantages could be obtained if the investment took the form of tax-exempt municipal bonds. If someone who was subject to a 50 percent top rate of income tax could borrow simultaneously at 12 percent, for example, and invest in tax-exempt bonds yielding 10 percent, the net interest cost of 6 percent would be four percentage points lower than the tax-free yield. To be sure, the law barred a deduction for interest on debt incurred explicitly to purchase or carry tax-exempt bonds, but someone with other assets who carefully arranged the transaction could avoid that limitation. Banks and other financial institutions successfully reduced their income taxes by holding both tax-exempt bonds and taxable securities and loans, while charging all their interest costs and operating expenses against the taxable part of their portfolios. However, after 1981 this possibility was somewhat restricted.

Complex Shelters and Abuses—More sophisticated and complex tax shelter schemes were devised to take advantage of tax-avoidance opportunities. The staff of the Congressional Joint Committee on Taxation defined a tax shelter as "an investment in which a significant portion of the investor's return is derived from the realization of tax savings with respect to other income, as well as the receipt of tax-favored (or, potentially, tax-exempt) income from the investment itself." Generally, investors were not involved actively in managing a business; often they were receiving high income from salaries or professional fees. Features of tax shelters commonly included deferral of any taxable income that might ultimately be realized by concentration of deductible costs in early years and of income in later years, conversion of ordinary income into capital gains, and heavy use of borrowed funds.

A favorite form of organization was a limited partnership, which shielded the participants from any personal liability for the debts of the venture but passed through to them any losses resulting from an excess of deductible costs over taxable returns. Promoters advertised their offerings and sometimes attracted hundreds of limited partners. Many of the partnerships were engaged in real estate, oil and gas extraction, and farming. Partnerships, both limited and general, engaged in these activities reported large losses for tax purposes.

Congress and the IRS were only partially successful in their efforts to check abusive shelters that were structured to give investors larger benefits than those warranted by law. Critics argued that the problem could be solved only by more fundamental measures to lessen or eliminate differences in taxation of income from various sources. Some also suggested that widely held limited partnerships should be taxed as corporations, which they resemble more closely than traditional general partnerships.

INTERACTION OF TAXATION WITH INFLATION

As mentioned previously, interaction between the income tax and inflation may have been a major cause of the growing disaffection for that tax during the 1970s and early 1980s. It also had serious economic consequences. Traditional measures of business and investment income were distorted; questionable amendments to the tax law were rationalized as piecemeal adjustments for inflation; fairness and economic efficiency suffered.

Cost of Capital—Tax specialists and business executives indicated that depreciation allowances based on original cost (as provided by the tax law) understated the cost of capital consumed in the production process and, hence, caused profits to be overstated. This effect was especially great for capital-intensive industries with long-lived plant and equipment. The accelerated capital-cost recovery system enacted in 1981 was strongly supported as a means to correct this defect. But that provision could not adjust correctly for inflation, because, for one thing, the system arbitrarily assigned all depreciable property to only four classes whose components differed greatly in normal useful life. A second and more important reason was that the degree of acceleration of recovery of historical cost required to compensate for inflation depends on the inflation rate. An accelerated schedule that would compensate for a 10 percent inflation rate would be overly generous for a 5 percent rate but inadequate for a 15 percent inflation rate. In actuality, the inflation rate declined rapidly in 1981–84, which made the 1981 accelerated deductions increasingly generous.

Capital Gains—The exclusion from taxable income of 60 percent of so-called long-term capital gains also was frequently represented as an allowance for inflation. Since the tax law provided that gains were computed as the difference between the cost of an asset and the selling price, clearly, the true gains were overstated if inflation had occurred during the holding period. There was, however, a 50 percent exclusion long before inflation was recognized as a problem. It is possible that the increase in the exclusion to 60 percent in 1978 was motivated partly by concern about inflation.

Any uniform fractional exclusion can adjust correctly for inflation only by accident and only for a particular combination of nominal gain and inflation. Suppose, for example, that the price level doubles during the time an investor holds an asset. A nominal gain equal to 100 percent of the cost of the asset will just keep intact its real value; if the investor sells and realizes that amount of nominal gain, a 60 percent exclusion will still leave 40 percent of the fictitious gain subject to tax. However, if the nominal value of the asset increases by more than 167 percent during a period when inflation is 100 percent, a 60 percent exclusion will remove part of the real gain from the tax base

(0.60 × 167% = 100%). Of course, partial exclusion offers no relief for an investor who realizes a loss. In order to correct for inflation, it would be necessary to adjust the basis (usually the original cost) of the asset for the increase in the price level. Such an adjustment was proposed by various experts and in the Treasury's 1984 tax reform report.

Interest Income and Expense—Another aspect of the interaction between income taxes and inflation relates to the treatment of interest income and expense. Inflation forced nominal interest rates higher because lenders sought compensation for the loss of purchasing power of their claims, and borrowers were willing to pay high rates because they expected the nominal value of their output and assets to rise. But since the extent of inflation was unforeseen, the rise in nominal interest rates lagged behind inflation for several years; when inflation slowed, nominal interest rates declined less rapidly. Compensation for inflation received by lenders and paid by borrowers was not interest in the real sense but actually partial amortization of the debt. While interest receipts are properly included in the income of lenders and interest payments on debt incurred for business or investment purposes are properly deducted in ascertaining net income, debt amortization should not enter directly into income calculation. (In accounting terms, amortization affects the balance sheet but not the income statement.) But the income tax made no distinction between the components of nominal interest payments. On one hand, lenders were overtaxed and often suffered negative real after-tax returns, and borrowers, on the other hand, were undertaxed. Therefore, lending was encouraged and borrowing discouraged.

Depreciation Allowances—Although some economists called attention to the inequity and inefficiency of the treatment of interest income and expense, these problems received much less attention than did the overstatement of profits, owing to the practice of basing depreciation allowances on historical cost. To obtain an accurate picture, it is necessary also to account for changes in the real value of debt and claims. Economists Jeremy Bulow and John Shoven found that after adjustment for inflation of all principal items in corporate accounts, aggregate real profits of nonfinancial corporations sharply fluctuated from year to year in the inflationary period 1973–79; but, for the period as a whole they somewhat exceeded nominal profits based on historical cost.

A correct adjustment of interest income and expense for inflation would be technically more difficult than adjustment of depreciation allowances and capital gains and losses. In principle, creditors should be allowed to include in their income calculation a negative item that is equal to the decrease in the real value of their claims; debtors should be required to include a positive item that is equal to the decrease in the real value of their indebtedness. Combining these adjustments with the amount of nominal interest receipts and payments would produce a correct net figure. Such adjustments, however, would be highly inconvenient because of the multiplicity of claims and frequent changes in their amounts. A very rough adjustment could be made by excluding a fraction of interest income, disallowing an equal fraction of interest expense, and setting the fraction annually in light of prevailing interest rates and inflation. The Treasury proposed such a scheme in its tax reform report of 1984. However, that adjustment would not allow for differences in nominal interest rates attributable to differences in the time when the loan was made and differences in the risk component of interest rates.

COMPLEXITY AND SIMPLIFICATION

Tax experts, as well as the general public, complain about the complexity of the income tax. Paid professionals are hired by 40 to 50 percent of individual taxpayers to prepare their income tax returns. Other citizens spend much time assembling information, studying instructions, and completing returns that often have to be supplemented by separate schedules. Talented and well-paid lawyers and accountants devote attention to the tax problems of high-income individuals and corporations. An overworked IRS tries to cope with a flood of information and with ingenious tax-avoidance schemes.

Much of the effort devoted to tax compliance—and avoidance—and to tax administration is socially unproductive. The extent of the waste, however, may well be exaggerated by critics. In a complex economy, a fair and effective income tax cannot be truly simple. But much of the complexity is caused by special provisions that are not essential features of income taxation. Base broadening could be supported as a simplification program. A particularly significant simplification measure would be the elimination of the difference between the taxation of capital gains and other income, which necessitates many provisions of the Internal Revenue Code and regulations intended to limit the conversion of ordinary income into preferentially taxed capital gains. Other reform measures, however, can increase complexity. Among these are proposals to tax fringe benefits of employees, substitution of economic depreciation allowances for the arbitrary accelerated capital-cost recovery system, and adjustment of capital gains and losses for inflation.

Interest groups and Congress universally have endorsed simplification but have been unwilling to pay much for this goal in terms of their primary objectives. Indeed, to attain their purposes, they readily have accepted complications instead.

Proposals for a Consumption or Cash-flow Tax

During the 1970s and early 1980s, many economists and some lawyers argued that an income tax was inferior to a consumption tax. They advocated replacing the individual income tax with a direct tax on consumption. This proposal must be distinguished from the familiar sales tax or value-added taxes. A direct tax on personal consumption, usually called an expenditure tax, would be assessed, like the income tax, on the basis of individual returns and would include provisions for personal exemptions and graduated rates.

The idea was not new. It had been advanced by distinguished economists in the nineteenth century but had been dismissed as impracticable. A combination of circumstances revived interest in the expenditure tax and led to sympathetic consideration of it in a staff report issued by the Treasury in the closing days of the Ford administration (*Blueprints for Basic Tax Reform,* 1977), in a study prepared for an official Swedish tax commission (published in Swedish in 1976 and in an English translation in 1978), and in the 1978 report of the unofficial—but well regarded—Meade committee created by the Institute for Fiscal Studies in the United Kingdom.

ARGUMENTS FOR AN EXPENDITURE TAX

Treatment of Savings—The traditional academic argument for an expenditure tax is that it would eliminate the unfair double taxation of savings that occurs under an income tax. Most simply stated, the charge is that an income tax hits savings twice, once when income is originally received and again when interest is received on the portion that is saved. A more subtle statement is that an income tax favors those who choose to consume early as compared to those who choose to postpone consumption but that an expenditure tax is neutral to both groups. In the absence of taxation, it is reasoned, the present values of immediate consumption and future consumption are equal since interest received on savings is sufficient to offset the discount that has to be applied to postponed consumption. An income tax, however, reduces the net amount of interest received and brings the discounted value of the future consumption below the value of immediate consumption. An expenditure tax, in contrast, equally cuts immediate and postponed consumption.

At an abstract level, the arguments in favor of an expenditure tax raise issues that extend beyond this chapter's purpose. Much of the discussion of these issues is an exercise in persuasive definitions and pejorative terminology. Nevertheless, the substance of the case should be considered seriously since it is endorsed by able theorists. The arguments derive from the previously mentioned principle that identifies fairness and efficiency in taxation with neutral treatment of the allocation of resources that result from actions of individual participants in markets. In this instance, the principle is pressed to the point of holding that individual taxpayers should be allowed to decide, perhaps not *how much* they finally pay, but *when* they pay. The advantage that an expenditure tax grants to savers who postpone consumption is that they postpone tax payment and receive interest on the deferred tax. The Treasury, meanwhile, must either pay interest on additional debt or raise taxes on others.

The decisive question is: which is a better measure of ability to pay—income or consumption? Income has the advantage of being more comprehensive. Income measures one's command over economic resources; saving is a personal decision that does not lessen one's capacity to contribute to the support of the commonwealth.

Difficulty of Application—A second, more pragmatic argument in favor of a consumption tax is that, contrary to earlier opinion, a consumption tax can be applied more easily than an income tax. Two difficulties of income taxation are emphasized. First, inflation causes distortions of the measurement of income from capital, particularly depreciation allowances, capital gains and losses, and interest income and expense. Second, capital gains are taxed when assets are sold or otherwise transferred rather than as the gains accrue, resulting in discouragement of socially desirable transactions and accumulation of untaxed wealth. A consumption tax deals with the difficulties, not by resolving them, but by avoiding them. In that sense, it is neater and simpler than the detailed adjustments for inflation previously mentioned (and an adjustment for tax postponement in respect of capital gains, not covered in this chapter).

As for practicability, the argument for a consumption tax is unpersuasive. Commercial accounting and established tax rules are directed toward measuring income, not consumption. It is true that, rather than by direct accounting, consumption could be assessed as the residual difference between the sum of cash inflow and outflow to meet business and professional expenses and to acquire physical and financial earning assets. Nevertheless, for the majority of taxpayers, burdens of recordkeeping and reporting would be increased. The IRS would have great difficulty when checking taxpayers' returns. Special provisions would be needed to cope with the transition from an income tax to an expenditure tax. International complications would occur.

From the preceding analysis, it can be concluded that the greatest shortcoming of the U.S. tax system arises not from a mistaken choice of income taxation as the centerpiece, but from defective application of income tax principles.

Concluding Remarks

A review of the U.S. tax system reveals many offenses against fairness, efficiency, and simplicity. Never ideal, over time the federal tax system became less equitable, less progressive, more complex, and more inefficient. The deficiencies, though real, surely were exaggerated in the public mind. People were misinformed about taxation and took inconsistent positions on tax policy. The dissatisfaction with the federal tax system increased in the 1970s, at the same time that opinion polls and other evidence revealed growing alienation from the national government and other institutions. General forces, as well as specific tax developments, must have been responsible.

Tax experts may tend to be overly critical of the federal tax system and to apply puristic standards. Those who elaborated proposals for radical changes may have diverted attention from more attainable reforms. Other experts who pressed only for incremental improvements often failed to convince politicians because they attached more value than the politicians did to neutral taxation and were unwilling to examine in detail the advantages and disadvantages of tax provisions and other measures to advance social and economic objectives.

When compared with the systems of other industrial countries, the U.S. tax system in 1985 could be judged fairly favorably. The most attractive features of the U.S. federal tax system were the leading role of the individual income tax, which, though flawed, was superior to other major taxes, and the absence of a broad sales tax or value-added tax, which in Europe accounted for a large and growing fraction of revenue. Most of the defects of the American system could be remedied, or greatly alleviated, by adoption of proposals that have already been advanced.

Alvin C. Warren, Jr.

2
The Individual Income Tax

Introduction

There has been considerable interest in recent years in "flat tax" and "modified flat tax" proposals designed to reform the individual income tax by broadening the base of the tax and reducing rates, sometimes to a single rate. Reform along these lines has long been advocated on the grounds that such reform would improve the equity of the income tax, reduce economic inefficiency induced by the tax, and simplify the tax system.

This chapter investigates the weaknesses of current law and examines the three leading proposals for change: the 1984 U.S. Department of Treasury report, *Tax Reform for Fairness, Simplicity, and Economic Growth;* the Bradley-Gephardt bill, the "Fair Tax Act of 1985," sponsored by Senator Bill Bradley (Democrat, New Jersey) and Representative Richard Gephardt (Democrat, Missouri) with support from many Democratic members of Congress; and the Kemp-Kasten bill, the "Fair and Simple Tax Act of 1985," sponsored by Representative Jack Kemp (Republican, New York) and Senator Robert W. Kasten, Jr.,

ALVIN C. WARREN, JR., *is professor of law at the Harvard Law School and previously held the same title at the University of Pennsylvania Law School. He serves as chairman of the Committee on Tax Structure and Simplification of the American Bar Association Section of Taxation and as a member of the Advisory Group of the American Law Institute Federal Tax Project. Professor Warren also has written numerous articles for prestigious law and tax journals.*

(Republican, Wisconsin), supported by many Republican members of Congress.

Evaluation of the current income tax and proposals for change requires a concept of income against which the current or proposed tax base can be evaluated. The concept of personal income most widely accepted for tax purposes is the Haig-Simons definition, which describes the potential tax base as the sum of an individual's consumption and saving during the year. As Henry Simons explained in his 1938 classic, *Personal Income Taxation*:

> Personal income may be defined as the algebraic sum of (1) the market value of rights exercised in consumption and (2) the change in the value of the store of property rights between the beginning and end of the period in question.

While it may not be possible to translate this broadly sweeping formulation directly into an administrable tax system, the underlying concept of income can definitely provide guidance on a variety of issues that arise in the design of a practical tax base. For several decades, the Haig-Simons formulation has provided the intellectual foundation for the movement that has come to be called a "comprehensive income tax."

The Haig-Simons definition of income (consumption plus saving) also illuminates the differences between an income tax and a personal consumption tax, which would reach only the consumption portion of the income tax base. Although the current Internal Revenue Code levies what is called an "income tax," many of its provisions can be understood only as attempts to remove certain categories of saving from the tax base. In chapter 5, Joseph Stiglitz presents the arguments for substituting a personal consumption tax for an income tax. The case for retaining the individual income tax is threefold. First, saving should be included in the tax base for reasons of fairness. As Joseph Pechman indicates in the Introduction, a personal consumption tax would, in effect, remove capital income from the tax base. Second, gains in economic efficiency that might be achieved by switching to a consumption tax are highly uncertain. Third, the current condition of the income tax should not be considered the best possible income tax, nor should Congress be assumed likely to enact the best possible consumption tax. There simply is no reason to believe that a personal consumption tax would be immune to the erosion of the tax base that has afflicted the income tax for over a half century.

The remainder of this chapter is organized around the major structural provisions of current law. In each case, the analysis describes deficiencies of the current regime, outcomes under a truly comprehensive income tax, and approaches taken by the Treasury's proposal, the Bradley-Gephardt bill, and the Kemp-Kasten bill. Because of the vastness of the Internal Revenue Code, this survey is necessarily illustrative, rather than exhaustive.

Three conclusions emerge from this analysis: (1) The current personal income tax is hardly comprehensive and deviates substantially from the underlying idea of income. The deviations constitute what have been termed "tax preferences" or "tax expenditures," which Congress often has enacted in order to further some nontax purpose. The current system can be described roughly as a "high-rate, narrow-base" system, while the alternatives under review are "low-rate, broadly based" systems. (2) The Treasury's proposal, the Bradley-Gephardt bill, and the Kemp-Kasten bill are all useful starting points for the conversion of the present system to a comprehensive income tax. Of the three, the Treasury's proposal goes furthest in implementing that ideal. (3) But all three proposals, even the Treasury's recommendations, fall short of fully converting the Internal Revenue Code into a comprehensive income tax. They should be regarded as ways to begin that process—not end it.

Tax Rates and Filing Units

TAX RATES

Tax rates for individuals currently range from 11 to 50 percent. Prior to the Economic Recovery Act of 1981, individual rates ranged from 14 to 70 percent; before 1964, the maximum individual rate was 91 percent. The rate structure under current law is further complicated by a zero-bracket amount (in effect, a standard deduction), personal exemptions, additional exemptions for the blind and elderly, a refundable credit for a limited amount of earned income, a special deduction for

"two-earner" married couples, an alternative minimum tax on
tax preferences, and special provisions for "averaging" income
over several years.

Each of the three major proposals for change would reduce
tax rates substantially and simplify the complicated rate structure. The Treasury's proposal would tax individual income at
three rates—15, 25, and 35 percent. The Bradley-Gephardt bill
would enact a "normal tax" of 14 percent on taxable income,
which would be supplemented by "surtax" rates of 12 and 16
percent on adjusted gross income, for maximum marginal rates
of 14, 28, and 30 percent. The Kemp-Kasten bill would tax
individuals at the single, nominal rate of 24 percent, although
the effective tax rate also would depend on an exclusion of 20
percent of employment income that is phased out gradually as
income rises. The maximum effective rate for individuals
would be about 28 percent.

Reducing rates and broadening the tax base as mandated by
the proposals would simplify the income tax system. For example, all three proposals would repeal the deduction for two-
earner couples, modify the current exemption structure, and
modify or repeal the averaging provisions. The Treasury's
proposal and the Bradley-Gephardt bill also would repeal the
minimum tax for individuals, while the Treasury's proposal
and the Kemp-Kasten bill provide that the exemptions, zero-
bracket amount, and earned income credit would be indexed
for inflation. Most important, reduction of the rates would
make possible elimination of preferential provisions that narrow the tax base, as detailed later. Reduced rates also could lead
to a reduction in tax planning that is designed to avoid the
current law's high marginal rates. Because marginal tax rates
would be reduced under all these proposals, distortions in taxpayer behavior that are often said to be caused by the income
tax might be reduced also.

Rate reduction and base broadening are attractive on two of
the principal grounds for judging tax policy—simplicity and
economic efficiency. Rate reduction is also attractive on the
third ground—fairness—because the concomitant base broadening would reduce unequal treatment of similarly situated
taxpayers. Rate reduction would reduce the nominal pro-

gressivity of the rate schedule, but the effect of base broadening would have to be considered in a full evaluation of the distributional effects of the proposals. Each proposal is said by its designers to leave unchanged the distribution of the tax burden among income classes. Although taxpayers within each class would experience change in their individual tax burden, the degree would depend upon the extent to which they had benefited from preferential provisions under existing law.

THE FILING UNIT

Under current law, individual taxpayers are separate taxpaying units, with the exception of married couples who file joint returns. A great deal of tax planning currently involves shifting income to family members in lower tax brackets, often through the use of family trusts. The major alternatives to the current regime include sole reliance on individual returns (to eliminate the relevance of marital status) and broadening the taxable unit to include other family members (to avoid income shifting within the family).

The Treasury's proposal would tax unearned income received by children under fourteen years of age from property received from their parents at the marginal tax rate applicable to the parents. It also would revise the treatment of family trusts to eliminate much of the advantage of income shifting through such devices. Neither the Bradley-Gephardt bill nor the Kemp-Kasten bill makes any fundamental changes in the nature of the filing unit.

A primary simplification advantage of a low-rate tax system could be to eliminate incentives for taxpayers to allocate income and losses among parties facing different tax rates. The approach suggested by the Treasury would reduce substantially such incentives in the family context and still preserve the remaining progressivity of the low-rate system. While they would be an improvement over current law, the Treasury's proposal would introduce new complexities into the tax law, such as the need to determine whether property was received from a parent. It may well be that additional simplicity could be achieved by moving even further in the direction of a family filing unit in a comprehensive income tax.

Gross Income

The Haig-Simons definition of income suggests that all receipts that could potentially increase consumption or saving should be taken into account under the income tax. Section 61 of the Internal Revenue Code seems to embrace this result by indicating that "gross income means all income from whatever source derived." Unfortunately, the reach of Section 61 is severely circumscribed by a variety of exclusions from gross income. Some of those exclusions are specifically authorized by the code; others have developed as a matter of practice in the years since the income tax was first enacted. All three of the leading proposals for income tax reform would eliminate many of these exclusions, moving the income tax base closer to the comprehensive base suggested by the Haig-Simons concept of income.

FRINGE BENEFITS

One of the largest categories of untaxed income under current law—employer-provided fringe benefits—can be subdivided into specific statutory exclusions, other fringe benefits, and deferred compensation.

Specific Statutory Exclusions—For many years, the Internal Revenue Code has contained a significant number of specific exclusions for employer-provided fringe benefits, such as group term life insurance, employer contributions to accident and health plans, rental values of parsonages, meals and lodging furnished for the convenience of the employer, group legal services plans, qualified transportation, "cafeteria" plans (which allow employees to choose among various benefits), educational assistance programs, and dependent care programs.

The Treasury's proposal would limit tax exclusions for employer-provided health insurance and repeal those for employer-provided group term life insurance, death benefits, legal services, dependent care services, transportation expenses, educational assistance, cafeteria plans, employee awards, military allowances, and parsonage allowances. The Bradley-Gephardt bill takes a similar, but less comprehensive, approach, while the Kemp-Kasten bill generally leaves these exclusions intact. If all income is to be treated the same, no matter what its source, elimination of these statutory exclusions is surely the first step toward comprehensive tax reform.

Other Fringe Benefits—The Tax Reform Act of 1984 enacted statutory treatment for many fringe benefits that previously had not been the subject of specific legislation. In general, the act excluded five categories of fringe benefits from the tax base, provided that certain requirements (generally including nondiscrimination) are met: (1) no-additional-cost services, (2) qualified employee discounts, (3) working-condition fringe benefits, (4) *de minimis* fringe benefits, and (5) qualified tuition reductions.

The 1984 provisions permit many forms of income, such as free airline travel for airline employees and free college tuition for children of university employees, to go untaxed. None of the current reform proposals addresses the fringe benefits that fall in this category, and all leave intact some exclusions that would be eliminated under a truly comprehensive income tax base.

Deferred Compensation—The Internal Revenue Code also contains numerous and detailed provisions for special treatment for deferred compensation. For "qualified" plans, employees may defer inclusion of income set aside for future receipt (generally on retirement), even though employers may currently deduct their contributions to such plans and no one is taxed on investment income produced by the deferred compensation in the interim. Amounts contributed to individual retirement accounts (IRAs) and "Keogh Plans" for the self-employed also benefit from similar treatment. The justification for these provisions presumably is the social benefit generated by encouraging a strong private pension system.

None of the current reform proposals makes major changes in the taxation of deferred compensation, even though exclusion of current earnings saved for retirement is more consistent with a consumption tax than with a comprehensive income tax. Full implementation of the concept of income in the tax base would require the current taxation of all compensation, whether it is deferred or not. That approach might be simpler than current law, because the elaborate provisions that grant preferential treatment would be repealed. As suggested in the Treasury Department's 1977 *Blueprints for Basic Tax Reform*, a still simpler approach that would accomplish roughly the same result would be to defer taxing the employees until they receive their retirement payments while taxing the retirement fund on income earned in the interim on invested employer contributions.

However, both of the suggested approaches are inconsistent with the nontax policy reasons that originally led to special treatment of resources set aside to produce retirement income. Assuming that the preferential treatment of deferred income is to remain part of the income tax, the current provisions could be simplified greatly and should be reexamined in that light in any proposal for comprehensive reform, rate reduction, and simplification. The Treasury's proposal includes a number of recommendations for harmonization and simplification of these provisions.

CAPITAL INCOME

The Internal Revenue Code currently excludes capital income in a variety of forms from the individual income tax base. For example, individuals are not taxed on the first $100 of dividend receipts. Interest on bonds issued by state and local governments for governmental and other purposes has long been exempt from taxation. Income from life insurance savings is also subject to special treatment. Interest or other investment income accruing in the hands of a life insurance company under an annuity, life insurance, or endowment contract is not currently taxed to the policyholder or the insurance company. Amounts paid to a beneficiary under a life insurance policy by reason of the death of the insured are also not taxable, except in certain situations where the policy has been transferred for value. In other cases, amounts received under annuity, life insurance, and endowment contracts are taxed to the extent that they exceed the premiums paid, with the cost basis prorated in the case of annuities.

Because of the resulting distortions in taxpayer choices, special treatment for only certain categories of capital income are objectionable on the grounds of efficiency. (See chapter 3 for details.) If all taxpayers are not equally able to choose among investments that are taxed differently, special treatment is also objectionable on the ground of fairness. Under a comprehensive income tax, all capital income would be treated in the same manner to the extent feasible. Many of the special exclusions of current law would be limited or repealed under the reform proposals. For example, all three proposals would eliminate the current limited exclusion for some dividend income, the tax-free build-up of interest on life insurance policies, and the tax exemption for state and local bonds when the borrowed funds are not used for a governmental purpose. Full implementation of the comprehensive income tax also would eliminate the exemption for such bonds when the funds *are* used for a governmental purpose.

OTHER EXCLUSIONS

Other statutory exclusions under current law that arguably might be subject to tax under a broad-based income tax include certain prizes and awards (such as the Nobel Prize), unemployment compensation, certain social security benefits, gifts and inheritances, compensation for injuries or sickness, amounts received under accident and health plans, scholarships and grants, and gains from the sale of a principal residence by individuals fifty-five years old or more.

The Treasury's proposal would repeal some of these exemptions, including the current tax-exempt threshold for unemployment insurance compensation, the exemption of workers' compensation payments, black lung and certain veterans' disability payments, the exclusion of scholarships and fellowships in excess of tuition, and the exclusion for prizes and awards. The Bradley-Gephardt and Kemp-Kasten proposals also repeal certain of these exclusions, but they do not go as far in that direction as does the Treasury's.

IMPUTED INCOME FROM HOUSEHOLD SERVICES

The Internal Revenue Code has never taxed the economic value or "imputed income" created by the performance of services within the household. As a result, individuals who decide to leave the household to work in the marketplace may find their taxable income increased by more than the increment in

value produced by shifting personal services from the household to the marketplace. The special deduction for two-earner
couples mitigates this effect under current law, as does the
credit for child care. Under an ideal comprehensive income
tax, economic activity in the home would be treated no differently from economic activity outside the home. None of the
current reform proposals would tax the provision of imputed
income within the household, and it seems unlikely that the
Internal Revenue Code would ever reach such income. However, the tax system should not create a significant disincentive
for in-home workers to enter the marketplace. In a regime of
low tax rates, it may be that the remaining disincentive would
not be great, but the matter deserves further consideration,
especially since in some cases the reform proposals would eliminate the special treatment for two-earner couples and child
care under existing law.

CONCLUSIONS REGARDING GROSS INCOME

By reducing rates and broadening the base, all three reform
proposals offer useful starting points for fundamental reform
of the income tax. Of the three, the Treasury Department's
proposal goes furthest toward implementing a comprehensive
income tax base, but even it does not implement such a base
fully. Any of the proposals would be a significant improvement
over current law, given the desirability of taxing income, rather
than just consumption.

Personal Deductions and Credits

TRADITIONAL RATIONALES

Personal deductions under an income tax are usually defended on one of two grounds. First, the expenditure reduces
taxpayer net worth without increasing personal consumption,
thus diminishing "income" in the Haig-Simons sense. For
example, deductions for medical expenses have been defended
as not giving rise to the type of personal consumption falling
within the definition of income. From this viewpoint, restoring
a taxpayer's physical condition to a state of normalcy is not
regarded as a gain producing a tax liability.

The second rationale for certain personal deductions is that such deductions encourage socially desirable expenditures by the taxpayer. The deduction for charitable contributions provides an example of a provision that is sometimes defended on this ground. This rationale also provides the basis for the suggestion that some personal deductions should be replaced with credits so that the level of government support does not vary with the taxpayer's marginal tax rate. This second rationale is fundamentally inconsistent with comprehensive taxation of income and depends upon a willingness to use the income tax as a means to subsidize certain activities.

MEDICAL EXPENSES AND CASUALTY LOSSES

Medical expenses are currently deductible to the extent that they exceed 5 percent of adjusted gross income. The Bradley-Gephardt and Kemp-Kasten bills would increase this floor to 10 percent. Otherwise, none of the current reform proposals would modify this deduction significantly. The cost of medical services should be deductible under a comprehensive income tax if such services are not considered consumption. While that characterization is generally apt, there are surely some medical services, such as some cosmetic surgery, that involve a substantial consumption component. Broad-based reform of the income tax might include a clearer statutory definition of medical services to prevent taxpayers from deducting personal expenses as medical expenses. The task of distinguishing between personal and medical expenses is currently relegated to the Internal Revenue Service (IRS) and the courts.

Like medical expenses, casualty losses reduce a taxpayer's net worth without increasing consumption and should be deductible under a comprehensive income tax. However, because the casualty deduction reduces the burden only of uninsured losses, nondeductibility of premiums for casualty insurance on nonbusiness property may distort normal economic incentives to purchase such insurance. Current law reduces the possibility of this distortion by limiting the deduction to losses that exceed $100 each and aggregate to more than 10 percent of adjusted gross income. Of the current reform proposals, only the Kemp-Kasten bill would repeal the deduction for casualty losses. By that repeal, the bill would apparently tax an individual's weekly salary even if it were stolen as soon as it was received, a result that is hardly consistent with levying a tax on income.

CHARITABLE CONTRIBUTIONS

Within certain limits, contributions to qualified charitable organizations can be deducted from gross income under current law. Contributions of appreciated property yield the donor an additional benefit in certain cases; not only is the full value of the property deductible, but also the previously unrealized capital gains on the gift are not taxed. This "double benefit" is available for gifts of real property, intangible property (such as shares of stock), and tangible property when the exempt donee uses the tangible personal property to further its exempt purpose. Thus, a gift of an appreciated painting to an art museum would qualify for the double benefit; a gift of the same painting to a hospital might not. The Treasury's proposal makes two significant changes in the treatment of charitable contributions. First, deductions would be limited to those in excess of 2 percent of adjusted gross income. Second, the double benefit from contributions of appreciated property would be eliminated. The Bradley-Gephardt and Kemp-Kasten bills do not make major changes in this area.

Purely from a tax perspective, whether or not charitable contributions should be deductible depends on whether or not they are considered enough like consumption to the donor to be included in the tax base. From a broad social perspective, it is sometimes argued that the deduction is an efficient means of government subsidy for private charity, since the loss of a dollar in government revenue results in more than a dollar of receipt by the charity. Finally, it is sometimes argued that the double benefit is less egregious than it seems since donors always can choose to retain their assets until death. As explained later, all previously unrealized appreciation is eliminated at death because donees of testamentary gifts step up their basis to the value of the property on the donor's date of death. If donors of charitable contributions would retain the contributed assets until death, there is arguably no double benefit from the contribution because the income tax would never have reached the appreciation in value.

On the other hand, charitable contributions can be viewed as involving a consumption component sufficient to render them nondeductible under an ideal comprehensive income tax. If the federal government plans to subsidize private charities with public funds, the budgetary process provides a more appropriate means.

HOUSEHOLD EXPENSES AND CHILD CARE

Current law provides a nonrefundable credit for an individual who pays employment-related dependent and child care expenses. The Treasury's proposal and the Bradley-Gephardt bill would replace the credit with a limited deduction; the Kemp-Kasten bill repeals the credit. A deduction for such expenses is justified if they are considered costs of earning income. However, no deduction would be warranted if household and dependent care expenses were considered personal expenditures or work-related expenses borne by such a large percentage of the taxpaying population that no deduction is necessary to differentiate among taxpayers. Dependent and child care expenses then would be in the same category as the costs of commuting, lunches at work, and business clothing that can be worn elsewhere.

INTEREST PAYMENTS

Considered by itself, interest arguably should be deductible under an income tax in all cases, because interest payments have the same effect as interest forgone by drawing down savings. The income of a taxpayer who withdrew $1,000 from a savings account to take a vacation would have been reduced by the forgone interest receipts. Consider a second taxpayer who borrowed $1,000 to take the same vacation and used the interest receipts from savings to pay the interest due on the vacation loan. The second taxpayer would be in the same economic position as the first and, therefore, should be able to deduct interest payments against interest receipts.

The appropriate treatment of interest payments for taxpayers without assets is more controversial. One view is that yet another taxpayer, who has no assets and uses borrowed funds to finance the same vacation trip, also should be able to deduct interest payments since such payments are items of "negative income," which reduce potential consumption without increasing the taxpayer's wealth. Other analysts would limit the interest deduction to cases where the taxpayer has income-producing assets.

Tax Arbitrage—However, interest cannot be considered in isolation because not all investment income is fully taxable under current law. Such tax preferences create the possibility of "tax arbitrage" when tax-preferred income is combined with full deductibility of interest. One objection to this combination is that transactions that would not be profitable before taxes can yield after-tax profits. For example, taxpayers in the 50 percent tax bracket could borrow at 14 percent to invest at a tax-exempt rate of 10 percent because the after-tax receipt of 10 percent would exceed the after-tax interest cost of 7 percent. This simple example does not capture the full dimensions of the problem of tax arbitrage for a variety of reasons, including the potential response of the capital markets. If, for example, the tendency of the markets to equate after-tax returns from capital resulted in the pretax return on the exempt asset falling to 7 percent, there no longer would be any advantage for a 50 percent taxpayer to borrow at 14 percent in order to invest at 7 percent. The extent to which the capital markets can be relied upon to make such adjustments is a matter of considerable dispute.

One area in which the use of borrowed funds to acquire tax-preferred assets is permitted—and common—is the debt-financed purchase of an owner-occupied residence, which is an asset that produces an economic return in the form of housing services. These services are directly consumed by the homeowner and are not subject to the income tax. The exclusion of this economic return from the tax base results in preferential treatment of homeowners, as compared to renters. Full deductibility of mortgage interest makes that preference available to taxpayers who purchase homes with borrowed funds, as well as those who pay cash.

Current Law—The previous analysis suggests that interest payments should be fully deductible under a broad-based income tax, except where necessary to prevent tax arbitrage and, perhaps, when the indebtedness is incurred to finance consumption. Current law contains a number of limitations on the deductibility of interest that are designed to prevent individuals from coupling full interest deductibility with income that currently is not fully taxed. These provisions are less than satisfactory because they do not apply to all forms of preferred income and because they generally require that borrowed funds be traced to preferred assets.

Proposals for Reform—Each of the major tax reform proposals would impose additional limitations on the deductibility of interest. The Treasury's proposal would limit the deductions for interest not incurred in connection with a trade or business, and not related to debt secured by a principal residence, to investment income plus $5,000. The Treasury apparently concluded that the possibility of tax arbitrage requires substantial interest limitations, except in the case of owner-occupied residences.

The Kemp-Kasten bill does not deal specifically with the problem of tax arbitrage, but it does eliminate the deductibility of "consumer interest," which is defined as interest that would not be otherwise deductible (for example, business expense) and is related to neither residential property nor educational expenses. For purposes of the surtax, the Bradley-Gephardt bill restricts the deductibility of nonbusiness interest, including home mortgage interest, to investment income, presumably on the theory that the disallowed excess interest is related either to untaxed receipts or to consumption. For taxpayers without investment income, the Bradley-Gephardt bill effectively converts the deduction for home mortgage interest into a credit by limiting it to computation of the 14 percent normal tax. This limitation does not achieve simplification and is not justified by the concept of income, although it may be explained as a compromise between the allowance of full deduction or total disallowance.

None of these proposals is likely to simplify the law. None would be needed under a completely comprehensive income tax base that reached all forms of current income. Given the strong social policy for homeownership in the United States and the continued preferential treatment of certain types of income, some provisions along the line of the Treasury's proposal are probably necessary to prevent tax arbitrage.

STATE AND LOCAL TAXES

Because the public goods and services provided by state and local governments are not included in gross income, none of the currently deductible taxes is a cost of taxable income. Moreover, the deductibility of one tax—the general sales tax—is especially difficult to administer and requires either the use of complicated tax return tables or detailed records. As in the case of interest payments on home mortgages, the deductibility of the real property tax results in currently deductible expenditures that relate to an untaxed economic return. Under a comprehensive income tax, none of these state and local taxes would be deductible. That is the approach taken by the Treasury's proposal, which would repeal the itemized deduction for all state and local taxes. The Kemp-Kasten bill retains only the deduction for real property taxes; the Bradley-Gephardt bill repeals only the deduction for sales and personal property taxes.

BUSINESS DEDUCTIONS FOR PERSONAL EXPENSES

As the previous review suggests, a recurring issue under the income tax is the dividing line between personal and business expenses. The Treasury's proposal includes new provisions designed to deal with some troublesome areas. The proposal denies deductions for all entertainment expenses except for business meals furnished in a clearly business setting; limits deductions for business meals on a per meal and per person basis; limits deductions for meals and lodging away from home; extends rules for allocating travel expenses between personal and business expenses; and denies deductions for seminars held aboard cruise ships. Neither the Bradley-Gephardt bill nor the Kemp-Kasten bill contains comparable provisions.

CONCLUSIONS REGARDING PERSONAL DEDUCTIONS

Because the surtax rates are applicable to the excess of adjusted gross income over $25,000 and the normal tax of 14 percent is applied to taxable income, the personal deductions that are retained under the Bradley-Gephardt bill are limited to income that is taxed at 14 percent. In effect, personal deductions that are not taken into account in determining adjusted gross income are converted into credits that return 14 percent of their value to the taxpayer. In effect, personal deductions that are made into credits are those for child care, charitable contributions, state and local income and real property taxes, medical expenses, and employee business expenses. As indicated earlier regarding interest, credits for such expenditures cannot be justified as implementing a comprehensive income tax; such credits must be defended as either accomplishing a governmental subsidy for preferred activity or reflecting a compromise between full deductibility and none at all.

As in the case of gross income, the Internal Revenue Code's current treatment of personal deductions deviates substantially from a comprehensive income tax. None of the reform proposals would fully eliminate these deviations, but each would move in that direction, with the Treasury's going the furthest.

Capital Gains and Losses

CURRENT LAW

Under current law, 60 percent of long-term capital gains is excluded from the taxable income of individuals. They may deduct capital losses without limitation against capital gains, but against only $3,000 annually of ordinary income, carrying forward any excess indefinitely.

Gains or losses are taken into account only when "realized," generally on the sale or disposition of an asset. Even if realized, gains and losses will not affect current tax liabilities if they are not "recognized." For example, realized gains on the sale of a principal residence are not taken into income if the sale proceeds are reinvested in another principal residence within a specified period. Because a form of saving is omitted from the tax base, deferral of accrued gains until realization and recognition effectively subjects such gains to consumption, rather than income, tax treatment.

In general, the basis for determining gains or losses is the taxpayer's cost with no adjustment for inflation. (Like assets, liabilities are not adjusted for inflation under current law.) Donees of lifetime gifts carry over the donor's basis, but donees of testamentary gifts step up their basis to the value of the property on the donor's date of death. This step-up of basis permanently removes from the tax base any gains that are not realized prior to the donor's death.

The realization criterion originally was adopted by the Supreme Court as essential to the meaning of "income" in the Sixteenth Amendment to the Constitution, which authorized the enactment of the modern income tax. The requirement of realization is often defended today as necessary to avoid annual valuation of assets and the taxation of individuals without liquid assets to pay the resulting taxes. Full implementation of the Haig-Simon concept would require a tax base that reflected all changes in asset values as they occurred.

RATIONALE FOR PREFERENCE

The preferential treatment accorded capital gains is usually defended on one of four grounds. First, the preference can be justified as a means of mitigating the sharp disparity in treatment between realized and unrealized gains. Without preferential treatment, holders of appreciated assets, the argument runs, would be deterred from selling them by high marginal tax rates. Second, the preference can be seen as an approximate offset for the failure of the income tax to increase cost basis by inflation. Third, the preference can be seen as a crude means of mitigating the particularly high marginal rates that would be applicable to capital gains that were "bunched" into a single year of realization, even though they had accrued over a number of years. Fourth, the preference can be seen as mitigating the inclusion of capital income in the tax base and permitting a sort of consumption tax treatment of at least some forms of saving and investment.

The realization and capital gains provisions of current law are widely regarded as unsatisfactory. The realization criterion and the special treatment given capital gains and losses have produced a web of complicated statutory provisions and a bewildering array of judicial decisions as taxpayers have sought to achieve the advantages of deferral and capital gains and avoid the detriments of capital losses. The step-up of basis at death has a substantial effect on the willingness of taxpayers to transfer assets prior to their death. In addition, the failure to adjust basis for inflation means that tax is sometimes due on gains that are merely a result of general price inflation rather than an actual increase in taxpayers' wealth.

THE REFORM PROPOSALS

Capital Gains and Losses—The Treasury's proposal eliminates preferential treatment of capital gains. Losses on "investment assets" would be deductible against gains on such assets plus $3,000 of other income, and the excess would be carried forward. The Bradley-Gephardt bill repeals preferential treatment of capital gains and permits deduction of capital losses only to the extent of capital gains plus $3,000 annually, and any excess is carried to the next year. The Kemp-Kasten bill also eliminates preferential treatment of capital gains, but it permits full deductibility of capital losses, to which the minimum tax would be applied.

Elimination of the special treatment of capital gains and losses, in conjunction with the adoption of low tax rates, would result in substantial simplification of the tax system. Retention of the concept of capital gains as a limitation on the deductibility of capital losses, as permitted by the Bradley-Gephardt bill, would not achieve maximum simplification. However, full deductibility of capital losses against all income, as allowed under the Kemp-Kasten bill, would permit taxpayers to defer realization of their gains and to reduce the amount of other income taxed each year by realizing capital losses; the bill attempts to mitigate this possibility by applying the alternative minimum tax to the amount of capital losses deducted. Some limitation on deductibility of losses would be necessary to prevent taxpayers from realizing losses while deferring gains. A simpler limitation than the current definition of capital gains could be devised for this purpose, as indicated by the Treasury's proposal to develop such a limitation based on the concept of "investment assets."

Inflation Adjustments—The three reform proposals take notably different approaches to the need to adjust basis for inflation. The Bradley-Gephardt bill makes no adjustment at all, a position that will continue to create problems as long as inflation remains a significant fact of economic life. The Kemp-Kasten bill adjusts the basis of capital assets, but gives the taxpayer the opportunity to forgo the adjustment and accept a 40 percent exclusion, resulting in a maximum effective tax rate of 17 percent. This proposal does not provide an inflation adjustment for liabilities, and it is not clear that adjustments to only a part of the tax base for inflation are better than none at all. Thus, a taxpayer who borrowed $100 to purchase an asset that tripled in value as a result of inflation would have no taxable income even though $200 in additional cash would be retained after using some of the $300 in sale proceeds to pay off the original loan. Failure to adjust liabilities while adjusting the basis of assets would treat taxpayers in accordance with their true economic positions only if the rate of interest correctly anticipated the rate of inflation and interest deductibility was denied for the inflation portion of payments denominated as "interest."

If inflation remains a serious problem, the Treasury's general approach—adjustment of liabilities as well as gains—is surely the preferable one. Unfortunately, the method chosen by the Treasury to adjust liabilities—modification of the interest deduction—is itself flawed. Under this proposal, deductible interest would be reduced by an inflation factor that does not depend on the amount of borrowed funds. For example, consider an individual who borrows $100 at 16 percent and lends it at 20 percent; that individual clearly has $4 in income in current dollars. But under the Treasury's proposal, interest would be deductible and included only to the extent that it exceeded the fractional portion of interest attributable to inflation. If inflation were thought to account for 25 percent of interest, taxpayers would include and deduct only 75 percent of interest payments. In the previous example, interest receipts of $15 would be included and interest payments of $12 would be deducted, yielding taxable income of $3, even though it is clear that the taxpayer obtained gains of $4. Further work needs to be done on the implementation of the Treasury's proposal to adjust liabilities as well as assets for inflation.

The Realization Criterion—Many of the complexities of the current tax system can be traced to the need to define realized income. While new problems of valuation and liquidity would arise, a tax system that directly implemented the Haig-Simons definition of income by taxing changes in market value would eliminate many of these difficulties. A broadly based reform of the income tax coupled with substantial rate reduction might be an opportunity to experiment with taxation of some forms of unrealized appreciation. The process of comprehensive income tax reform at least should consider the possible advantages of a tax on some unrealized appreciation.

If unrealized appreciation is not to be taxed at present, full implementation of the concept of income would require both that basis be increased to take account of inflation and that taxable gains be increased by an interest charge to take account of the deferral of taxation until realization. Although these adjustments are attractive in theory, they could be extremely complicated in practice. In any case, they, too, should be considered as part of a comprehensive reform effort.

Tax Shelters

"Tax shelters" typically combined preferential treatment of an asset with full deductibility of interest incurred on indebtedness used to acquire the asset. Real estate shelters, for example, offer accelerated depreciation deductions for acquisitions made with borrowed funds and full deductibility of interest payments on those funds. Farming benefits from special accounting rules that permit use of cash accounting to defer income.

As indicated previously, the Treasury's proposal would limit further the availability of the interest deduction. In addition, provisions that now limit the amount of deductions a taxpayer may take with respect to an investment to the amount the taxpayer actually has "at risk" would be extended to all investment and business activities, including real estate. The Bradley-Gephardt and Kemp-Kasten bills contain no particular provisions devoted to tax shelters.

Because there would be no preferential treatment for particular categories of assets on which to build a shelter, tax shelters would not be a problem under a truly comprehensive income tax. The Treasury's proposal and the Bradley-Gephardt bill would enact depreciation systems that more closely reflect the actual decline in asset value, thereby reducing the potential for shelters. All three proposals would eliminate other preferences for some categories of business income, thereby further reducing the potential for tax shelters. Nevertheless, none of the reform proposals would enact a truly comprehensive tax base. Extension of the at-risk provisions, as proposed by the Treasury, would therefore be a salutary part of a reform proposal.

Conclusions

The attraction of a comprehensive income tax for individuals depends on the judgment that the annual sum of consumption and savings provides an appropriate basis on which to allocate the tax burden in society. Advocates of consumption taxation argue that that allocation should be made solely on the basis of how much is consumed, ignoring what is saved. The case that saving should be ignored is not convincing, particularly if savings or wealth are not otherwise taxed by a wealth or transfer tax.

The current income tax falls far short of the ideal of a comprehensive income tax for individuals; the narrowed tax base requires high marginal tax rates to generate sufficient revenue. The Treasury's proposal, the Bradley-Gephardt bill, and the Kemp-Kasten bill all would broaden the tax base substantially and reduce rates. The Treasury's proposal goes the furthest in the direction of an ideal comprehensive income tax, but even it falls short of that ideal. Rather, the Treasury's proposal implements the Haig-Simons definition within the constraints of the realization criterion and certain overriding nontax policies, such as encouragement of homeownership and retirement savings. Compared with current law, any of the three proposals would be a significant improvement. Among the three, the Treasury's proposal is to be preferred as a way to begin reform and simplification of the individual income tax.

Alan J. Auerbach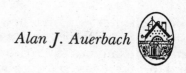

3

The Corporation Income Tax

In recent years the corporation income tax in the United States has accounted for less than 10 percent of federal budget receipts—a stark contrast to the 1950s and 1960s, when such taxes regularly contributed well over 20 percent of federal revenue. Yet, partly because most private nonresidential investment and industrial production are done by corporations, the corporate tax still lies at the heart of the tax reform debate. This attention is justified since, while corporate tax revenue has declined, the distortions associated with the tax have not. Legislative changes that, individually, may have had some economic merit when enacted have combined to produce a tax system that few would support were it to be reintroduced today in its entirety. In its current form, the corporate tax distorts economic decisions among assets in which firms choose to invest and among financial sources that firms may use, affects the timing of investment decisions, favors some firms over others, and causes an unnecessary dependence of investment incen-

ALAN J. AUERBACH *is a professor of economics at the University of Pennsylvania and a research associate at the National Bureau of Economic Research. Previously, Dr. Auerbach taught at Harvard University and at Yale University. In addition to other professional activities, he serves as associate editor of the* Journal of Public Economics *and was a consultant to the Treasury Department in the formulation of its 1984 tax reform proposal. Dr. Auerbach is the author of numerous articles in prestigious national economics and law journals, and he recently served as editor (with M. Feldstein) of the* Handbook of Public Economics.

tives on the rate of inflation. Yet all of these results occur with a minimal overall tax burden actually being placed on corporations.

This chapter explores how the corporate tax has made its historical transition from a stable revenue source to its current state and examines the reasons that it is important to look beyond the aggregate statistics above to understand the incentives firms face today because of the corporate tax. After an examination of these incentives, various potential reforms—ranging from outright repeal to structural reform to measures that would transform the corporate tax into a withholding mechanism for the individual income tax—will be examined and evaluated.

Corporate Taxation during the Postwar Period

In fiscal year 1983, corporation income taxes represented a postwar low of 6.2 percent of federal revenue, compared to 48.1 percent for individual income tax receipts. Comparable numbers for earlier years were, respectively, 27.3 percent and 43.9 percent in 1955, 20.3 percent and 44.6 percent in 1963, and 15.6 percent and 44.7 percent for 1973. While the individual income tax has been a stable source of revenue, the corporate tax has steadily declined in importance. (The revenue gap created by this decline has been filled primarily by the rapid increase in social security taxes.)

Some have suggested that much of the decline in corporate tax revenue comes not from corporate tax cuts but rather from the decline in corporate profitability that occurred during the 1970s. As a fraction of national income (gross national product less depreciation and indirect business taxes) corporate profits, corrected to include inventory valuation and capital consumption adjustments, were 13.8 percent in 1955, 13.5 percent in 1963, 10.0 percent in 1973, and 8.5 percent in 1983. Not all of this decrease reflects a drop in profitability. Some of the decline in profits is due to the increased debt-equity ratios that were observed over the same period, along with the higher nominal interest rates associated with inflation. Both of these factors lead to the absorption of a greater part of the return to corporate capital by interest payments. However, if the decline in corporate profits were the primary explanation for the decline in corporate tax revenue, an examination of corporate taxes *relative* to corporate profits should fail to show the same historical decline in taxes. Instead, a comparable decline is reflected in corporate taxes as a percent of corporate profits. According to statistics presented by Joseph Pechman in *Federal Tax Policy*, this figure was 42.2 percent in 1955, 38.0 percent in 1963, 30.9 percent in 1973, and 13.1 percent in 1982. Thus, change in the tax treatment of corporate profits has played a significant role in the decline of corporate tax receipts during the postwar period. To understand the way in which this change has occurred, it is necessary to describe the structure of the corporate tax in some detail.

The U.S. federal corporation income tax is essentially a flat rate tax of 46 percent, reduced from 48 percent in 1978 and 52 percent in 1964. However, the key legislative changes in the tax treatment of corporate income have occurred not through these rate cuts, but through two other channels—depreciation deductions and the investment tax credit.

DEPRECIATION DEDUCTIONS

A tax on true economic income, in keeping with the Haig-Simons definition of cash flow plus changes in wealth, would allow a deduction from taxable income for reductions in the value of capital assets used in producing income. Such depreciation deductions are a normal part of the corporate tax structure. Since 1954, however, depreciation deductions have been seen also as a vehicle for changing the effective corporate tax rate and, it was hoped, the incentive to invest. An "effective" corporate tax rate means a tax rate that would lead to the same tax payments by corporations as that actually accomplished through the narrowing of the tax base by the use of investment incentives rather than a direct lowering of the statutory tax rate. Tax lifetimes for depreciable assets have been shortened, or the rate of deduction over such lifetimes increased, in 1954, 1962, 1971, and 1981. (There have also been infrequent moves in the opposite direction, as in 1984, but these have been relatively unimportant quantitatively.) While economic depreciation is difficult to measure, these changes were not enacted with the purpose of reflecting economic depreciation more closely.

THE INVESTMENT TAX CREDIT

The second major instrument used to reduce corporate tax payments has been the investment tax credit. Since 1962, businesses have received a subsidy, in the form of taxes forgiven, of 7 percent of the purchase price of new machinery and equipment (increased to 10 percent in 1975). Both the acceleration of depreciation allowances and the investment tax credit have found favor because they have more "bang per buck," more of a reduction in the effective tax rate on income from new investment per dollar of federal revenue lost. Unlike a cut in the corporate tax rate, these tax incentives do not reduce the effective rate of tax on income from other sources of corporate income, including preexisting depreciable capital.

INFLATION

Together, corporate rate reductions, accelerated depreciation, and investment tax credit would have resulted in an even more marked decline in the effective corporate tax rate and corporate tax collections were it not for one important factor—inflation. Because the corporate tax is essentially a proportional tax with a single rate, its revenue rises in proportion to its base. Unlike the progressive individual income tax, the effective corporate tax rate does not rise simply from the growth of income. However, price level changes do more than raise the level of corporate profits, distorting their measure in a way that may overstate them. This distortion has three major components. First, because many corporations carry their inventories on a first-in/first-out basis, the cost of goods sold is understated during periods of rising prices. Second, because depreciation allowances, even if accelerated, are based on historical asset cost, they are smaller than if such allowances were based on actual replacement cost. However, as already stated, part of the reduction in these corporate profits can be attributed to the rise in nominal interest rates associated with the inflation of the 1970s. Not included in corporate profits as usually calculated are the capital gains of corporate borrowers that result from the decline in the real value of debt obligations; moreover, this income is not taxed. Thus, in exchange for higher tax-deductible nominal interest costs, corporations receive tax-free income when there is inflation. Although the degree is uncertain, evidence suggests that inflation increases the effective tax rate on corporations. In addition, such tax base distortions are also present in the individual income tax as applied to capital income. Because households are net creditors, the effect of taxing nominal interest on debt is to raise taxes as a percentage of real household income. Because capital gains are taxed according to nominal realized gains, those gains are overtaxed by inflation.

Thus, the trend toward lower corporate taxes is the result of numerous legislative changes that were primarily aimed to that end, partially mitigated by the increase in inflation that was experienced until the early 1980s. Had corporation income tax collections in fiscal year 1983 borne the same ratio to those of the individual income tax as they did in fiscal year 1978 (when the ratio was .33), revenue from the corporate tax would have been $58.7 billion higher than it was—30 percent of the 1983 federal deficit.

The Recent Tax Acts

A growing willingness to change the provisions of the tax code that affect business arose in recent years, and major changes in depreciation allowances were enacted in 1981, 1982, and 1984. The combined effect of these provisions has been to lower corporate tax collections to a level where serious discussion about abolishing the corporate tax could take place.

THE ECONOMIC RECOVERY TAX ACT

The 1981 changes in the corporate tax contained in the Economic Recovery Tax Act (ERTA) were the most important of the entire postwar period. A clean break was made between depreciation allowed for tax purposes and actual economic depreciation by the creation of "capital recovery classes" for depreciable assets, and most equipment was able to be written off over three or five years; most structures, over fifteen. One of the reasons offered for these changes was their necessity to offset the increase in inflation that had occurred in the 1970s because of the eroded purchasing power of depreciation deductions taken in years following asset purchases.

Because of the short period over which equipment could be written off, the combined effects of the investment tax credit (equal to 6 percent for three-year equipment, 10 percent for five-year equipment) and depreciation deductions were to provide investment-related tax savings in excess of those that would be provided by treating capital purchases as current expenses and immediately deducting the entire cost. In turn, this implies that there is no net positive tax burden facing new capital investments. The analogy has been made that once full expensing has been granted, government assumes what is basically a partnership role in the enterprise and shares equally (a share equal to 46 percent in 1984) in investments and their returns. For example, consider an investment project that costs $10 million and will forever yield $2 million a year. This project's before-tax rate of return is 20 percent. With a 46 percent tax rate and immediate write-off, the out-of-pocket cost to the investor is only $5.4 million, and the after-tax return is $1.08 million per year—a rate of return again equal to 20 percent. Since the actual effect of the 1981 cut was to provide tax benefits in excess of those associated with an immediate write-off, the impact added a government subsidy to this partnership-like arrangement—the after-tax return on investment *exceeded* the before-tax return.

Another important provision of the ERTA was the liberalization of leasing provisions to facilitate the transfer of tax benefits among corporations. The vehicle used for this change, referred to as "safe-harbor" leasing, was justified as a means to allow firms without taxable income sufficient to benefit directly from the increased depreciation allowances to gain indirectly instead by selling the allowances to firms with taxable income.

THE TAX ACTS OF 1982 AND 1984

The Tax Equity and Fiscal Responsibility Act of 1982 (TEFRA) and the Deficit Reduction Act of 1984 (DEFRA) scaled back some of the perceived excesses of ERTA. TEFRA introduced a schedule under which safe-harbor leasing would be phased out, and it called for a reduction in depreciable basis equal to half the amount of investment credits received by investors. DEFRA increased the tax lifetime of buildings to eighteen years. Nevertheless, the basic tax structure introduced in

1981 remained fundamentally in place. Furthermore, since inflation later decreased, the generosity of the depreciation provisions was magnified still further, since the real value of future depreciation allowances increased.

Economic Effects of the Corporate Tax

The preceding section described the process by which the corporate tax arrived at its current structure. This section explores the variety of ways in which the tax influences economic behavior, especially decisions related to capital investment.

THE INCENTIVE TO INVEST

The statistics previously cited regarding the decline in corporate tax collections as a fraction of corporate profits might suggest that there may have been a concomitant rise in the incentive to invest since corporations saw less and less of their before-tax profits being claimed by the federal government. For several important reasons, however, such aggregate statistics comparing tax collections to profits in a given year may fail to capture changes in the relevant *marginal* tax rate on income from new capital. Perhaps the most important of these limitations is the fact that the tax burden on any firm in any given year is dependent not only on the firm's gross revenue but also on the depreciation allowances and investment tax credits to which the firm is entitled. In turn, these have come to depend increasingly heavily on dates of previous investments since an accelerated write-off causes the value of an asset's successive depreciation allowances to diminish rapidly. For example, a fast-growing firm may have a much lower tax burden than one with a slow growth, even if both have the same rate of profit on their investments, since the former has a higher ratio of depreciation allowances to income in each year.

Marginal Investment—Yet this difference is largely irrelevant when considering the marginal investment decision, which concerns *additional* taxes paid relative to additional income received if the investment is undertaken. In other words, regardless of a firm's current ratio of tax payments to income, its decision as to whether or not a new investment should be undertaken should depend on the after-tax flows the project would generate. The tax component of these flows relates to the project's depreciation class and whether or not it qualifies for investment tax credit—not on the current ratio of taxes to income.

A second problem with aggregate statistics is that they mask differences among assets in their tax treatment. Because current law treats some investments much more favorably than others, it biases the choice of investments by individual firms and favors those firms that, because of their particular production processes, heavily utilize the tax-favored assets.

As an alternative to the use of aggregate tax rates based on observed tax collections, hypothetical tax rates on different types of new investment can be calculated by determining what fraction of an asset's before-tax return, over its life, will be collected in taxes under current economic conditions and current tax law. The calculations also may be viewed as a determination of the tax rate that, if applied to a base of the firm's true economic income, would provide the same incentive to invest in the particular asset as the existing tax system actually does. Therefore, the rate's divergence from 46 percent shows how much the actual tax base differs from actual income; a tax rate below 46 percent indicates a narrower base. Such effective tax rates for different fixed asset classes are presented in Table 1. For the case in which investments are taken to be financed by equity funds only (i.e., no interest deductions are included in the computations), a real after-tax rate of return of 4 percent is assumed, and the inflation rate is set equal to its 1983 value. The 19.4 percent aggregate tax rate is a weighted average of the rates for different assets based on relative amounts of investments in different classes undertaken by corporations; the first twenty asset classes are equipment; the last fourteen, structures.

Table 1 clearly shows the distortion in the choice among assets present in the current tax code. Under present economic conditions, *all* types of equipment face *negative* tax rates; the prospective investor can expect to gain a net reduction in tax liability over the course of the asset's life. Naturally, this outcome requires that other taxable income be present to be offset, a complication that will be covered later. Structures, on the other hand, face *positive* tax rates. This is even true of public

TABLE 1. EFFECTIVE TAX RATES IN PERCENT

Asset Class	1984
1. Furniture & fixtures	− 9.1
2. Fabricated metal products	− 7.9
3. Engines & turbines	− 7.1
4. Tractors	−12.7
5. Agricultural machinery	− 8.2
6. Construction machinery	−13.4
7. Mining & oilfield machinery	−12.9
8. Metalworking machinery	− 9.9
9. Special industrial machinery	− 8.6
10. General industrial machinery	− 9.9
11. Office & computing machinery	−21.0
12. Service industry machinery	−12.9
13. Electrical equipment	− 9.6
14. Trucks, buses, & trailers	−19.5
15. Automobiles	−28.9
16. Aircraft	−14.2
17. Ships & boats	− 6.8
18. Railroad equipment	− 6.3
19. Instruments	−11.6
20. Other equipment	-11.6
21. Industrial buildings	39.7
22. Commercial buildings	35.9
23. Religious buildings	33.7
24. Educational buildings	33.7
25. Hospitals	35.4
26. Other nonfarm buildings	42.5
27. Railroads	22.6
28. Telephone & telegraph	27.1
29. Electric light & power	26.2
30. Gas	12.2
31. Other public utilities	14.4
32. Farm structures	35.5
33. Mining, shafts & wells	22.2
34. Other nonresidential structures	37.4
Aggregate	19.4

utility structures, which receive relatively favorable tax treatment. Finally, the overall tax rate of 19.4 percent suggests that, even without additional interest deductions, the tax base is less than 50 percent of what it would be under a true income tax, because the current, smaller base is being taxed at 46 percent

(the statutory corporate rate) and yielding an effective rate of
tax on all income of less than half this nominal rate.

These distortions in investment choices also translate into a
bias among industries, as can be seen by the statistics in Table 2,
in which the tax rates in Table 1 and information on asset mix
by industry are used to compute aggregate tax rates on investment for each of the forty-four industries.

These industry-level tax rates range from a high of 37.1 percent for water supply, sanitary services, and other utilities to a
low of −20.2 percent for street railway, bus lines, and taxicab
service. Six of the industry groups face negative tax rates on
their combined investments, and that certainly raises the question of whether firms in such industries will pay taxes in the
future.

What is the justification for a tax system under which income
generated by investments in industrial machinery is taxed at
−9.9 percent while income from investment in industrial
buildings is taxed at 39.7 percent? What kind of industrial policy is embodied in the tax rate variation shown in Table 2?

The Cost of Distortive Corporate Taxation

DISTORTIONS WITHIN THE CORPORATE SECTOR

When a tax system treats different assets differently, there
are obvious incentives for the shifting of capital toward these
types of investments and the firms making them. Aside from
the question of who gains or loses from such shifts, there is the
one of how much is lost by society *as a whole* because private
incentives are being distorted. When firms face differential
asset taxation, the asset with the highest after-tax return normally will not be the one with the highest pretax or social rate of
return. Investors ignore that part of the return that they cannot
keep (a fully rational decision), but this part of their return, the
tax revenue, is still available to society as a whole. The choice of
projects with the highest after-tax returns will result in those
with the highest before-tax returns being undertaken only if
the returns on available projects face the same rate of tax. For
example, if there are two projects, one yielding 10 percent and
the other yielding 11 percent before-tax, society as a whole gets
a greater return if the latter project is undertaken. However,

TABLE 2.   EFFECTIVE TAX RATES BY INDUSTRY IN PERCENT

Industry Number	1984
1. Food & kindred products	23.8
2. Tobacco manufacturers	20.3
3. Textile mill products	19.1
4. Apparel & other fabricated textile products	21.8
5. Paper & allied products	12.4
6. Printing, publishing, & allied industries	25.8
7. Chemicals & allied products	14.9
8. Petroleum & coal products	31.3
9. Rubber & miscellaneous plastic products	13.8
10. Leather & leather products	25.0
11. Lumber & wood products (except furniture)	20.9
12. Furniture & fixtures	26.1
13. Stone, clay, & glass products	20.2
14. Primary metal industries	23.1
15. Fabricated metal industries	18.7
16. Machinery (except electrical)	20.1
17. Electrical machinery, equipment, & supplies	20.5
18. Transportation equipment (except motor vehicles & ordinance)	27.9
19. Motor vehicles & motor vehicle equipment	14.8
20. Professional photographic equipment & watches	23.2
21. Miscellaneous manufacturing industries	21.9
22. Agricultural production	7.8
23. Agricultural & horticultural services, forestry & fisheries	3.5
24. Metal mining	32.1
25. Coal mining	8.8
26. Crude petroleum & natural gas extraction	28.5
27. Nonmetallic mining & quarrying (except fuel)	1.0
28. Construction	− 5.6
29. Railroads & railway express service	9.3
30. Street railway, bus lines, & taxicab service	−20.2
31. Trucking service, warehousing, & storage	−13.8
32. Water transportation	− 6.4
33. Air transportation	−12.7
34. Pipelines (except natural gas)	13.4
35. Services incidental to transportation	− 0.1
36. Telephone, telegraph, & miscellaneous communication services	12.9
37. Radio broadcasting & television	23.3
38. Electric utilities	20.7
39. Gas utilities	11.6
40. Water supply, sanitary services, & other utilities	37.1
41. Wholesale trade	8.3
42. Retail trade	23.5
43. Finance, insurance, & real estate	34.9
44. Services	18.4

the effective tax rates on the projects may differ. If they do, and if the latter project faces a higher tax rate, it may deliver a lower after-tax return and, hence, not be undertaken. If the two projects face the same tax rate, their relative ranking after-tax will preserve the preference for the latter project.

As it exists today, differential tax treatment causes a suboptimal choice of investments to occur from the social viewpoint—one of the costs of the current tax system. While some distortion of behavior is inevitable for practically any tax system, this particular set of distortions is avoidable and represents a cost that society bears unnecessarily.

The extent of this cost can be quantified by estimating the extent to which the overall capital stock could be reduced without a loss in production, if the current corporate capital stock were allocated efficiently among different assets. This represents the fraction of the capital stock being wasted because of the distortions to asset allocation caused by the present tax system. According to estimates, this social loss was 3.25 percent of the capital stock in 1984. This finding indicates that the effect of removing the distortions would be equivalent to a one-time increase in the corporate capital stock of roughly $75 billion, in terms of the increase in capital productivity. Despite the fact that corporate revenue is so low, this percentage figure is high by historical standards. If the extra capital would earn a before-tax rate of return of 8 percent (a conservative figure), this misallocation of corporate capital reduces before-tax income by $6 billion annually, about 16.7 percent of corporate tax receipts.

DISTORTIONS BETWEEN CORPORATE AND NONCORPORATE SECTORS

In addition to the distortions caused by the differential treatment of assets within the corporate sector, another problem is that investment opportunities there face a different overall tax burden than those outside the corporate sector, especially in the housing sector. Even under the present circumstances, as a result of the favorable tax treatment accorded owner-occupied housing, the incentives to invest in housing are greater than those to invest in corporate capital. This results because housing investment's income, which consists of the imputed rental income earned by the homeowners plus the capital goods on the house, is essentially untaxed and full deductibility of mortgage interest is maintained. Previous studies have considered the social cost of the distorted allocation of capital between the corporate and noncorporate sectors (the latter primarily housing) and found that, generally, this additional distortion in the social allocation of capital is at least as costly as that associated with distorted allocation of capital *within* the corporate sector.

Tax Losses under the Corporate Tax

As depreciation schedules have become more accelerated over the years, more firms have found themselves without taxable income against which to claim deductions. This is easy to understand. Under current tax law, an investor purchasing an asset in the five-year recovery class receives an immediate deduction of 15 percent, a deduction of 22 percent after one year (both on a basis equal to 95 percent of purchase price), and an immediate investment tax credit. Gross receipts in the first year of at least 56.9 cents per invested dollar ([15 + 22] v 0.95 + 10/0.46) would be required to absorb these tax benefits, even without accounting for the fact that investment credits cannot be used to offset all taxable income. Firms without substantial existing sources of income and fast-growing firms are likely to have to carry losses back or forward. Carrying losses forward, however, essentially offsets the benefits of accelerated depreciation. This problem provided an impetus for the introduction of safe-harbor leasing under ERTA in 1981.

Under the typical arrangement of this scheme, the purchaser of the tax benefits (the lessor) received the investment tax credit and depreciation deductions in exchange for an initial "down payment," plus a stream of future tax liabilities. The transaction involved a paper loan by the seller of the tax benefits (the lessee) to make up the difference between the down payment and the full price of the asset. The tax obligations of the lessor reflected the fact that the paper lease payments received exceeded the paper interest payments by an amount equal to the principal repayments made to the lessee. In addition to the down payment, the lessee received a stream of future decreases in tax liability mirroring those of the lessor.

However, this provision for tax benefit transfer was criticized and soon repealed, partly because of the politically unpopular appearance of some profitable lessor companies, who paid little or no corporate taxes by purchasing other firms' tax deductions, and partly because some of the firms using the mechanism to sell their tax benefits were not the high-growth firms envisioned by some as the provision's chief beneficiaries, but, instead, firms whose lack of taxable income derived from poor past earnings performance.

Under such a tax law, this second problem is inevitable since tax losses can come not only from low income but also from high investment and its associated deductions and credits. Aside from the question of desirability, it is difficult to design a system of partial tax loss refundability that distinguishes between the causes for a firm's lack of taxable income. Without any such system, however, the tax system's incentives can be even more perverse. It has been estimated that under current tax law firms without taxable income generally face a higher cost of capital than firms with taxable income because of their inability to utilize the generous investment-related benefits in the years immediately following an asset's purchase. This discrimination applies regardless of the reason for the lack of taxable income. Although there is little empirical evidence on the subject, this problem of tax losses also has been cited as one of the motives for firms to merge, since a firm not able to use its tax benefits will seek to combine with another that can.

The Corporate Tax and the Stock Market

Many may share the view that what's good for the stock market is good for investment and vice versa. However, this view is incorrect when one is considering the impact of the tax code. It is possible, even likely in some cases, for changes in the tax code to have opposite effects on investment and firm value; policies that increase investment can also act to depress the value of corporate equity. The key distinction is between *average* and *marginal* after-tax profitability of corporate assets. The former is relevant for equity valuation; the latter, for investment decisions.

As an extreme, but not totally absurd, example, imagine that

Congress enacted a one-time tax on the value of corporate assets, to be paid by all corporations, and used the revenue thus generated to establish a trust fund whose future revenue would facilitate a reduction in the corporate tax. What would happen to equity values and investment? Since paying the tax would reduce their asset base, equity values would decline by the wealth taxes paid by the corporations. At the same time, the incentive to invest would have increased, since investments offering a given before-tax return would now yield a higher return after taxes. Owners of corporate equity would be worse off, but investment would increase.

Though this may seem far too extreme a case, there exist actual policies that differ from this one primarily in form rather than substance. When enacted, the investment tax credit, for example, was primarily limited to new investment; it was argued that a greater revenue efficiency—"more bang for the buck"—would result. Not only did old assets receive no such tax benefits, but the capital stock expansion that followed the credit's introduction probably drove down the before-tax return to all capital. In turn, this could be expected to have lowered the value of the stock market when the credit was introduced, in anticipation of what was to follow. The same logic applies to the acceleration of depreciation allowances, from which benefit existing assets were excluded.

INCENTIVES FOR INVESTMENT

At any given time, the effects of the tax code can be separated into two parts—on the incentive to invest and on the value of the firm. Any change in the corporate tax affects both measures. In the examples previously discussed, the two effects pushed in opposite directions, but this need not always be the case. However, only the incentive to invest, which relates to the marginal tax rate on new investment, is relevant for current and future corporate decisions. The second part is not irrelevant more generally but is a matter of income distribution rather than changes in economic incentives and should be seen more as a question of fairness and equity: should the owners of corporate equity bear a greater tax burden? Whether the answer is "yes" or "no," it has nothing to do with whether or not the objective is to stimulate investment. As shown previously, an increase in the investment tax credit would lower the marginal tax rate and encourage investment, but it could also lower the value of corporate equity. A similar effect would be expected from the introduction of accelerated depreciation allowances restricted to new investments. Conversely, a corporate tax cut would encourage investment and raise stock values, since its benefits would be extended to existing sources of income, while, at the same time, the relative advantages of new investments from accelerated depreciation would be reduced by the lower rate at which depreciation allowances could be deducted. Therefore, old assets would gain more in tax reductions than they would lose through a before-tax return lowered by the competition of more new capital. Whether this outcome is viewed as preferable may depend on the composition of one's portfolio. As a way of spending tax dollars to encourage investment, however, it is less efficient since a greater fraction of the revenue loss is absorbed by firms who do little or no investment.

As the corporate tax has come to include the investment tax credit and ever more accelerated depreciation allowances, this distinction between old and new capital becomes more important. For example, a new piece of equipment in the five-year depreciation class receives deductions and credits with a present value close to fifty after-tax cents per dollar invested. After five years, the same asset, though perhaps nearly as productive, has no such tax benefits remaining.

It can be calculated that the existing corporate fixed capital stock is currently worth approximately 66 percent of its replacement cost solely because of the tax distinction between new and old assets. The present value of tax deductions and investment tax credits that owners of existing capital can expect to receive on these assets is so much smaller than what they would receive on comparable new assets that the resulting after-tax cash flows are 33 percent lower in present value. Rational asset pricing in the stock market would be expected to reflect this discount. The predicted decline in market value since 1980 attributable to tax changes represents about half this full discount, about 17 percent of the total replacement value of the fixed corporate capital stock. This drop in value occurred while the marginal tax rates on new investment were declining and the tax-related incentives to invest were increasing.

THE CORPORATE TAX AND FOREIGN COMPETITION

The United States has recently experienced foreign trade deficits of enormous magnitudes, exceeding $100 billion annually. Many economists have suggested that the immediate cause was the strong dollar and that the indirect cause was perhaps the historically high real interest rates that result from government credit demands induced by unprecedented federal budget deficits and tight monetary policy. Others have concentrated on the potential competitive advantages enjoyed by foreign competitors, especially the Japanese. The success of Japan in exporting steel and automobiles, two especially depressed American industries, makes the United States particularly sensitive to Japanese-American differences. While many competitive differences between the United States and Japan have been considered, the one relevant question here is whether or not Japanese businesses enjoy a lower cost of capital than their American counterparts.

In an influential 1983 study, entitled *High Cost of Capital: America's Industrial Handicap*, George Hatsopoulos offers measures of real capital cost before-tax in the United States that were much higher than his measures for Japan and argues that much of this difference was due to the corporate tax provisions in the United States. Hatsopoulos estimates that the real before-tax cost of capital services in the U.S. in 1981 was 18.76 percent, including the cost of asset depreciation, and 12.36 percent, excluding this cost. (This latter number may be considered as the before-tax rate of return a project must earn for the firm undertaking just to meet its capital cost.) In contrast, he estimates that Japanese companies faced a real cost of capital of only 5.54 percent in 1981, *including* depreciation, and slightly less than zero, *net* of depreciation. Hence, his work suggests a difference in the real costs of capital of approximately thirteen percentage points between the United States and Japan.

Hatsopoulos also offers estimates of the cost of funds after taxes in the two countries, where the gap in costs persists. He finds that the real cost of funds after taxes in the United States was approximately +6.4 percent in 1981, while it was −1.8 percent in Japan in the same year. This difference of over eight percentage points in the after-tax cost of capital is the primary reason why before-tax costs of capital differ, since a much larger before-tax difference would be necessary to provide an after-tax difference of 8 percent. Thus, the immediate source of the cost of capital difference between the two countries is the *after-tax* cost of funds—the overall return, adjusted for inflation, that is received by owners of corporate securities in their respective countries. It is extremely difficult to understand how this difference can be attributed to corporate tax differentials since it is a difference in costs that corporations must meet *net* of taxes. Furthermore, given the low U.S. effective corporate tax rates, complete repeal of the corporate tax could close only a small fraction of this gap.

If these estimates are accurate, then the relevant question is why, in an integrated world capital market, Japanese firms have access to cheaper funds than American firms do. This is an important question since the effects of such a gap in capital cost, regardless of the root cause, could be devastating to U.S. investment in the long run. However, the appropriate policy response depends crucially on where the gap originates. If financial costs differ in the two countries, there is an implication that there must be important barriers to the free flow of capital funds from Japan to the United States. Otherwise, the relatively attractive rates here would draw away funds from Japanese industry until rates in Japan rose to a competitive level. If there are such restrictions of capital flows, this is a problem of foreign policy, not tax policy.

Reform of the Corporate Tax

The corporate tax has declined as a source of revenue, but it still distorts behavior, and it is a prime candidate for tax reform. How should alternative reform proposals be evaluated? There are a number of relevant criteria. Under present circumstances, the revenue effect is perhaps the most obvious. Equally important to consider is the impact on the incentive to invest and the extent to which the distortions among assets and firms are reduced. Finally, the effect on the value of corporate equity, as distinct from the incentive to invest, is a good measure of how much of the lost tax revenue is effectively transferred to owners of corporate equity. A program that engenders a larger transfer is likely to have less "left over" to stimulate new investment.

REPEAL

In 1983, President Ronald Reagan struck a chord in the minds of many when he proposed abolishing the corporate tax. Indeed, this is a simple proposal. Aside from the total corporate tax revenue loss that would occur, there would be the beneficial impact that all assets would face the same effective corporate tax rate (zero) as would all firms, regardless of whether or not they had positive income. However, this would be an extremely inefficient way of reducing marginal tax rates since the value of existing equity would rise substantially to reflect the extension of the same zero tax treatment to all existing sources of corporate income. This transfer would be roughly $750 million based on the current degree of tax capitalization previously cited and the size of the net corporate fixed capital stock of well over $2 trillion. Hence, repeal would lead to allocative efficiency and increased investment incentives, but it would entail great revenue cost.

CASH-FLOW TAXATION

One of the reforms of the individual tax base often discussed, at least among economists, is the shift from taxing income to taxing consumption expenditures. Such a tax has also been called a cash-flow tax since households would be taxed on receipts (income plus the proceeds of asset sales) less asset purchases. The tax treatment would resemble that currently accorded Individual Retirement Accounts (IRAs) in the United States and, as with IRAs, would remove the tax on the return to savings. Investments would be made out of before-tax dollars, and principal and accumulated interest, when withdrawn, would also be treated as before-tax. Therefore, without changes in the individual's marginal tax rate, the after-tax and before-tax returns would be the same. For example, $100 invested would cost a taxpayer in the 40 percent bracket only $60 and, at a 10 percent rate of return before-tax, generate proceeds one year later of $100 before-tax and, if withdrawn, $66 after-tax—a 10 percent after-tax return.

The same principle could be applied at the corporate level, as was discussed by England's Meade committee in its report, *The Structure and Reform of Direct Taxation*. Such a proposal would be accomplished through the replacement of depreciation deductions and the investment tax credit with the ability to expense investments immediately. Compared to current treatment, this would represent a marginal tax increase for equipment, but a sharp decrease for other corporate investments. At the same time, financial investments would be treated symmetrically, preserving interest deductions but *including* borrowing in the tax base. Thus, in place of investment credits and depreciation allowances, firms would be allowed immediate write-off of the portion of new investments financed by equity.

Some firms would gain and others lose under cash-flow taxation, depending on their asset and financial mixes. But all firms would face a zero marginal tax rate on all investments, just as they would under outright repeal. The primary difference would be that by not removing the tax on income from existing corporate capital, the $750 million windfall associated with repeal would be avoided. However, without some companion provision for the sale or transfer of tax benefits, the greater acceleration of investment deductions would worsen the problem of insufficient taxable income to use these deductions that faces many investing firms.

One proposed alternative to tax benefit transfer, accomplished briefly through safe-harbor leasing, would be to offer firms that are forced to carry unused tax benefits forward a nominal interest rate on these benefits and to allow such benefits to accrue indefinitely without the current fifteen-year expiration limit. This provision would lessen the penalty placed on firms in a temporary loss position without opening the Internal Revenue Service to the assaults of fictitious companies with nonexistent investments and tax losses. While this type of reform of the treatment of tax losses could be applied under any version of the corporate tax, it would be especially relevant under any system with heavily front-loading investment deductions, such as the current system and, especially, one with a cash-flow tax instead.

TAX SIMPLIFICATION SCHEMES

Several proposals to simplify the tax system and broaden the tax base have been made in recent years, and some include major changes in the corporate tax. Two proposals for revamping the corporate tax were introduced in Congress in 1983, and the Department of the Treasury's own plan was unveiled at the end of 1984. One of the congressional bills, the Bradley-Gephardt "fair tax," is especially like the Treasury's plan in its treatment of the corporate sector. Both plans would lower the corporate tax rate (to 30 percent and 33 percent, respectively) and restore the lost revenue by eliminating the investment tax credit and basing depreciation allowances on more realistic estimates of economic depreciation. However, the proposals differ in two important respects. The Treasury's plan also would permit the eventual deduction of 50 percent of dividends paid and provide price-level indexation for depreciation allowances and interest deductions. As stressed previously, since the sensitivity of effective corporate tax rates to inflation is due to the lack of such indexing, such provisions will eliminate this dependence. Further examination of the impact of the partial dividends-paid deduction will be deferred until the general consideration of tax integration proposals.

The Fair Tax—Because of the similarity of the Bradley-Gephardt fair tax plan and the Treasury's plan, the effects of only the first need to be reviewed in further detail. In terms of its costs and benefits it, like the Treasury's proposal, lies somewhere along the road to repeal from the current system—there would be fewer distortions, but windfalls would occur. The distortions would be almost entirely eliminated, but under repeal perhaps half of the windfall gains for corporate shareholders would remain.

To allow consideration of the impact on distortions in investment incentives, Table 3 presents estimated effective tax rates under the Bradley-Gephardt proposal for the same assets and under the same economic assumptions as those for the current tax system presented in Table 1. The range in effective tax rates is reduced from between −28.9 percent and +42.5 percent to between 14.8 percent and 42.1 percent. The change is even more striking across industries, shown in Table 4. Compared to the current tax system (Table 2), industry-level tax rates range from 24.2 percent to 33.1 percent, instead of from −20.2 percent to 37.1 percent. These changes lead to a substantial reduction in the estimated "capital wastage" cost due to a distorted asset mix. From the current 3.25 percent of the capital stock, it is estimated that all but 0.10 percentage points of this cost would be eliminated—a result virtually as good as could be achieved were the corporate tax simply repealed.

TABLE 3. EFFECTIVE TAX RATES IN PERCENT

Asset Class	Bradley-Gephardt
1. Furniture & fixtures	25.8
2. Fabricated metal products	23.4
3. Engines & turbines	30.1
4. Tractors	14.8
5. Agricultural machinery	24.1
6. Construction machinery	33.0
7. Mining & oilfield machinery	32.3
8. Metalworking machinery	27.4
9. Special industrial machinery	24.9
10. General industrial machinery	27.4
11. Office & computing machinery	42.1
12. Service industry machinery	32.3
13. Electrical equipment	26.8
14. Trucks, buses, & trailers	29.1
15. Automobiles	24.2
16. Aircraft	23.8
17. Ships & boats	29.9
18. Railroad equipment	28.2
19. Instruments	30.3
20. Other equipment	30.3
21. Industrial buildings	31.0
22. Commercial buildings	27.6
23. Religious buildings	25.8
24. Educational buildings	25.8
25. Hospitals	27.2
26. Other nonfarm buildings	33.5
27. Railroads	25.4
28. Telephone & telegraph	30.2
29. Electric light & power	29.2
30. Gas	29.2
31. Other public utilities	33.4
32. Farm structures	27.3
33. Mining, shafts & wells	18.3
34. Other nonresidential structures	28.9
Aggregate	28.4

TABLE 4. EFFECTIVE TAX RATES BY INDUSTRY IN PERCENT

Industry Number	Bradley-Gephardt
1. Food & kindred products	29.4
2. Tobacco manufacturers	29.2
3. Textile mill products	28.0

TABLE 4. EFFECTIVE TAX RATES BY INDUSTRY IN PERCENT

Industry Number	Bradley-Gephardt
4. Apparel & other fabricated textile products	29.3
5. Paper & allied products	27.6
6. Printing, publishing, & allied industries	29.2
7. Chemicals & allied products	28.2
8. Petroleum & coal products	30.0
9. Rubber & miscellaneous plastic products	28.7
10. Leather & leather products	28.7
11. Lumber & wood products (except furniture)	28.8
12. Furniture & fixtures	29.5
13. Stone, clay, & glass products	29.1
14. Primary metal industries	29.3
15. Fabricated metal industries	29.4
16. Machinery (except electrical)	30.1
17. Electrical machinery, equipment, & supplies	29.8
18. Transportation equipment (except motor vehicles & ordinance)	29.9
19. Motor vehicles & motor vehicle equipment	29.8
20. Professional photographic equipment & watches	30.7
21. Miscellaneous manufacturing industries	30.0
22. Agricultural production	24.2
23. Agricultural & horticultural services, forestry & fisheries	23.8
24. Metal mining	30.8
25. Coal mining	31.3
26. Crude petroleum & natural gas extraction	23.2
27. Nonmetallic mining & quarrying (except fuel)	31.5
28. Construction	31.8
29. Railroads & railway express service	26.9
30. Street railway, bus lines, & taxicab service	26.9
31. Trucking service, warehousing, & storage	29.0
32. Water transportation	29.9
33. Air transportation	24.0
34. Pipelines (except natural gas)	33.1
35. Services incidental to transportation	29.2
36. Telephone, telegraph, & miscellaneous communication services	28.7
37. Radio broadcasting & television	29.4
38. Electric utilities	29.0
39. Gas utilities	29.2
40. Water supply, sanitary services, & other utilities	28.9
41. Wholesale trade	28.6
42. Retail trade	28.1
43. Finance, insurance, & real estate	28.1
44. Services	28.6

There also would be windfalls associated with the proposal since reductions in the corporate rate would be enjoyed by all, not just those making new investments. Estimates show that the tax discount present in the market valuation of the corporate stock would be, roughly, halved and reach again its pre-1981 level. This tax revenue leakage is evidenced elsewhere. As shown in Table 3, effective marginal tax rates, in the aggregate, would rise approximately nine percentage points under the Bradley-Gephardt plan, even though government revenue estimates suggest it would be, roughly, revenue neutral. This would occur because some of the revenue is being given away; to prevent an overall loss in revenue, marginal tax rates must be increased.

This proposal, like the Treasury's plan, could be made more efficient through a scheduled phase-in of the corporate rate reduction. This provision would limit the extent to which existing income sources would benefit from the tax cut. Phased reduction in rates also could be coupled with a phased deceleration of depreciation allowances resulting in two additional benefits. First, it would make more credible the government's commitment to lowering rates as scheduled, for this would be the *quid pro quo* for the continued phase-out of accelerated depreciation. Second, the prospect of depreciation allowances being reduced on future *new* investment would provide firms with an additional incentive to invest during the years of the phase-in period, while relatively accelerated depreciation allowances were still available. Estimates suggest that such a phase-in would not only raise revenue but also would provide a greater incentive to invest during the phase-in period, because firms would act to make their investments and get their largest depreciation deductions at the highest possible tax rates.

TAX INTEGRATION

If one were designing a tax system *de novo*, one might very well eschew a separate corporate tax and, instead, prefer to tax corporations' individual owners based on their own circumstances rather than those of the corporations. If it were easier to collect taxes from corporations because of their size and sophistication, they might be used as withholding agents for individual capital income taxes as employers serve today for wage and salary income. But this would not constitute an argument for retaining an entirely separate tax on corporations.

This is essentially the notion behind proposals to integrate corporation and personal income taxes. "Full" integration proposals would remove the corporation income tax, attribute all corporate earnings to shareholders, and continue to collect taxes from corporations only for withholding purposes. Though this proposal is conceptually straightforward, it would be difficult to institute in practice. There are many other schemes in the "partial" integration category.

Dividend Relief—Such proposals would continue to tax retained earnings at the corporate level, but would tax dividends only at the individual level, either by allowing corporations a deduction for dividends paid or by allowing shareholders a credit against taxes based on dividends received. The credit method would have individuals "gross-up" dividends received to include the corporate taxes on the earnings from which the dividends were paid, count this larger number as income, but allow a credit against individual taxes for corporate taxes already paid. Therefore, the corporate tax on distributed earnings would be converted into a withholding tax. However, the difference would be that tax-exempt and foreign shareholders who do not pay U.S. income tax would have no taxes to offset with the credits so earned. This is the proposal's main difference from the approach that allows corporations a deduction for dividends paid. (The Treasury's recent proposal would allow a partial deduction of 50 percent rather than a full deduction of dividends paid.) This treatment of foreigners, however, might run afoul of existing tax treaty provisions against substantial withholding taxes on capital income.

New Equity Relief—The primary argument for dividend relief is that dividends are now double taxed—both at corporate and at individual levels. While true, this view ignores the fact that most dividends come from earnings generated by investments from retained earnings, which come from before-tax dollars. As a result, there is an initial offset to the stockholder level of dividend taxation. Dividends are eventually taxed, but on earnings from investments from funds for which dividend taxes were avoided. Hence, at least one level of the "double taxation" argument is suspect. For example, suppose an individual shareholder is in the 40 percent tax bracket. If the corporation retains $100 more of earnings to purchase additional assets, this reduces the investor's after-tax income by $60. If the new investment yields 10 percent, after corporate taxes it will permit a permanent dividend increase of $10 a year, resulting in increased after-tax income of $6 a year for the investor. This amounts to a 10 percent return on the initial out-of-pocket investment of $60; the dividend tax does not further reduce the after-tax corporate rate of return.

This same logic does not hold, however, when the equity funds are generated by the sale of new shares, since there is no coincident avoidance of dividend taxes. Thus, it is investment through equity issues that is discriminated against, not all equity-financed investment. Some proposals have recognized this distinction, notably one contained in the appendix to a recent study on the corporation income tax produced by the American Law Institute (ALI). This proposal would allow firms a dividends-paid deduction based on the fraction of new equity in their total equity base (new equity defined as equity funds raised through new issues after the scheme's effective date).

THE EFFECTS OF INTEGRATION

As the preceding exploration indicates, integration may have effects other than those often assumed. In particular, to the extent that equity funds come from retentions, a cut in the total tax rate on dividends through a dividend-relief scheme would have little, if any, effect, because the benefit received when future earnings are distributed would be offset by the smaller dividend tax forgone when the investment was originally made. Using the same numerical example as before, with a dividend tax rate of 20 percent or zero, no effect on the after-tax rate of return would arise. For the remaining equity investments, those financed with new shares, dividend relief *would* provide an incentive to invest, just as the ALI scheme would. The primary difference between the approaches would be the cost, the latter being larger by an amount equal to the increase in stock values associated with the removal of taxes on future dividends traceable to funds already within the corporation. The differences between the two approaches are completely analogous to the difference between corporate tax repeal and corporate cash-flow taxation. In this case, it is the removal of dividend taxes on income from existing sources, rather than corporate taxes, that would result in a windfall, but the implications are the same.

Full integration, like dividend relief, would remove the double taxation of dividends. It would differ by replacing the corporate tax on retentions present under both current law and dividend relief schemes with the individual income tax. Hence, to the extent that such rates are similar, its effects, including the windfall, would be analogous to those of dividend-relief schemes.

An additional technical problem with any of the integration schemes discussed arises when considering the treatment of so-called "preference" income—income shielded from taxation through the use of tax credits or accelerated depreciation, for example. If a company has a surfeit of such tax benefits, as many do, what credits, if any, should its shareholders receive under a gross-up-and-credit system? If they do receive credits, they are being permitted credits for taxes never paid. If they do not receive credits, then no tax relief for dividends paid is being granted. Similar problems arise under the other schemes. In general, it is difficult to implement a system designed to integrate two income taxes when the corporate tax has moved so far from income as its base.

Conclusions

The corporation income tax has declined as a source of revenue but not as a source of distortion. This is not the result of a single change in policy, but of several independent historical changes that make even less sense when viewed as a whole than they might have when originally viewed in isolation. The corporate tax today imposes a small aggregate burden on new corporate investment, but the burden ranges substantially across particular investments. This is the source of much of the distortion caused by the tax, although the differential treatment of corporations according to their taxable income status is also a source, as is the overall distortion in the allocation of capital between corporate and noncorporate uses.

Because of the capitalized tax differential in the value of existing corporate assets, reform proposals that would include a corporate rate reduction involve a transfer of tax revenue to the owners of existing assets. Similar problems arise with certain tax integration proposals. The ultimate cost of such transfers is that, for a given total tax collection, *effective* marginal tax rates must be increased to pay for them. Alternatives do exist, however, that would limit such wealth transfers without sacrificing the major benefits of reform—namely, simplicity and a reduction in the distortions currently present.

Irwin Friend

4

Effects of Taxation on Financial Markets

In exploring the impact of taxation on financial markets, this chapter's major focus is on the differential effects of different kinds of taxes on the principal types of financial assets and liabilities, on markets and institutions which deal in these instruments, and on the economy as a whole as a result. Obviously, any increase in total taxes lowers the funds available for private saving and investment, as well as private consumption, and, other things being equal, adversely affects financial markets. However, it will be assumed that the total levels of government expenditures and taxes are held constant. Hence, the concern here is not with the effects of increasing or decreasing the total level of taxation, but with the differential impact of different taxes on total saving and, therefore, on financial markets and on the channeling of current and accumulated saving into major types of financial instruments, markets, and institutions. After examining the effects of different taxes on total saving, the effects of these taxes on the major types of assets

IRWIN FRIEND *is the Edward J. Hopkinson Professor of Finance and Economics and the director of the Rodney L. White Center for Financial Research at the Wharton School of the University of Pennsylvania. Dr. Friend is a past president of the American Finance Association. He has written many articles for numerous prestigious international journals and several books; his most recent is* The Structure and Reform of the U.S. Tax System.

and liabilities and the related markets and institutions will be considered. Special attention will be paid to the rationale for and consequences of the capital gains tax, because it has been one of the most controversial taxes since the inception of the federal income tax and is frequently alleged to have a unique role in the market for risky assets, particularly common stock. This tax, like several other taxes affecting financial markets, would undergo a major change under the tax proposal made public by the U.S. Department of the Treasury at the end of 1984.

Effects of Taxation on Saving

Since the rate of private saving determines the overall real value of changes in—and the level of—household and business net worth and also has a pervasive effect on all types of assets and liabilities, the analysis of the effects of taxation on financial markets should begin with an examination of effects on saving. Because this chapter's primary interest is in aggregate or realized saving (saving equal to investment for the economy as a whole) the effects of taxation must be considered not only on the propensity to save but also on the propensity to invest. Only private saving should be considered here since it is assumed that government revenue and expenditure and, therefore, government saving are held constant.

For a given level of federal government revenue and expenditure, the primary tax mechanisms that have been used, either implicitly or explicitly, for affecting the propensity to save have been the allocations of total taxes between taxes on capital income (levied directly on individuals or indirectly through corporations) and taxes on labor income. While the main concern here is with the after-tax interest sensitivity of saving and investment propensities, and ultimately realized saving, the effects of shifting taxes from capital income to labor income (or vice versa) on the incentive to work or on the burden of taxation on different socioeconomic groups cannot be completely ignored. Thus, if lower taxes on capital income do, as commonly perceived, increase realized saving, they still might be undesirable if they depress work incentives or if they make the tax structure regressive since upper-income groups receive a much larger share of capital than of labor income. Some "supply-side" economists might question the implicit assumption that a decrease in tax rates is not likely to increase the demand for and income of both capital and labor sufficiently to offset the adverse effect of lower tax rates on the government deficit, but there is no evidence, including the federal government's recent experiment in supply-side economics, that would support their position.

Before examining relevant theory and empirical evidence on the effect of capital income taxation on aggregate saving, it should be noted that recent estimates by Joseph Pechman indicate that, as a result of changes in the tax structure over the last decade, capital income is no longer taxed more heavily than labor income. In fact, Pechman's estimates of the current tax burden imply that for most economic groups labor income is somewhat more heavily taxed than capital income—a finding characterizing marginal as well as average tax rates. These estimates also indicate that, when all forms of taxation are combined, the present tax structure is only moderately progressive and less progressive than it was a decade earlier.

While there is no consensus among economists about the after-tax return elasticities of private or aggregate saving, my own assessment, documented in the technical literature, indicates that neither relevant theory nor empirical evidence provides much support for the belief that higher after-tax rates of return on assets stimulate the private sector's propensity to save. There is evidence that a redistribution of after-tax income from the lower- to the upper-income groups, regardless of its form, would increase the private sector's saving-to-income ratio, at least in the short or intermediate run but not necessarily in the long run. Thus, it might be possible to stimulate the aggregate propensity to save by shifting the overall burden of taxation (on both labor and capital incomes) from the upper- to the lower-income groups. However, there is no strong evidence that the effect on saving of this regressive shift would be either large or sustained

In view of the substantially higher propensity to save by corporations than by individuals, a shift in taxation from corporations to individuals would probably increase the aggregate propensity to save, at least in the short and intermediate runs. A rise in the corporate saving-to-income ratio would probably be partly offset by a decline in the household saving-to-income ratio, reflecting lower direct saving by stockholders. However, except perhaps in the long run when higher corporate saving is associated with higher household wealth, it is unlikely that the offset will be anywhere near complete. Yet, it should be noted that the fairly pronounced shift in taxes over the past decade from capital to labor income and from corporations to individuals, together with the general decline in the progressiveness of the tax structure, especially for the top income group, was associated with a decline in the ratios of income to personal, private, and total saving to their lowest levels since the postwar adjustment in the late 1940s. This was true in spite of the specific additional saving incentives provided by IRA, Keogh, and similar plans.

While the impact of capital income taxes on saving behavior via an after-tax return effect is not entirely clear, even in direction, both theory and empirical evidence seem to indicate a negative impact of the cost of capital on investment. However, for risky investment the cost of capital is not necessarily positively related to the level of income taxes, as might be expected. Theoretical considerations do suggest a positive effect of higher corporation income taxes on the cost of capital and, therefore, a negative effect on stock prices and investment. However, this is not necessarily true of higher personal income taxes, at least in the short run, since under certain plausible assumptions (including personal tax credits for investment losses) investor risk is decreased more than expected return. The required rate of return on risky assets thereby may be reduced by higher personal tax rates. Conversely, both theory and empirical evidence point to a positive relation between the cost of capital and the level of corporation income taxation and, hence, a negative relation between the cost of capital and the magnitude of investment tax credits and depreciation deductions. Even in this instance, however, the effectiveness of changes in corporation income taxation on investment would be limited in the long run by the apparent long-run ineffectiveness of such changes on saving incentives.

Combining these different strands of theoretical and empirical evidence relating to separate effects of capital income taxation (corporate and personal) on saving and investment behavior, it is apparent that a reduction of capital income taxes, especially at the corporate level, initially would stimulate investment over the cycle. However, the long-run effect on capital formation is likely to be moderate if the assessment of the apparently low after-tax interest elasticity of saving is correct. Maximizing the effect on investment would require strongly regressive changes in the tax structure, such as the combination of eliminating corporation income taxes and either raising taxes on labor income or substituting flat consumption taxes for progressive income taxes. Such changes would probably raise corporations' propensity to invest in both the short and long run and stimulate aggregate saving, at least in the short and intermediate runs, in view of the higher saving propensity of the upper-income groups. Thus, it is possible—but by no means certain—that a significant increase in capital formation could be effected, at least for a number of years, by a substantial increase in the regressiveness of the tax structure.

It should be emphasized, however, that in the long run the apparently low after-tax interest elasticity of saving would limit any increase in capital formation and, therefore, realized saving that might be associated with a more regressive tax structure or with the substitution of taxes on labor income for those on capital income. Moreover, any beneficial effect of such changes in the tax structure on economic growth as a result of the stimulation of investment might be offset, at least in part, by weakened labor incentives when lower taxes on capital income are financed by higher taxes on labor income. More importantly, changes in the structure of taxes are not likely to greatly affect the aggregate level of realized saving.

Effects of Taxation on Financial Instruments

Although total saving does not seem to be affected substantially by the structure of taxes, the demand for and supply of different financial instruments are quite sensitive to the large variations in effective tax rates applicable to the income from these instruments. While there is a substantial amount of econometric evidence to this effect, perhaps the evidence more convincing to many is the observed major shift of funds in recent years from one type of institution or investment to other types. The shift has occurred in response to fluctuations in relative after-tax returns as a result of the elimination of regulatory constraints on interest rates or the introduction of preferential tax treatment for certain forms of saving. Such shifts, of course, have no necessary implications for total saving.

COMMON STOCK

Thus, the extremely low effective tax rate on capital gains, which has been estimated to be in the neighborhood of 5 percent for common stock, probably has increased significantly the demand for and price of such securities. It would also be expected to decrease the corporate dividend payout ratio and correspondingly raise earnings retention. Surprisingly, there is no evidence of such an effect in U.S. time series data available since World War I in spite of the major increase in the tax advantage of capital gains over dividend and other ordinary income during this period.

CORPORATE BONDS AND PREFERRED STOCK

Similarly, the preferential treatment provided to the issuance of corporate bonds instead of stock, a result of the exemption of interest payments from corporate income taxes, has served to stimulate the issuance of bonds at the expense of stock, to depress the supply of new stock, and to bolster stock prices yet again. The corporate tax advantage of bonds is appreciably greater than the personal tax advantage of stock. Just as it is surprising, given the tax structure, that corporations pay out so much in dividends, it is almost as surprising that corporations do not issue more bonds. However, the risk aversion of management, whose investment risk in their company's stock (associated with both human and nonhuman wealth) cannot be diversified away as easily as for other investors, may help explain the relatively low corporate debt ratio in the United States, but it does not clarify the low earnings retention.

With one notable exception, the tax treatment of preferred stock is less favorable than that of bonds and common stock. Bonds have the same type of corporate tax advantages over preferred stock that they have over common stock. This has resulted in a marked decline in the issuance of preferred stock as compared with bonds subsequent to the 1920s, when corporate tax rates were low and, therefore, not a major factor in financing decisions. Common stock has the same type of personal tax advantages over preferred stock that it has over bonds since most return from preferred stock, like that from bonds, is subject to ordinary income tax rates rather than capital gains tax rates.

The one tax advantage preferred stock has over bonds is that dividends received by corporations from investment in preferred, as well as common stock, are subject to a low rate of taxation. As a result, many corporations favor holding preferred stock in their portfolios rather than bonds. Aside from control purposes, corporations favor holding preferred rather than common stock because of its generally higher quality rating. As a result of these differential tax rates, individuals hold relatively small amounts of corporate bonds and preferred stock. Corporate bonds are held mainly by insurance organizations and other institutions that are tax-exempt or taxed at preferential rates. Preferred stock is held mainly by taxable financial and nonfinancial corporations. Corporate common stock is held by individuals, tax-exempt institutions, and by other corporations for control purposes.

GOVERNMENT BONDS

Substantial amounts of long-term U.S. government bonds are owned by all major sectors of the population, including taxable as well as nontaxable corporations, institutions, and individuals. In spite of the general absence of any major tax advantages associated with income from such bonds, this widespread ownership is attributable to these bonds' high marketability and their great appeal to risk-averse investors who want to insure a given flow of income for a prolonged period.

Tax-exempt state and local government obligations are owned mainly by individuals, commercial banks, and insurance companies other than life insurance companies. For obvious reasons, they are not held to any appreciable extent by tax-exempt institutions. In recent years, federal income tax exemption has been granted not only to general obligations of municipalities and revenue bonds associated with the financing of traditional types of public works but also to revenue bonds issued by private industrial corporations and to bonds for financing private housing, hospitals, and universities, all under the auspices of municipalities.

MORTGAGES

Mortgages, largely for residential housing, constitute the remaining major type of financial investment whose demand and supply are greatly affected by differential taxation. They are held mainly by savings and loan associations and other savings institutions and to a lesser extent by commercial banks and individuals. The deduction of mortgage interest payments and the noninclusion of imputed rental income on owned homes in the calculation of taxable income greatly increases the demand for owned homes and for mortgage financing. Prior to the changes in the corporate tax law under the Reagan administration, the taxation of income and expenses associated with homeownership was more favorable than the corresponding taxation for business investment and stimulated investment in housing at the expense of plant and equipment. After changes in corporate taxes had lowered substantially the marginal tax rates on most new investment, it was not clear how the effective marginal tax rates compared on income from investment in housing and income from business investment. The average corporation income tax rates have remained higher than those on income associated with housing investment, especially when allowance is made for the double taxation of corporate income. However, both average and, even more so, marginal effective tax rates vary greatly for different corporate activities and investments.

It should be noted that while it is generally possible to determine the qualitative differences in the incidence of the tax structure on different financial instruments, it is much more difficult to estimate the quantitative differences. Since one reason for this difficulty is the existence of tax-exempt institutions and other investors with widely different effective tax rates, computation of effective marginal tax rates is subject to a major margin of error even when the relative importance of institutional and other holdings of the different instruments is known. Another reason is the set of complications introduced by uncertainty, which obscures even the direction of the effect of income taxes (with loss offsets) on the demand for risky assets. Third, it is extremely difficult to hold risk constant when attempting to estimate the effect of taxes on two groups of financial investments subject to different tax rates.

State and local taxation generally does not have as significant an effect on investment in different assets as do federal income and capital gains taxes. The major state and local taxes bearing on the form of investment are the real estate tax, which serves as a partial offset to favorable federal tax treatment of such assets, and, less important in its aggregate amount, the personal property tax. State income taxes are also of some importance in certain states. Personal property and state income taxes, from the viewpoint of the financial markets, constitute an annoying impediment to market efficiency even though the total amounts involved are not large. Thus, securities issued by municipalities within a state are normally exempted from state personal income and personal property taxes, and preferential tax treatment is sometimes accorded to corporations paying a franchise tax to the state. Therefore, there is a tax or noneconomic incentive to invest in a relatively nondiversified or unnecessarily risky portfolio. Less importantly, but a nuisance from the viewpoint of the financial markets, it is possible in some states to avoid personal property taxes by shifting some assets (e.g., shares in no-load mutual stock funds or shares in money market funds) into bank deposits for one day at the end of the year.

The obvious question that arises is: what are the implications of differential taxation of the various types of financial instruments? Clearly, the financial institutions and markets that specialize in tax-favored instruments benefit at the expense of other institutions and markets, at least until the economy fully adjusts to the differential taxes and equilibrium with competitive returns is achieved for all investors and business organizations. However, more fundamentally, differential tax rates on different financial instruments or financial institutions interfere with their basic objective—to funnel current and accumulated saving into those investments perceived as offering the highest rate of economic (before-tax) return for a given degree of risk and for the lowest possible transaction cost. Preferential taxation may stimulate activity in economically inefficient markets and institutions and contribute both to an inefficient allocation of economic investment and to nonoptimal portfolios for investors. The quantitative cost in loss of allocational efficiency associated with differential taxes of income from different financial or economic sources is virtually impossible to estimate with any precision. However, crude efforts to estimate these losses in specific cases (e.g., the double taxation of corporate income and the preferential corporate tax treatment of bond interest as compared with dividend payout) have suggested that such costs could be sizable. In any case, there is no obvious reason why such costs should be borne.

The differential taxation of the various types of financial instruments also has an undesirable effect on the corporate capital structure, artificially stimulating the issuance of bonds and raising the corporate risk exposure, although, as noted earlier, its effect does not seem to be as large as anticipated. When equity is used, the current structure of taxes encourages internal financing through retention of earnings rather than external financing through capital markets. It is frequently argued, though it is not clear how validly, that allocational efficiency would be improved if new equity financing were systematically exposed to the discipline of the competitive capital markets.

Also, differential taxation of several major classes of financial investments may have a significant impact on the burden of taxation on different income groups, as well as on other groups in the population. Stock which is taxed more favorably than fixed-interest-bearing obligations is owned mainly by the wealthy. This is especially true for stock whose returns come largely from capital gains and for investors who can afford not to realize their gains.

Effects of Capital Gains Taxes on the Stock Market

In the past, capital gains have been treated as ordinary income on occasion and subjected to preferential tax rates at other times; the degree of preferential treatment has varied widely over different periods. The treatment of capital losses also has varied greatly in different years, ranging from no allowance for such losses to limited and full deductibility from capital gains or other income. Long-term and short-term capital gains have also been treated differently for tax purposes, their specific provisions subject to substantial changes from time to time. In particular, provisions relating to the holding period that distinguishes short-term from long-term capital gains have varied significantly.

Currently, for assets held longer than six months, 40 percent of realized net gains are included in adjusted gross revenue for tax purposes, and 50 percent of losses from short-term transactions are deductible from taxable income. Only realized gains are subject to taxation, and capital gains taxes can be completely avoided if the assets are held until the owner's death. As a result, the effective rate of capital gains taxation is much smaller than the normal rate on realized gains. Thus, as noted earlier, for several years in the past the effective capital gains tax on common stock is estimated to have been only about 5 percent.

As distinguished from their treatment in taxable income, all real capital gains, which consist of net gains adjusted for inflation, would be considered as part of economic income. This would be true for unrealized as well as realized gains. In the presence of inflationary price movement, nominal capital gains should be adjusted downward (and may be negative) since only the value (in current dollars) of the change in real assets should be included in income. The effective tax rate on capital gains as a whole is, in most periods and for most taxpayers, substantially less than it would be if all real capital gains, both realized and unrealized, were included in both taxable and economic income. This is not necessarily true in periods of rampant inflation when owners of financial assets, including equities and debt, may suffer large real losses. However, the likelihood of sizable losses on common stock that result from unexpected inflation has been reduced substantially by changes in corporate taxation that resulted in a more rapid write-off of plant and equipment expenditures; also the rate of inflation has moderated greatly.

Many reasons have been advanced for the preferential tax

treatment of capital gains. Perhaps the most important is that it is widely believed that the more favorable this treatment, the better for saving and investment. From this point of view, private saving is supposed to be stimulated by the higher after-tax rate of return achieved by lower taxes on all forms of capital income, and the effective cost of capital to all forms of investment is lowered. However, as indicated earlier, there is no strong theoretical or empirical reason for the belief that a decline in personal income taxes will have a substantial, sustained effect on the propensity to save or on the cost of capital. While there are strong theoretical and empirical grounds for expecting the cost of capital to be positively related to the level of corporation income taxes so that a reduction in such taxes probably would stimulate investment, the long-run effect on capital formation is likely to be moderate if the after-tax interest elasticity of saving is as low as evidence suggests. Moreover, as also noted earlier, for a given overall level of taxation, any favorable effects on capital formation of lower marginal tax rates on capital income would be counterbalanced by unfavorable effects on labor incentives of higher taxation of labor income.

Taxation of real capital gains has been considered so far to be approximately equivalent in impact on capital formation to the same amount of taxes on any other form of capital income. This is not necessarily true theoretically in view of the greater uncertainty associated with capital gains than with ordinary income and the more asymmetric impact of capital gains taxation. It has been shown on theoretical grounds that a reduction in capital gains taxes (or a shortening in the holding period) can either increase or decrease saving. Empirically, the evidence regarding the impact of the level of capital gains taxation on capital values—and, hence, on the cost of capital—is scanty and not conclusive. Thus, for common stock, which has been subject to more analysis of price effects of capital gains taxation than other capital assets, evidence available from time-series analysis is weak and inconsistent. The problem with time-series analysis lies in the difficulty of using the small number of changes in the relevant tax laws to explain extremely volatile movements in stock prices. Basically, the case for a substantial impact of capital gains taxation on stock prices has yet to be proven or refuted, but there is no strong reason for believing that the effect of such taxes on stock prices is markedly different than that of other forms of capital income taxation.

A second important reason advanced for preferential tax treatment of, at least, unrealized capital gains, normally a much larger component of the total than realized gains, is the great difficulty of measuring a high proportion of unrealized gains and of financing the tax payments that would be associated with these gains without forcing undesirable and costly asset liquidation. Such problems are generally unimportant for readily marketable securities, but they are important for nonmarketable securities and owned homes, two other major forms of assets held by individual taxpayers. For all assets, including marketable securities, the desirability of adjusting nominal capital gains in a period of marked inflation introduces a further complication.

Another argument frequently adduced in support of more favorable tax treatment of capital gains than of other income is that capital gains are an especially important part of the returns on risky ventures, which are claimed both to play a particularly important role in economic growth and to be discriminated against by the capital markets. However, available evidence points to no such discrimination, which, if it existed, presumably would involve a higher risk-adjusted required rate of return on unseasoned new stock than on new stock issues or on new outstanding shares of seasoned companies. Even without a risk adjustment, the realized rates of return on unseasoned stock issues from the 1920s to the 1970s were, on the average, no higher—and some evidence even suggests may have been lower—than on seasoned stock issues. Presumably, a risk adjustment would reinforce this finding.

There is one other respect in which capital gains taxation is frequently claimed to have an adverse effect on financial markets and economic efficiency—i.e., depressing market liquidity. The theoretical rationale for this claim is that since capital gains taxes can be substantially reduced by holding the assets for a period in excess of six months and can be avoided altogether if carried over into taxpayers' estates, taxpayers have a strong financial incentive to hold the asset for at least six months, even if nontax economic considerations would lead them to switch their funds into more attractive investments. Such a constraint on their investments would presumably lead to a less efficient allocation of economic resources, though it is extremely difficult to determine the magnitude of the effect and more difficult still to assess its economic importance. It even has been argued that the discouragement of short-term realization of capital gains is economically desirable as a means of reducing market speculation, but there is no strong theoretical or empirical support for this position.

A substantial amount of empirical analysis has been devoted to the effect of the holding-period provisions in the tax laws on the timing and amount of capital gains realizations and on the implications for tax revenue collected, but the analytical results are again inconclusive. Virtually all of them show a significant positive effect of liberalized holding-period provisions (i.e., permitting the more favorable taxation of long-term capital gains to apply to short-term holding periods) on accelerating realizations. However, the results differ widely on the size of the effect and on whether or not the greater realizations are sufficient to offset the lower levels of effective tax rates or whether or not the level of increased realizations found at the time of capital gains tax changes is likely to carry over to longer periods of time.

When the results in these different studies are considered, it appears that capital gains taxes do inhibit realizations, and, therefore, probably introduce some allocational inefficiencies. However, it is not clear that the effect is sizable in the long run, important in the short run, or sufficient to offset the loss in tax revenue associated with lower tax rates.

On one hand, evaluation of available evidence suggests that the only significant reason for taxing real capital gains (i.e., capital gains adjusted for inflation) differently from other income is the inadvisability of forcing realization of the gain and, in the absence of realization, the difficulty of measuring the gain for many assets and financing the tax payment on that gain. On the other hand, differential taxation of different assets results in allocational inefficiencies and distributional inequities. One reasonably satisfactory solution to this problem would be to tax all realized real capital gains at the ordinary income tax rates and to insure that all real capital gains are ultimately considered realized, whether at the time of a gift of an asset to a charitable organization or at the time of death.

While the preceding exploration suggests that there is no particularly good reason for treating real capital gains more favorably than other income, capital gains taxation does introduce a number of problems not associated with the taxation of ordinary income. As a result, it should be pointed out that if taxation is shifted from an income to a consumption base, the problem of appropriate capital gains taxation would disappear in the long run but only at the expense of a new set of problems, including major transitional difficulties.

Effects of Taxation on Different Financial Institutions

Financial institutions as a whole—including commercial banks, savings and loan associations, savings banks, credit unions, and insurance companies—are subject to a number of different tax rules from those for nonfinancial corporations. These rules are generally more favorable than for other companies, but they differ widely among the major institutional groups. Credit unions are now tax-exempt. Banks and other thrift institutions are permitted special bad debt reserve deductions that significantly lower their effective tax rates. The most favorable tax deductions are provided to thrift institutions which specialize in residential mortgage financing, and clearly distort investment allocations. Moreover, this favorable tax provision is of benefit only to profitable thrift institutions and also raises questions of equity as well as of allocational efficiency.

As noted by the U.S. Department of the Treasury in an analysis of its November 1984 tax proposal, *Tax Reform for Fairness, Simplicity and Economic Growth*, "The special bad reserve rules are clearly a large subsidy for most savings and loan associations and commerical banks, and a significant distortion from the measurement of economic income." It should be made clear, however, that many nonfinancial corporations also effectively receive large subsidies in connection with current tax treatment of new investments.

Banks, thrifts, and certain other financial institutions receive an additional significant tax preference over other institutions because of their ability to invest their depository funds in tax-exempt obligations without losing the deduction for the entire interest paid on deposits or other short-term obligations used to finance their investments in tax-exempts. The exclusion from income of Federal Savings and Loan Insurance Corporation payments to thrift institutions in connection with reorganization is another special tax treatment accorded to savings institutions.

Insurance companies also receive substantial tax preferences. Current law permits life insurance policyholders to earn tax-free income on premium payments in excess of costs. Such income is reflected in an increase in the company's insurance reserves, which shield the investment income from taxes at the company level. Since payments of a life insurance policy at death of the insured are excluded from income of the beneficiary, the investment income on the policy can escape tax permanently. This preferential tax treatment of income earned on investment in life insurance, which the Treasury describes as "the largest tax distortion in the financial services area," is a tax-deferral or tax-avoidance mechanism that has been used primarily by individuals in high-income brackets. Lower-income taxpayers who buy term insurance would receive no tax benefits since there is no investment component in such policies.

There are other significant tax advantages received by life insurance companies and their policyholders. Perhaps most important among these are the advantages provided by life insurance policies with fixed borrowing schedules that are frequently marketed mainly as tax shelters. Another significant advantage possessed by life insurance companies is that tax-deferred annuities can be purchased only from them. In addition, life insurance companies benefit from an initial over-statement of reserves allowed under current law and from a special deduction equal to 20 percent of their otherwise taxable income. Again, a number of these tax advantages of life insurance companies, such as those associated with a fixed borrowing schedule and with tax-deferred annuities, are primarily beneficial to the upper-income groups.

Property and casualty insurance companies, like life insurance companies, are also subject to favorable tax treatment, and a wide range of special tax rules are applicable to their income. Mutual property and casualty company policyholders receive additional tax benefits, and a number of nonprofit organizations engage in the property and casualty, as well as other insurance, business without any tax liability.

Enough has been said about the differential tax treatment of the various groups of financial institutions to suggest the types of inequities and allocational inefficiencies that would be associated with these disparities in taxation. It is difficult to attach a numerical magnitude to the implicit tax subsidies and even more difficult to assess the economic importance of the associated distortions. The resulting inequities and allocational inefficiencies may be substantial; however, they could be largely avoided at little cost except, perhaps, in the transitional period.

Some Policy Implications

Both on efficiency and equity grounds, the same tax rates should apply as a general rule to all sources of economic return, whether the return comes from investment in housing or plant and equipment, from stock or bonds, from capital gains or ordinary income, or from deposits in commercial banks and other depository institutions or policies in life insurance companies. This does not mean that there may not be products or periods when national policy considerations would lead to differential taxation on different forms of economic activity (e.g., the consumption of cigarettes, liquor, or gasoline). However, such exceptions should be kept to a minimum, should require a strong justification, and would not appear to be desirable in the taxation of returns earned on investment in financial instruments or in financial institutions.

While the source of economic return generally should not be a basis for differential taxation, the economic status of the taxpayer, which measures the ability to pay, may legitimately be used as a basis for payment of different tax rates by households in upper- and lower-income groups. The justification for such differences in tax rates, which currently contribute to a moderate progressivity in the overall tax structure, is ethical rather than economic. The basic economic argument against progressivity is its association with high marginal tax rates and the possible adverse incentive effects of such rates on saving, investment, and labor. However, as discussed earlier, the evidence regarding these effects suggests that they are not large, especially for saving and investment.

The Treasury Department proposal for reform of the federal income tax system would improve substantially the taxation of the capital markets as well as of economic activity generally. If that proposal were enacted, financial institutions would be taxed more equitably, and a high proportion of the inefficiencies and inequities associated with unequal taxation of institutional groups would disappear.

The Treasury's proposal also would effect significant improvement in the taxation of different financial instruments and, in particular, the taxation of corporate income and resulting dividends and capital gains. The current major differences in the tax rates paid by different corporations, which depend on their investment policy and capital intensity, would largely disappear so that stock values would approximate more clearly the before-tax productivity of corporations rather than their tax treatment. Because of an explicit adjustment for inflation, the major disparities between taxable and economic income of corporations in periods of high inflation would be greatly diminished. The exemption of half the dividends paid by a corporation from corporate income would greatly reduce the current differential tax advantages of bonds over stock and of retained over distributed corporate earnings and may be regarded as a step toward the ultimate elimination of the double taxation of corporate income. Assuming the Treasury's estimates of the distributional effects of these proposed tax changes are correct, these improvements would involve no shift in taxation from corporations to individuals or from upper-income to lower-income groups. In fact, according to the Treasury, the share of the total federal income taxes borne by corporations would be increased moderately from the greatly reduced share of recent years.

The Treasury's proposal would introduce two significant improvements in capital gains taxation. It would adjust realized capital gains for inflation and then tax the adjusted gains at the normal rather than the preferential tax rate and would eliminate the tax deductions for unrealized real gains on property contributed to charitable organizations. From the viewpoint of economic efficiency and equity, one major gap in the Treasury's proposed tax treatment of capital gains is that no provision is made for the taxation of unrealized capital gains, not even at the time of death of the taxpayer. Although it may not be practical to tax unrealized capital gains systematically as they accrue, there does not seem to be any justification for not taxing them at some suitable time, such as at death. It also might be noted that although the indexation of realized capital gains as recommended by the Treasury may be desirable, indexation would make more sense if applied to the taxation of all capital gains, both realized and unrealized. Otherwise there may be an incentive for taxpayers to postpone realization on their more successful investments and use their less successful investments, which show tax losses when adjusted for inflation, as a basis for minimizing taxes.

Further, it should be noted that indexation of capital gains can be regarded as an insurance by the federal government that stock will constitute a satisfactory inflation hedge. As long as taxpayers possess sufficient other income, any inadequacies of stock as an inflation hedge would be underwritten by the government, which would assume the risk of stock losses attributable to inflation.

The federal government's tax policy could also contribute to economic efficiency in general and to the demand for risky assets in particular by a symmetric tax treatment of capital income and losses both for corporations and individuals. The market for financial assets seems to price unique (or specific-asset) as well as common (or market) risks, but the government need not concern itself with unique risks (unless extremely large). As a result, government assumption of unique risks associated with the taxation of returns from capital assets should contribute to efficient asset pricing. If higher returns associated with higher risks are to be taxed at the same rate as risk-free returns, even the assumption of market risk by the government in its tax policy can be justified on the grounds that losses associated with such risks should receive a tax offset.

The ultimate improvement in the taxation of income from the most important marketable risky assets (namely, corporate securities and, especially, common stock) would require full integration of corporation and personal income taxes. Initially, this might entail a substantial reduction in ordinary corporate tax rates, to be offset by elimination of special corporate tax preference (the so-called corporate tax-expenditure items) along the lines suggested by recent "flat-tax" proposals. The subsequent move to full integration could be accomplished by one of two approaches. The first would involve gradual reduction of corporate taxes from the lower base set by the flat tax proposals until set at zero, at the same time offsetting the reduction by the inclusion of a pro-rata share of corporate retained earnings in stockholders' personal tax bases. A second approach would also gradually eliminate the double taxation of corporate income but retain corporate taxation as a convenient withholding device. Whatever approach is used, it will be necessary to insure that there are no undue windfall gains to corporate shareholders and that regressivity is not introduced into the tax structure.

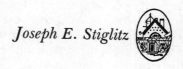

Joseph E. Stiglitz

5
The Consumption-Expenditure Tax

Though there is virtual unanimity that the tax system ought to be changed—that it is inequitable and generates costly inefficiencies in the economy—there is no unanimity on how it should be changed. Some individuals are concerned particularly with inequities and believe that many rich individuals pay less than their fair share. Others are concerned with inefficiencies and believe that the present tax system pays too high a price for a relatively small amount of progressivity. However, there is widespread agreement that present tax laws are overly complex, so complex that it is often difficult to tell who—other than the tax lawyers and accountants—are the real beneficiaries of many special provisions. This complexity leads to tax avoidance and evasion, inequities, and inefficiencies. Some complexity is the result of special provisions enacted on behalf of special interest groups or designed to provide certain incentives (e.g.,

JOSEPH E. STIGLITZ *is professor of economics at Princeton University. Previously, he was the Drummond Professor of Political Economy at Oxford University and the Oskar Morgenstern Distinguished Fellow and Visiting Professor at the Institute for Advanced Studies and Mathematica. The recipient of several fellowships and national honors, he has served as a consultant to departments in the federal government, state governments, international organizations, and public companies. Dr. Stiglitz also serves as an editor of many distinguished economics journals and has published over 150 papers in prestigious international journals.*

to conserve energy and to save). Nonetheless, some complexity is inherent in any tax structure that attempts to make distinctions between capital and labor income and between capital gains, dividends, and interest and that attempts to introduce a reasonable degree of progressivity. The question is: is it possible to reform and simplify the tax structure and still obtain the redistributive objectives of the current tax system? On this, there is no agreement.

This chapter is concerned with one group of proposals for reform—those substituting a consumption tax for the present income tax. Though proposals for such a tax long have been favored by academics (Irving Fisher, Nicholas Kaldor, and Milton Friedman, among others), only recently have they received widespread interest by those in government, including the U.S. Department of the Treasury, which produced an excellent study in 1977 *(Blueprints for Basic Tax Reform)*, and a special committee headed by James Meade in the United Kingdom, which produced a similar study in 1978 *(The Structure and Reform of Direct Taxation)*. Of course, this is only one of several possible reforms of the tax structure; others attempt to make the present income tax more comprehensive. The 1984 Treasury report *(Tax Reform for Fairness, Simplicity, and Economic Growth)* takes the latter approach. There is an interesting contrast between these two approaches: while one of the central tenets of the comprehensive income tax is the comprehensive taxation of income from capital, the central feature of the consumption tax is the exemption of that income.

To present an evaluation of the consumption tax, the impetus behind the current concern for tax reform will first be examined. General "principles of tax reform" will also be reviewed, and arguments for and against the consumption tax, as well as some important problems regarding its implementation, will be studied. The final section will summarize conclusions concerning the desirability of the consumption tax and, in particular, whether or not it provides a better approach to tax reform than the comprehensive income tax.

The Impetus for Reform

The impetus for a major reform in the U.S. tax system comes from widespread belief that the system carries high administrative cost; that, in spite of this high cost, compliance is decreasing; that it is riddled with inequities; and that high marginal tax rates and myriad special provisions give rise to significant inefficiencies and may be important contributors to the marked slowdown of U.S. productivity growth apparent in recent years.

ADMINISTRATIVE COST

The major brunt of the administrative cost of the U.S. income tax is borne by taxpayers. In 1977 the government estimated that the direct cost of completing federal tax forms comprised 78 percent of the total cost of all federal reporting requirements; the public spent about 613 million hours completing tax forms.

The laws are so complex that nearly 50 percent of all taxpayers used tax preparers in 1977. Joel Slemrod of the University of Minnesota estimated that taxpayers spent between $17 and $27 billion on compliance costs in 1982—5 to 7 percent of the revenue raised by the federal and state income tax systems combined. He estimated that the number of hours spent on filing tax returns had grown to between 1.8 and 2.1 billion and that between $3 billion and $3.4 billion was spent on professional tax assistance. But even these numbers provide an underestimate of total compliance cost; they do not include the cost of extra bookkeeping required to comply with the tax laws.

COMPLEXITY

The complexity of the tax code contributes to the high administrative cost, the low level of compliance, the widespread sense of inequity, and the inefficiencies associated with the tax. There are many indicators of this complexity. Robert Hall and Alvin Rabushka point out:

> The entire Code of Federal Regulations, all general and permanent laws in force in the United States, has 50 different titles filling more than 180 volumes. Title 26, the Internal Revenue Code, is responsible for 14 of these volumes, of which 8 are just for the income tax. Title 26 occupies 14 inches of library shelf space. The eight volumes for the income tax fill 5,105 pages, cost $65.00 per set, and weigh 12 pounds 2 ounces. The 1981 Economic Recovery Act amended some 89 separate sections of the tax code. To explain these changes, the staff of the Joint Committee on Taxation published a 411-page booklet. . . . (*The Flat Tax*, 1985)

The complexity is also reflected in the difficulties that even the IRS suffers in accurately assessing tax liabilities. Ralph Nader's Tax Reform Research Group created a tax schedule for a fictional couple and sent it to twenty-two IRS offices. The tax liabilities assessed by the different offices differed markedly, from a high refund of $811.96 to a tax underpayment of $52.14. IRS studies have shown error rates of 82 percent for commercial firms working on tax returns of individuals with low incomes and a 72 percent rate for people trained and employed by IRS when handling relatively simple tax problems.

The difficulty that individuals have in knowing whether or not they are complying with the law is another indication of its complexity, illustrated by the fact that individuals who go to court to challenge IRS decisions generally win; the IRS recovers only about 33 percent of what it claims. Instances where different courts have ruled differently on similar issues make the taxpayer's plight even more difficult.

COMPLIANCE

To collect its taxes, the federal government relies on a combination of voluntary compliance and the threat of prosecution for outright fraud. To assist individuals whose sense of moral responsibility might be too weak to induce them to report all their income, the government requires that employers report wages paid to their workers and that firms report dividends and interest paid to shareholders and bondholders. However, the government has only limited facilities to scrutinize cash transactions, and the ability to avoid taxes by the use of cash has encouraged the growth of what has been called the "underground economy." Though precise estimates of its size are difficult to make, some observers believe it may involve as much as 25 percent of the work force and 15 percent of the gross national product and includes not only drug dealers, but also babysitters, domestic help, carpenters, gardeners, and those who sell merchandise on the street.

The IRS estimates that of the $750 billion that individuals were supposed to pay in taxes in 1982, $100 billion will not be paid. This does not include those who reduce their tax liabilities by taking advantage of the loopholes; this $100 billion represents those who do not report all of their income. The extent of noncompliance has been growing more rapidly than tax revenue. From $29 billion a decade ago, it is expected to grow to $180 billion by 1985.

Some observers believe even these estimates are conservative. The decrease in compliance may be partly a result of the increasing complexity of the tax code and the sense that it is inequitable, partly a result of the increased marginal tax rates which make compliance more expensive, and partly a consequence of the decreased likelihood of apprehension. While the government audited 2.59 percent of the tax returns in 1976, in 1981 it audited only 1.55 percent of all returns; by 1984 the percentage was down to just over 1.30 percent. Even audits fail to uncover all taxable income; in one study it was discovered that experienced IRS auditors discovered only one out of four dollars that subsequently appeared in reports on wages paid by employers and on dividends and interest paid by firms.

Even after reporting their income, many individuals do not pay their taxes. Presently, the IRS claims that taxpayers owe more than $27 billion in back taxes, a threefold increase from the $8.3 billion in 1977.

TAX AVOIDANCE

Tax avoidance (taking advantage of all the loopholes in the tax structure) results in significant erosion of the tax base and has increased rapidly in recent years. There are tax shelters (investments designed to take advantage of special provisions of the tax code in order to reduce liabilities) in many industries. It might have been thought that the Economic Recovery Tax Act of 1981, which reduced the maximum tax bracket from 70 to 50 percent, would have decreased the demand for tax shelters. However, at the same time the act's generous provisions for depreciation, leasing, and research and development increased the benefits of certain categories of tax shelters, and this step more than offset the effect of the reduction in the marginal tax rates. The consequences were predictable: impressive growth in research and development, equipment leasing, and, in particular, real estate tax shelters. Robert Stanger, a tax shelter expert, suggested that the act might be more aptly called "the Real Estate Benefit Act."

The line between tax avoidance and evasion is not always easily defined. Thus, in 1983, IRS agents audited 96,000 returns that took advantage of tax shelters and obtained an additional $1.8 billion in revenue; they estimated as much as $7 billion might be obtained when audits of an additional 350,000 returns were completed.

Whether as a result of tax avoidance or tax evasion, the net effect is that certain industries, such as real estate, are effectively exempt from taxation. Thus, reported *losses* in partnerships (the usual form of tax shelters) in real estate and insurance more than doubled from 1980 to 1981—$3.6 billion to $7.6 billion. Indeed, the two industries combined (including partnerships and sole proprietorships) showed an overall loss of $50 million in 1981.

Principles of Tax Reform

To understand how to reform the tax system, it is important first to understand what gives rise both to tax avoidance and the inefficiencies and inequities associated with avoidance. Why taxation in general is distortionary also needs to be understood.

THE NATURE OF TAX AVOIDANCE

There are three major methods of tax avoidance: income splitting, tax deferral, and tax arbitrage. In a progressive tax system, splitting income reduces the family's total tax burden between, for example, a parent and child. Trusts play a particularly significant role here. Tax deferral is important because the present discounted value of tax liabilities can be reduced by postponing taxes. The most common form of tax deferral is deferred compensation, but there are other examples, such as installment sales. When receipt of income is deferred in order to defer taxes, the individual effectively avoids paying taxes on the implicit interest income. Tax arbitrage takes advantage of different rates facing the returns to different categories of investment and facing different individuals. For instance, if an individual borrows to buy an appreciating asset, the interest payments can be deducted against ordinary income, and only

40 percent of the gains are taxed. Opportunities for tax avoidance, both by tax arbitrage and deferral, are so great that, in a perfect capital market, individuals could eliminate all tax on capital income and, in the absence of provisions limiting loss offsets and interest deductions, would be able to eliminate all taxes on wage income as well. Even with restrictive provisions limiting interest deductions and loss offsets, taxpayers may be able to eliminate a significant fraction of their tax liabilities on wage income.

Of course, there is cost associated with tax-avoidance activities, and a taxpayer weighs benefits against costs. Benefits are critically dependent on the magnitude of the *marginal* tax rate as well as the probability of discovery and the nature of the penalty imposed if discovered. In part, the probability of discovery is a function of the number of other offenders; when there are many tax avoiders for a given IRS budget, it is less likely that any single individual will be caught. Thus, by inducing more individuals to engage in avoidance, high marginal tax rates have a multiplier effect on the level of tax avoidance. Moreover, the complexity of the tax code contributes to tax avoidance not only by opening loopholes, but also by making it more difficult to assess large penalties for those who take advantage of the system.

SOURCES OF AND INDUCEMENTS TO TAX AVOIDANCE

Marginal Tax Rates—What lessons for tax reform follow from this brief description of tax avoidance? First, the extent of tax avoidance, as well as the general level of distortions associated with taxation, increases significantly with the *marginal* tax rate. As a first approximation, the deadweight loss associated with a tax increases as the square of the marginal tax rate. (The deadweight loss is the measure of the *excess burden* of a tax, the loss in efficiency relative to an ideal nondistortionary tax raising the same revenue.) Therefore, tax systems should be designed with low marginal rates. The tax code often seems perverse; there are high marginal rates with low average rates and, therefore, low revenue. Because of numerous special provisions of the individual income tax code, relatively high tax rates have to be imposed on the remaining fraction of taxable income in order to obtain the requisite revenue. Because of generous provisions for accelerated depreciation and the investment tax credit, the net revenue raised by the corporate income tax may be relatively low, but high tax rates, at the margin, still may have large distortionary effects.

Progressivity and Capital Taxation—Second, as earlier noted, tax-avoidance schemes are primarily associated with (1) the progressivity of the tax schedule and (2) the taxation of capital, particularly the taxation of different kinds of capital income at different rates. Reducing the level of marginal tax rates would reduce individuals' incentives to engage in tax evasion and avoidance; reducing differences between the tax rates faced by different individuals would reduce the incentive for tax avoidance through income splitting; reducing or eliminating the differential treatment of different types of income would reduce the incentive and ability to engage in tax arbitrage.

Complexity—Third, the complexity of the tax code arises from many of the very same sources that give rise to tax avoidance. Whenever different income categories are taxed differently, individuals will attempt to ensure that their incomes receive the most favorable tax treatment. It seems a general rule that delineating clear distinctions is harder in law than theory. For instance, distinction between capital gains and interest is less clear than it may appear. A promise to pay $100 in ten years is clearly a bond. But if the bond is issued with no interest payments, its current price will be low (about $50 at a 7 percent interest rate). Is the increase in price over the next seven years (from $50 to $100) treated as capital gain or is it disguised interest? Though Congress has enacted legislation to deny individuals the opportunity to take advantage of this particular ruse, clever tax lawyers and acountants are always on the search for more subtle ways of converting ordinary income into capital gains; even when the IRS is successful in stopping a particular practice, it is at the cost of an ever increasing complexity to the tax code.

Often there are conflicts between writing a tax law that is easy to understand, but provides opportunities for clever lawyers and accountants to develop tax-avoidance devices, and writing a tax law which prevents these tax-avoidance devices, but which makes the tax law impenetrable to even well-educated individuals who are not tax specialists.

INEQUITIES AND INEFFICIENCIES

Tax avoidance and tax evasion, besides making the tax system less progressive than it otherwise would be and less equitable (since some individuals are in a better position to take advantage of these tax-avoidance schemes and to evade taxes than are others), introduce important inefficiencies. Not only should the costs of designing and implementing these schemes (accountants' and tax lawyers' fees) be treated as deadweight losses, but there are further such losses resulting from resource allocation distortions to which they give rise. For instance, the tax shelter provided by cattle may have led to excessive investment in cattle. In another instance, at one time a glut of railroad boxcars developed when investments in this commonly "fashionable" tax shelter boomed.

It has been noted repeatedly that special provisions of the tax code give rise to inequities, inefficiencies, and tax avoidance and lead to high marginal tax rates, which bring additional inefficiencies, inequities, and tax-avoidance activities. It should be emphasized that at least some of these provisions are not merely the result of lobbying by special interest groups. In fact, persuasive "objective" arguments can be made in their behalf. This is true of two groups of provisions in particular—those that were introduced to increase the tax system's equity and those that were introduced to increase the economy's efficiency. For instance, there is a widespread view that those who are seriously ill, as reflected by their large medical bills, are less able to contribute to the support of government—less able to pay—than those with corresponding income but without medical expenses. Energy conservation credits were introduced because it was believed that private incentives to conserve energy were insufficient. There is a long tradition of arguments for the use of such "corrective" taxes, dating at least back to the great early twentieth-century Cambridge economist A.C. Pigou.

BASIC ISSUES FOR REFORM

What has emerged clearly during the past two decades is that the tax system cannot do everything. If asked to do too much, it may not do well in meeting any of its objectives. Thus, the basic questions facing tax reform are:

(1) Are there ways of simplifying the tax system that do not sacrifice much of the distributive objectives, but gain significant economic efficiency?

(2) In almost any reform of the tax system, some groups will be hurt, and others will be aided. Though society as a whole may be helped, tax reforms are seldom "Pareto improvements" (changes which result in *all* individuals being made better off). Thus, are there ways of designing the transition from the old to the new system in which relatively few groups of individuals are significantly disadvantaged? This point is also important to make these reforms politically acceptable.

(3) The tax system has been viewed as a relatively efficient way for the government to pursue certain objectives. For the government to design a direct grant system to encourage energy conservation would have been extremely difficult. Encouraging energy conservation through the tax system seemed a particularly effective and administratively inexpensive way to pursue this national objective. Therefore, if a simplification of the tax system entails an abandonment of the use of broadly construed corrective or incentive taxes, are there other ways by which these objectives could be attained that will achieve at least the same degree of effectiveness as achieved at present?

The Consumption Tax

The question of whether consumption or income provides a better basis for taxation has been debated for over fifty years. Irving Fisher, one of the early great American economists, argued that it was more appropriate to tax individuals on the basis of what they take from society (measured by consumption) than on what they contribute (measured by income). To tax consumption, it is not necessary to monitor an individual's purchases of goods; it is necessary only to observe an individual's cash flow. Since income equals consumption plus savings, if one can measure income (total receipts) and savings, the level of consumption can be inferred. The measurement of income involves the kind of problem encountered in any analysis of income tax, distinguishing between legitimate business expenditures and consumption expenditures. The consumption tax does not solve these problems, but neither does it make them worse. The problem of measuring savings is also not particularly difficult. One simple method calculates the total value of purchases of securities less the total value of sales. The difference is the cash flow. For businesses, one simply measures the flow of funds from the "business" to the "individual" account. The major advantages of the consumption tax arise from the fact that *a consumption tax is equivalent to the exemption from taxation of income from capital*. In a world in which individuals consume all their incomes during their lifetimes and tax rates and interest rates are constant, a consumption tax is equivalent to a wage tax. This equivalence provides the alternative method of levying tax—on wage income. In this approach, the return to capital is not taxed, but no subtraction is allowed for savings. (The approach recommended in *Blueprints for Basic Tax Reform* was a modified cash-flow approach.)

If the return on capital were not taxed, there would be no necessity for individuals to attempt to avoid this tax. This hardly seems a persuasive argument for its repeal since noncompliance with any tax can be eliminated by elimination of the tax. But the concern noted earlier was that the provisions relating to the taxation of capital income reduced the effective tax liabilities imposed on wage income; deduction of interest and accelerated depreciation could be used to offset ordinary wage income. For some individuals, at least, the net effective tax rate on capital could be negative. If this were the major concern, it would be easy to alter the tax code to eliminate it. Individuals would not be allowed to offset wage income with business or capital losses.

A rather different set of concerns is that the attempt to take advantage of the favorable treatment afforded to some kinds of capital gives rise to inefficiencies and inequities. The fact that returns to different kinds of capital are taxed differently gives rise to potentially large distortions in the allocation of capital. Moreover, some individuals may be in a better position to take advantage of some of these provisions than others. As a result, effective tax rates on different individuals differ.

It is probably impossible to eliminate all forms of special treatment. For instance, although it would be easy to tax individuals with defined contribution pension schemes at the time the contributions were made, it would be extremely difficult to impose corresponding taxes on defined benefit pension schemes. These pensions must be taxed at the time they are received, and, thus, they represent a form of tax-exempt interest income. Still, altering the special treatment afforded capital gains and reducing the extent of accelerated depreciation would eliminate several commonly employed tax-avoidance schemes. Advocates of the consumption tax believe this is not enough; the remaining opportunities for tax avoidance still will be sufficiently great to cause serious inequities and inefficiencies.

The taxation of consumption would eliminate many of the prevalent methods of tax avoidance. As noted earlier, tax deferral is of value only because interest income is taxed; with interest income exempt from tax, the only advantage of tax deferral is to benefit from differing marginal tax rates that individuals might face at different times in their lives. Actually, most economists think that this outcome is desirable, because individuals should pay taxes on the basis of their lifetime income, not their year-to-year income. In addition, those kinds of tax arbitrage that arise from differential treatment of long-term capital gains and other forms of capital income would no longer be attractive; all capital income would be taxed at the same (zero) rate.

THE CONSUMPTION TAX'S EFFECT ON THE CORPORATE TAX

When the basis of taxation switches to consumption, justification for the corporation income tax becomes even weaker than it is at present. If it is individuals' consumption that is of concern, all that needs monitoring is the transfer of resources to and from the corporate sector. All the complexity of the corporate tax, including distortionary provisions for depreciation, could be eliminated, and corporations could no longer be used as vehicles for tax avoidance.

TRADITIONAL ARGUMENTS FOR THE CONSUMPTION TAX

Based on the consumption tax's advantages in terms of administrative simplicity, current arguments in its favor are in marked contrast to those that have traditionally been put forward. The most important traditional arguments are (1) consumption is a "fairer basis of taxation" and (2) consumption is a less distortionary basis of taxation.

There are two reasons that consumption is a fairer basis of taxation. First, it seems fairer to tax individuals on the basis of what they take from society (their consumption) than what they contribute (which corresponds to their income). Second, the natural time unit to use for taxation is the individual's life (not a day, a month, or a decade; we use a year simply because of its administrative convenience). The (present discounted) value of an individual's lifetime income (including inheritance) is equal to the (present discounted) value of his or her consumption plus bequests. Thus a lifetime income tax is equivalent to a consumption tax plus a bequest tax.

The argument that a consumption tax is less distortionary than an income tax, in its simpler form, is based on the observation that income taxation involves two distortions, between leisure and consumption and between present and future consumption, but a consumption tax involves only the first distortion. This argument is no longer taken seriously since one cannot simply count distortions. However, more recent theories have confirmed, at least partially, many economists' prejudices against the taxation of the return to capital.

RECENT SUPPORT FOR THE CONSUMPTION TAX

The modern theory of taxation focuses on the question: what is the set of Pareto efficient tax structures, i.e., given that the reason that the government does not impose lump sum taxes is that it cannot ascertain (except by observing income) who has a higher ability to pay, what are the tax structures under which no category of taxpayer can be made better off without making some others worse off? If the government imposes a redistributive consumption tax, should it additionally impose a tax on interest income? Recent analysis ("The Design of Tax Structures: Direct Versus Indirect Taxation," by A.B. Atkinson and J.E. Stiglitz, *Journal of Public Economics*, 1976) provides some weak support for the desirability of a consumption tax. Although in one central case a consumption tax was optimal, in other cases an interest subsidy seemed as likely to be desirable as an interest tax.

Subsequent work has provided somewhat stronger support for an interest income tax. Because capital and unskilled labor are interchangeable, an interest income tax, which discourages investment, has a positive effect on the before-tax income distribution. Since there are large distortions associated with redistributing income, generally it is desirable to introduce some small distortions to improve the before-tax income distribution.

A critical assumption in the Atkinson-Stiglitz analysis was that the source of differences in income is differences in individuals' abilities, which are reflected in differences in wages. If there are differences in abilities to invest capital, resulting in higher returns on some individuals' investments than on others', then a stronger case for a tax on the return to capital also can be made.

Some Aspects of the Design of a Consumption Tax

The recent resurgence of interest in the consumption tax has been motivated not so much by traditional issues of equity or efficiency previously reviewed. Instead, it has been motivated by a concern with the administrative complexity of the tax laws and by the belief that much of this complexity arises from taxation of capital.

Critics of the consumption tax feel that the sources of complexity in the current system are at least known; their fear is that only gradual discovery of administrative problems associated with a consumption tax will occur. Therefore, consideration has been given to a few of these possible obstacles.

During President Gerald Ford's administration, the Office of Tax Analysis of the Treasury Department, headed by Princeton economist David Bradford, gave careful consideration to a number of problems associated with the design of a consumption tax. The analysts became convinced that although there were some problems that required attention, overall, the administrative problems were much less than those prevalent under the present system.

HOUSING UNDER THE CONSUMPTION TAX

Housing presents a problem for the consumption tax, just as it does for the income tax. The theoretically appropriate way of dealing with housing under an income tax is to *impute* to income an amount corresponding to the services yielded by the house, i.e., to impute a rental value. Similarly, with the cash-flow approach to the consumption tax, the purchase of a house represents an investment, and the expenditures to purchase a house should be subtracted from income to determine the tax base. Later, however, services yielded by the house should be included as "consumption" and added to the tax base. But, given the difficulties of imputing services yielded by the house, the alternative procedure, whereby expenditures on the purchase of a house are not subtracted from income and services yielded by assets are not then added, has certain advantages. The major disadvantage arises when tax rates on consumption are progressive. When that occurs, an individual who sells securities to buy a house would appear to be dissaving (the reduction in ownership of securities is viewed as dissaving), and the value of this dissaving would be added to income to form an estimate of consumption. In fact, of course, the individual is simply changing the form in which assets are held; that is, one set of assets (securities) is substituted for another (housing). Thus, any system of consumption taxation must make special provisions for housing.

BEQUESTS

The second problem has to do with bequests and inheritance. Should these be treated as consumption by the donor and as income by the receiver? One view treats an individual and descendants as a single, extended family. In this view, transfers between parent and child should not be taxed; each consumption unit should be taxed only once. If a parent gives an asset to a child and the child sells the asset to consume goods, a tax will be levied on the child's consumption. The other view says that giving money to a child is no different from spending money in other ways. Presumably the parent does it to receive pleasure from it. From the parent's viewpoint, it is a "consumption" expenditure, and, therefore, a bequest should be taxed as if it were a consumption expenditure. At the same time, bequests should be treated as income to the child; if the child sells the asset to purchase consumption goods, the child will be liable to pay the consumption tax.

Obviously, different approaches may have different consequences. Some critics of the consumption tax are concerned that totally exempting bequests from taxation may lead to excessive concentration of wealth. Defenders of the consumption tax claim that if the concern is concentration of wealth, the problem should be attacked directly by imposing a progressive wealth tax, for instance. Critics of the consumption tax claim that wealthy individuals will find ways to avoid such a tax and the way to increase the likelihood that their fair share is paid is to tax both capital income and bequests.

PROBLEMS OF TRANSITION

Some economists have been concerned with the transition from the income tax to the consumption tax. To implement the cash-flow method of calculating consumption, savings and dissavings need to be calculated. To do this, an individual's assets must be identified. There is some concern that individuals might underreport their present assets, and their true consumption would exceed their reported consumption. But the extent to which this is a problem is moot.

To see this, recall the earlier statement that a consumption tax is equivalent to exempting interest income from taxation (that is, it is equivalent to a tax on wage income). Therefore, in principle, there are two equivalent ways of administering such a tax system—as a consumption tax on a cash-flow basis or as a wage tax on individuals when they receive their wage income but exempting returns received from investments made from it. The proposal advanced in *Blueprints for Basic Tax Reform* involves a hybrid of these two systems. There would be "registered" securities; purchases of registered securities would be treated as savings; sales, as dissavings. These would form the basis of the cash-flow approach. In addition, there would be "unregistered" securities, such as houses; the purchase of unregistered securities subtracted from income and their returns would not be taxed.

Since a tax was levied when the invested income was earned, the end effect is the same as if the individual simply has invested assets in unregistered securities. Just as investment in unregistered securities is not deductible from income, so the sale of unregistered securities is not recorded as part of income and, therefore, is not taxable. Viewed in this way, one could divide existing assets into the following two categories. (a) Pensions (where individuals have not already been taxed on their and their employers' contribution) would be treated as registered securities. (b) All other assets would be treated as partially registered, with individuals being able to deduct their bases (their cost of acquisition) from their consumption. Note that implementing this proposal requires no more information than is required for the current income tax system.

There are two objections to this approach. One is that to make the consumption tax palatable, rates must be lower; the only way to have low rates is to impose simultaneously what amounts to a capital levy, i.e., a tax on all previously accumulated assets. This has both equity and efficiency implications. Whether a capital levy seems fair depends on whether individuals have already paid a tax on the wage income from which the saving which financed the original acquisition of the asset was derived. Whether it induces distortions depends on whether individuals believe that this is a once-and-for-all event, or whether they worry that there might subsequently be another capital levy. In my judgment, the former issue appears to be more important than the latter.

There is a second transition problem: there are marked differences in the ratio of consumption to income for individuals in different stages of their lives. Thus, for retired individuals, who are dissaving, consumption typically exceeds income; for some younger individuals, income exceeds consumption. Thus, unless previously accumulated capital was exempt from taxation, older individuals at the time of the transition would be disadvantaged. Since, in the popular view, older individuals are poorer, this seems inequitable. But several points need to be kept in mind: those older individuals who will be particularly disadvantaged are not the poor (who have little capital to dissave) but the wealthier older individuals. Moreover, a consumption tax can be progressive (see below), so that poorer older individuals might actually pay a lower tax than under the present system. More importantly, one needs to ask: once one has agreed upon what an appropriate basis of taxation should be (e.g., whether income or consumption provides a fairer basis of taxation, a better measure of ability to pay), is there any reason that older individuals with the same income or consumption as younger should be treated differently from a younger person (particularly if their medical expenses are being taken care of by another government program, and consumption of medical services, at least when paid by third parties, is not taxed)? Note that this transitional problem is important only if a tax is imposed on consumption out of current capital. If it is exempt, the elderly are probably advantaged. (To the extent that they dissave from IRAs and other forms of saving which are already tax exempt, the appropriate treatment would be to impose a tax on their consumption.)

INCOME VERSUS CONSUMPTION AVERAGING

The consumption tax has some advantages over income tax averaging. During the previous analysis of the income tax, inequities that arise under a progressive tax when an individual's income varies from year to year were noted. Two individuals with the same lifetime incomes might face completely different lifetime tax burdens. Though there are provisions within the tax code for income averaging, these only partially solve the problem. But, for most individuals, fluctuations in consumption are much less than fluctuations in income. Indeed, with a progressive tax, individuals would have a further incentive to smooth their consumption levels. (Moreover, the hybrid system of registered and unregistered securities, described in the *Blueprints for Basic Tax Reform*, would provide individuals with a relatively easy vehicle for smoothing their "measured" consumption; it would thus provide a much better approximation to a tax based on the individual's lifetime consumption than the present system does to a tax based on the individual's lifetime income.)

CONSUMPTION TAXES AND REDISTRIBUTION

There is some concern that a consumption tax will not be sufficiently progressive. This concern arises from two misconceptions. First, it is frequently *assumed* that the appropriate measure of progressivity is the ratio of taxes paid to income. However, if one were convinced that the appropriate tax base was how much one took from the system, rather than contributed to it, then the ratio of taxes paid to consumption becomes the appropriate measure of progressivity. Second, there is no reason that steeply progressive rates cannot be imposed on consumption.

Nevertheless, many inefficiencies and much tax avoidance in the current tax system are motivated by the highly progressive rate structure. Many of these inefficiencies would remain if the switch to a highly progressive consumption tax were made. A flat rate consumption tax would have significant advantages. For instance, taxes always could be imposed at the source; there would be a flat percentage withholding of all expenditures on personnel (wages and fringe benefits). The individual's entire tax form could be put onto a postcard. A flat rate consumption tax has been strongly advocated by Stanford economists Hall and Rabushka. They believe that a 19 percent flat rate consumption tax (which includes, in effect, a capital levy) with a $6,800 exemption for a married couple with no children would generate essentially the same revenue as the current system.

Critics of the tax are skeptical. Because the tax base is smaller than that of the flat rate income tax, the tax rate would have to be higher than with the flat rate income tax. To some extent, the magnitude of the required tax rate depends on the magnitudes of the responses of labor and capital. If labor supply increases significantly in response to the lowering of the marginal tax rate and if savings are sufficiently encouraged that the growth of the economy is significantly improved, it is more likely that the 19 percent flat rate consumption tax would raise the requisite revenue; if labor supply elasticities and saving elasticities are low, then it is unlikely to do so.

Conclusions

Both the consumption tax and comprehensive income tax entail a much broader tax base than the present system. They both entail, for instance, the taxation of fringe benefits (other than pensions) and elimination of special treatment of special categories of expenditures (charities, state and local taxes, medical expenses). They differ in their effective treatment of capital income.

At present, the United States has a hybrid system. Some forms of capital income (IRAs, pensions, housing) are tax exempt, and some forms of capital income (long-term capital gains) receive preferential treatment. Most comprehensive income tax proposals attempt to eliminate the latter but do little for the former. It is difficult to tax housing. There are difficulties in taxing forms of pensions (though these are not insurmountable, particularly if one is willing to accept some measure of "rough justice"), and to tax some and not others seems both inequitable and distortionary. Thus, the choice remaining is basically between the exemption of all or a significant fraction of returns to capital.

Presently, a large fraction of capital income is tax exempt. Present provisions will probably eventually effectively allow for the exemption of all returns on life-cycle savings (including housing) plus the return on a limited amount of bequest-motive savings. There is no agreement among economists about the relative importance of life-cycle savings. Some believe that it accounts for as little as 25 percent of total savings; others believe that the total may exceed 80 percent. Since housing may account for as much as 33 percent of the total capital stock, the total amount of tax-exempt capital well may exceed 50 percent, even using conservative estimates of the importance of life-cycle savings.

What can be said about whether or not the remaining "taxable" portion of savings should be taxed? To tax some savings and not others may be both inequitable and distortionary. However, it may be better to tax what can be taxed. Although the present system may discriminate in favor of certain forms of income, such as low-paid household help that can escape the net of taxation, the fact that some wage income goes unreported and, hence, untaxed is no reason to exempt all wage income from taxation.

This much seems clear: to impose full taxation on capital on top of the corporation income tax is likely to discourage entrepreurship. Elsewhere it has been argued that because of the provisions for tax deductibility of interest, the corporation income tax can be viewed essentially as a tax on entrepreneurship and risk taking. Indeed, at the present time and with generous provisions for depreciation and investment tax credits, there is a net marginal subsidy to capital investment. To impose a 50 percent capital gains tax on top of a 46 percent corporate tax implies an effective tax rate of 73 percent, sufficiently high to have a markedly deleterious effect on incentives, particularly when combined with limited-loss offset provisions. If a comprehensive tax were introduced, it would make sense only if it were combined with integration of the corporation and individual income taxes (though clearly, the magnitude of the distortion will be lower if the tax rates are lower).

The administrative problems associated with the tax system undoubtedly would be significantly reduced by a move to a consumption base. But if there were base broadening under the comprehensive income tax sufficient to lower the maximum marginal tax rate to 35 percent, or even 25 percent, the incentives for tax avoidance would be sufficiently reduced to alleviate this major problem. However, both systems are imperfect. Under a consumption tax, if all previously accumulated capital is taxed, some taxpayers will pay a double tax; if all is tax-exempt, some will escape a single tax. Under the comprehensive income tax, some taxpayers will be in a better position to take advantage of the tax-favored forms of investment than will others. One tentative conclusion is that the differences between the appropriate forms of the two are not as significant as the differences between either and the present system. What is imperative is major broadening of the tax base, simplifying the tax code by eliminating the myriad special provisions, and lowering the marginal tax rates. Were these steps taken under a comprehensive income tax, it may be found that the remaining problems of capital taxation are so great that the only reasonable approach is the consumption tax.

George F. Break

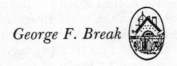

6
The Value-added Tax

Interest in the value-added tax (VAT) in the United States has ebbed and flowed since 1963, when the Fiscal and Financial Committee on Tax Harmonization in the Common Market (Neumark commission) recommended that the six European member countries replace their gross receipts or turnover taxes with an integrated set of value-added taxes. Certainly value-added taxation has developed and prospered in Europe, and to some degree the interest it has attracted in the United States simply may reflect the fact that taxes in faraway places often look better than those close at hand. To a much greater extent, however, this interest has been fueled by a recurrent series of fiscal difficulties and crises here at home. In the mid-1960s the Committee for Economic Development, concerned about low levels of business investment and exports, proposed a VAT as a substitute for the federal corporation income tax. In the early 1970s President Richard Nixon saw the VAT as a means of relieving growing pressures on the local property tax—

GEORGE F. BREAK *is a professor in the Department of Economics at the University of California at Berkeley and served as chairman there from 1969 to 1973. Previously, he taught at Pomona College in Claremont, California. Dr. Break has served as a consultant to both the federal and California governments. He is the noted author of numerous articles and of eight books, including:* Financing Government in a Federal System, Federal Tax Reform: The Impossible Dream? *(with Joseph A. Pechman), and* The Economics of Public Finance *(with Alan S. Blinder, Robert M. Solow, Peter O. Steiner, and Dick Netzer).*

pressures being built up by a combination of rising school costs and increasing public doubts about the equity of that tax. Later in the 1970s Al Ullman, then chairman of the House Committee on Ways and Means, recommended a VAT as a partial replacement for federal income and payroll taxes, and others saw the VAT as part of the solution to the incipient financial problems of the social security system. These problems, however, were dealt with in other ways, and the value-added tax once more slipped back into relative obscurity.

That respite, however, was short-lived. As the 1980s unfolded, two developments catapulted the VAT back into the tax reform arena. One was the persistence of unprecedentedly large federal budget deficits that neither economic growth nor federal spending restraint seemed able to reduce. The other development was an equally persistent public disenchantment with the federal income tax. In the annual public opinion polls taken by the Advisory Commission on Intergovernmental Relations (ACIR), for example, the percentage of respondents rating the federal income tax as the least fair of the four major sources of governmental revenue rose from barely 20 in the early 1970s to over 35 in the early 1980s. At both times only 15 percent or less of the respondents rated state sales taxes as the worst tax. However, these comparisons must be viewed with caution. State income taxes, which are structured in much the same way as the federal income tax, enjoyed an even lower unpopularity index, varying between 8 and 11 percent. The obvious implication is that it is not the structural weaknesses of state income taxes that determine reactions to them, but rather the low level of their rates. A more informative response was elicited by another question:

> Suppose the federal government must raise taxes substantially, which . . . would be the best way to do it—(1) have a form of a national sales tax on things other than food and similar necessities, or (2) raise money by reducing special tax treatment for capital gains and cutting tax deduction allowances for charitable contributions, state and local taxes, medical expenses, etc.?

In 1972, 34 percent of the respondents favored the first alternative and 40 percent, the second. In 1984 the percentages were 32 and 47, respectively. In neither year did a third alternative—the raising of individual income tax rates—attract much favor (7 percent in 1972; 10 percent in 1984). Income tax reform proved to be the preferred option in both years, but enactment of a national sales tax was clearly a respectable second.

What Is a Value-added Tax?

Value-added, as the name suggests, is a measure of the contribution or addition that a business firm makes to the nation's total economic output. It is equal to the firm's gross receipts from the sale of its own output minus the value of inputs it buys from other firms. Calculated another way, value-added is also equal to the firm's total payments to the factors of production—land, labor, and capital—employed in its operations. In principle, then, the base for a value-added tax could be computed either by the subtraction method (sales receipts minus input purchases) or by the addition method (the sum of wages and salaries, profits, and interest payments). In practice, a third procedure, known as the invoice method, is commonly used. This method follows the logic of taxing each firm on its gross receipts from sales with credits allowed against that liability for all taxes paid by its suppliers and invoiced on its purchases. The net tax due is the same as that arrived at by applying the tax rate directly to the value-added computed by the subtraction method, but the invoice approach offers the advantage of providing, up to the final stage of production, a matching set of records of tax payments made and tax credits claimed. These records are exceedingly useful in helping to control tax evasion.

The relationships involved in these calculations are illustrated in Table 1 for a simple three-stage production process. First-stage businesses purchase no inputs from other enterprises and sell their output of 200 to the second stage. These intermediate-level firms add value of 600 to their purchases and sell output of 800 equally to two final-level retailers. The first three lines of Table 1 illustrate the subtraction method, and in line 4 a 10 percent value-added tax is applied to the calculated base. Lines 5, 6, and 7 illustrate the application of the invoice method to the same three-stage production process. The final two lines show the taxes that would be due under the

TABLE 1.   VALUE-ADDED, RETAIL SALES, AND GROSS RECEIPTS TAXES IN A SIMPLE THREE-STAGE PRODUCTION PROCESS

	Stage 1	Stage 2	Stage 3 a	Stage 3 b	Total
1. Value of sales	200	800	500	500	2,000
2. Value of purchased inputs	0	200	400	400	1,000
3. Value-added (Line 1 minus Line 2)	200	600	100	100	1,000
4. Value-added tax (10% of Line 3)	20	60	10	10	100
5. Gross value-added tax due (10% of Line 1)	20	80	50	50	200
6. Tax credit on purchases (10% of Line 2)	0	20	40	40	100
7. Value-added tax (Line 5 minus Line 6)	20	60	10	10	100
8. 10% retail sales tax	—	—	50	50	100
9. 5% gross receipts or turnover tax (5% of Line 1)	10	40	25	25	100

two other major forms of sales tax. A 10 percent retail sales tax would produce the same total revenue but would be collected entirely from third-stage firms. As illustrated in line 9, an equal-yield turnover tax would appear to require only a 5 percent rate; but since it would provide strong incentives for vertical integration of firms, some higher rate would clearly be required. If the firms in this simple world integrated fully into a single stage of production, for example, they would reduce their collective gross receipts tax burdens from the 100 shown in line 9 to only 50. Avoidance of such distorting economic incentives was a major reason for the shift in Europe in the 1960s from turnover to value-added taxes.

CONSUMPTION AND INCOME VARIANTS

An important choice in the design of a value-added tax concerns the treatment to be accorded to business investments in capital assets. If the value of these purchases is allowed as a deduction under the subtraction method, or if the tax on them can be credited under the invoice method, the base of the VAT

will be personal consumption, which is the other main component of total current production in the private sector. If, on the
other hand, capital expenditure deductions must be spread
over the useful lives of the assets according to some depreciation pattern, the base of the VAT will be net income, since total
output minus depreciation equals consumption plus net
investment. The consumption variant is the form of VAT used
in Europe, and it is also the one that is of primary policy interest
in the United States. If income is to remain the main base for
the general tax revenue of the federal government, tax reform
should focus on improving the individual and corporation income taxes, and there would be, therefore, no need to add an
income-type VAT to the structure. On the other hand, the
development of a broad consensus favoring a reallocation of
federal tax burdens so as to place less weight on saving and
more on consumption could turn a consumption-variant VAT
into a prime contender among tax reforms. Two other strong
contenders would be a national retail sales tax, discussed later
in this chapter, and a personal consumption-expenditure tax,
discussed elsewhere in this volume.

ORIGIN- AND DESTINATION-BASED TAXES

A second important choice in the design of a value-added tax
is whether to place it on either an origin or a destination basis.
With an origin basis the levy is applied to the total production
of the taxing jurisdiction regardless of where it is used or consumed. By that logic exports are part of the tax base, but imports are not. The alternative approach uses a destination basis,
which excludes exports but includes imports since the tax base
is defined as the total consumption of the residents of the taxing jurisdiction, regardless of where the goods in question orig-
inate. It is this destination-based variety that is commonly used
in other countries and undoubtedly the one that would be
adopted for a national sales tax in the United States.

A retail sales tax is, by definition, a destination-based levy. Its
base is final sales to resident consumers, and these automatically include imports and exclude exports. A value-added tax,
in contrast, requires what are called "border adjustments" to
achieve the same result. Imports must be fully incorporated
into the domestic tax base, and exports must be fully freed of all

domestic VAT burdens. This is accomplished under the invoice method by granting exports a "zero-rating" status. If the stage 3b firms in Table 1 were exporters, for example, they would be registered for tax purposes, but a zero tax rate would be applied to their sales. By claiming credit for the taxes of 40 already paid on their purchase inputs, they would free their export sales of all VAT burdens. It is important to note that simply exempting exporters from the value-added tax would not achieve the same result. Exempt firms are not registered for tax purposes and pay no tax on their sales, but at the same time they can claim no tax credits for any VAT burdens embodied in their purchased inputs. In the Table 1 example, output flowing to consumers through exempt stage 3b firms would bear a tax of 40.

Exempt status under a VAT is particularly suitable for business enterprises too small to make collection of tax from them administratively feasible. If stage 3b firms in Table 1 fell in that category, for example, a value-added tax of 40 would still be collected in their purchased inputs, whereas a retail sales tax that granted them exempt status would leave their total sales—not just their value added—free of all tax burdens. Exemption of small firms at earlier stages of production could reduce compliance and administrative costs with no revenue loss to the government. If all stage 2 firms in Table 1 were small, for example, exempt status for them would relieve them of VAT burdens of 60 and add those same burdens to stage 3 firms if a flow-through of tax credits from stage 1 production were provided to them. Without that flow-through, exemption of stage 2 firms would mean the collection of VAT revenue of 50 from stage 3a and 3b firms since they would have no tax credits on their invoiced input purchases; the effective VAT rate on their total output would then be 12 percent.

TAX BASE AND REVENUE POTENTIAL

It is not to be thought that a national sales tax would succeed in reaching every single consumption expenditure in the United States. Certain items would be either completely exempted or lightly taxed—some for equity reasons, others for administrative reasons, and still others for political reasons. No one can predict exactly what the total tax base would turn out to be.

One can, however, list the main categories of consumption that might qualify for special tax status. Such a listing is presented in Table 2.

Quantification of the cost of these exemptions, however, must start with an estimation of the full base. The first step is to adjust the total personal consumption expenditures shown for the target year in the national income and product accounts ($2,156 billion) to a national sales tax basis by subtracting the foreign travel expenditures of U.S. residents ($22 billion) and adding the tourist expenditures of foreigners in the United States ($13 billion). The result is a total potential national sales

TABLE 2. POTENTIAL BASE AND PROBABLE EXEMPTIONS FOR A NATIONAL SALES TAX

(1983 Consumption Levels)		*In Billions of Dollars*	*Percent of Tax Base*
1. *Total Potential Tax Base:*	$	2,147	100.0
2. *Minimum Exemptions:*		455	21.2
a. Food furnished employees		6	
b. Food produced & consumed on farms		1	
c. Standard-issue military clothing		*	
d. Annual rental value of housing		363	
e. Domestic services		8	
f. In-kind services, financial intermediaries		51	
g. Handling expenses, life insurance		25	
3. *Additional Exemptions:*		750	34.9
h. Food for off-premise consumption		294	
i. Household utilities (except telephone)		115	
j. Medical care		238	
k. Legal, funeral, & burial services		25	
l. Local transportation services, bridge, road, & other tolls		8	
m. Theater & opera; nonprofit recreation services		5	
n. Private education & research		33	
o. Religious & welfare activities		32	
4. *Total Exemptions:* **	1,205	1,205	56.1

Source: Survey of Current Business (July 1984), Table 2.4, pp. 37–38.

*Less than $0.5 billion.

**Because column entries have been rounded, their sums may not equal the totals stated.

tax base of $2,147 billion, shown on the first line of Table 2. The next step is to identify candidates for favored tax treatment and to divide them into two broad groups. In the "minimum exemption" group the annual rental value of housing is the most important category, accounting for 17 percent of the potential tax base in 1983. In the "additional exemption" group, key items are food for off-premise consumption (14 percent of the total tax base), medical care (11 percent of the base), and household utilities (5 percent of the base). Altogether, the exemptions listed in Table 2 make up 56 percent of the tax base, with 21 percent in the "minimum" group and 35 percent in the "additional" category.

Compiling a list of potential tax base exemptions, however, is only the second step in estimating the probable yield of a national sales tax. Exemption would free a particular category of consumption from all tax burdens under a retail sales tax, but under a value-added tax it would not eliminate taxes paid at the preceding levels of production. Under a VAT that used exemptions rather than zero-rating, therefore, the potential tax base would be larger than it appears in Table 2.

Another equivocal area is the treatment of housing. While the annual rental value of the existing housing stock would undoubtedly be excluded from any national sales tax base, the value of new housing construction might well be included. In the 1983 context new housing amounted to $132 billion, which would have added 6 percent to the potential tax base shown in Table 2. Use of a broad tax base, it will be noted, would subject many necessities to taxation, thereby strengthening the case for some kind of tax relief for low-income groups. Use of a narrower base could lower the need for low-income relief, but only at the cost of higher administrative and compliance expenses.

All things considered, it is impossible to be precise about the probable yield of a national sales tax. A very tightly defined base that included the value of new housing construction might reach 85 percent of total consumption, while a loosely defined base might reach only 44 percent. At 1983 levels of consumption, then, each percentage point of tax would have a gross yield of somewhere between $9 and $18 billion. Net yields to the federal government would be lower, depending on the level of administrative expenses and the cost of any low-income relief that accompanied enactment of the tax.

SUMMARY

A value-added tax is simply one form that an impersonal tax on consumption might take. Another form, much more familiar to Americans, is the retail sales tax. Both levies are impersonal in the sense that they tax consumption directly, item by item, and persons only indirectly. In that respect they stand in sharp contrast to a consumption-expenditure tax that would tax persons directly on their total spending for consumer goods and services.

Who Bears the Burden of a Sales Tax?

Sales taxation, as practiced in this country, provides an interesting illustration of the ascendancy, if not indeed the triumph, of appearance over reality. Sales tax revenue is collected from retailers, but the intent is that it be paid by consumers. That intent is made explicit by having the tax stated separately on each sale of taxed output. The result is that the great majority of the general public believes firmly that sales tax burdens are borne by consumers. Whether these apparent incidence patterns are also the real ones is a question that has been debated by economists for a long time. Although critics of the ostensible impact have yet to convince a majority of their colleagues, to say nothing of the general public, they have made some points that deserve serious consideration.

The nature of the arguments made by critics of the standard consumer-burden theory of sales tax incidence can be understood by following the logic of a hypothetical illustration. Suppose that a national value-added tax is imposed on roughly half of total personal consumption expenditures, with its revenue dedicated to a reduction in the federal deficit. Prices of taxed products would rise, and the total consuming power of people would also rise to the extent that interest rates were lowered in response to the reduced level of government borrowing and to whatever monetary easing the Federal Reserve System chose to effect. Clearly, there are plenty of uncertainties here to argue about. If the spending power of consumers increased sufficiently, the tax-induced shift of output from the taxed to the nontaxed sector of the economy could occur with little or no decrease in wage or profit rates or in the prices of nontaxed goods and services. This is the scenario implicit in the standard consumer-burden theory of sales tax incidence. If, on the other hand, consumer spending power did not rise by much, output in the taxed sector would fall because of the higher prices in that sector, workers would be released from employment, and competition for jobs in both sectors of the economy would tend to drive down wage rates. Product prices in the taxed sector would ultimately rise by less than the full amount of the value-added tax, and prices in the nontaxed sector would be lower than they otherwise would be. Some consumers would be burdened, but others would be benefited. Some workers and some property owners would receive lower incomes than they otherwise would have received. This is a very different scenario, and it is, of course, the one stressed by the critics of consumer-burden incidence.

Exactly where the burdens of a new value-added tax would come to rest is far from obvious. Even if the second scenario prevailed, however, few people would be aware of the price and wage reductions brought about by the tax, and fewer still would attribute them to the right cause. That being the case, policy makers are probably well advised to assume that it is the apparent incidence of a sales tax that matters and to design their policies accordingly.

Would a Value-added Tax Be Inflationary?

A value-added tax, then, is both intended and expected to raise prices by the full amount of tax. In other words, a 10 percent VAT levied on half of total consumption should raise consumer prices by about 5 percent. That is a specific kind of inflation which in and of itself causes no problems. What is worrisome, however, is the risk that the tax would give rise to a more general wage-push inflationary spiral. That could happen if wages were widely indexed for inflation on the basis of a price index that included sales taxes in its calculation, as the Consumer Price Index (CPI) currently does. Enactment of a VAT would then trigger automatic wage increases on a broad scale, prices would increase in response to those cost increases, wage rates would rise still further, and so forth. That is not a prospect to be contemplated with equanimity. No good tax should be structured to allow some of its intended payers to shift its burden automatically to others.

Fortunately, there is a way of dealing with these potentially distorting effects of a national sales tax, and it is one that is attractive in a broader sense. Taxes that impose their burdens by raising prices are similar to inflation in their effects but quite different from it in their economic significance. This important distinction should be brought to public attention by the publication of official prices indexes that both include and exclude sales and excise taxes. Each kind is useful for its own specific purposes, and a general public discussion about what these are would be valuable. For the reasons just given, it is a tax-exclusive price index that should be used to index wages for inflation. Using the same kind of price measure to index the federal individual income tax structure for inflation would have the desirable effect of preventing an increase in one kind of federal tax from automatically reducing the yield of another kind. Conversely, use of a tax-inclusive price measure to index income-tested government transfer payments would significantly reduce the burdens of a national sales tax on low-income groups.

Why Should There Be a Value-added Tax at All?

Particular taxes may be justified on either of two broad grounds. One is that it is both equitable and efficient to allocate tax burdens in close relation to the benefits people receive from government programs financed by those taxes, thereby encouraging rational choice about the magnitudes of those programs. The other, which is especially appropriate when government benefits are intangible and diffuse, is to allocate tax burdens in close relation to the abilities of the people to pay them, regardless of how many—or how few—governmental benefits they receive. It is conceded that this separation of taxing and spending decisions in the minds of the public may create economic inefficiencies of various kinds, but the equity of basing tax burdens on personal abilities to pay is widely recognized and supported.

THE BENEFIT MODEL

Enactment of a national value-added tax could be justified under either the benefit or the ability model of taxation. Under the former, a VAT would be seen as a way to charge businesses for the myriad of federal government services that help to create a good, stable environment in which business can operate. Another federal levy that, in part, plays this kind of role is the corporation income tax, but the value-added tax is clearly the superior instrument. Businesses benefit from the free market whether they are incorporated or not and whether they make profits or not. There is much to be said for replacing the benefit portion of the corporation income tax, which also has an important ability portion, with a value-added tax. (A retail sales tax, incidentally, would not qualify for this purpose.) However, the rationale supporting the use of a VAT for this purpose has one important weakness. Because the government benefits in question cannot be measured quantitatively, little guidance is offered about where the tax rate level should be set, and much dispute could easily arise over a VAT that was seen mainly as a benefit levy.

THE ABILITY MODEL

It is as an ability-based levy that the sales tax finds its main justification. In such a role it must be evaluated according to the standard tests of equity and efficiency. The equity principle applies both to the equal treatment of equals (horizontal equity) and to the fairest distribution of tax burdens among differing ability levels (vertical equity). The main dispute centers on concepts of "fairness." Some argue for a proportional tax that exacts the same percentage of income at all income levels, and others argue for a progressive tax whose burdens increase in relation to income as income levels rise. Few openly advocate a regressive tax whose burdens become proportionately less as income increases. The efficiency test also has two main dimensions: (1) economic, having to do with the ways a tax encourages—or interferes with—the highest and best uses of the nation's resources, and (2) fiscal, pertaining to the collection costs imposed on both government and taxpayers. In a federal system of government the effects a tax has on intergovernmental fiscal relations are also important.

How Regressive Is the Sales Tax?

One of the most powerful arguments against the sales tax traditionally has been that the vertical distribution of its burdens is regressive. The very power of this criticism, however, has tempted many of its users to overstate its significance. The true variation of sales tax burdens in relation to family income is very difficult to specify, and it may well be considerably less regressive than often depicted. Whatever the true regressivity of sales tax burdens may be theoretically, in practice a sales tax does not need to have that effect on the great majority of people. Perhaps the best way to approach this issue is to paraphrase Gerard Brannon, who has provided some of the liveliest and most insightful discussions of the value-added tax: saying that the sales tax is regressive is like saying that lemonade is a sour drink; it all depends on how it is made, and the important task is to work out a palatable recipe. Various ways in which the vertical equity of a national sales tax can be enhanced are presented later. First, however, it is important to consider how sour a levy the unsweetened sales tax really is.

Sales tax burdens are conventionally measured in relation to the amount of income spent on taxable consumer goods and services by families at different income levels. If these computations are based on annual data, it is not unusual to find effective tax rates at the bottom of the income scale to be large multiples of those prevailing at the top. However, annual income data are, in fact, biased indicators of the regressivity of sales tax burdens. Many households at the extremes of the annual income distribution scale are there only temporarily. Since their consumption expenditures tend to be based on their more normal income levels, consumption tax burdens of low-income families show up as atypically high and those of high-income families as atypically low. While the direction of this bias has long been clear, its quantitative significance has not. As research on lifetime income patterns has accumulated, however, these uncertainties increasingly have been resolved. Whereas low-income families typically spend more on consumption than the amount of their annual incomes, families at the bottom of the lifetime income scale are net savers. More specifically, if families are ranked by income and then divided into ten equal groups (deciles) and if each group's effective sales tax rate is expressed as a ratio to the sales tax rate on the whole population, a rough picture of the differences between annual and lifetime income sales tax burden distribution can be tabulated as in Table 3. Sales tax burdens are still regressive when measured in relation to typical lifetime income patterns, but the degree of regressivity is considerably less than that shown by annual data.

A more important, but less certain, determination of the vertical distribution of sales tax burdens is the impact of the tax on the general price level. If the prices of taxed products generally rise by the full amount of the sales tax and other prices remain unchanged, the conventional burden patterns just illustrated give a true picture of the regressivity of sales tax burdens. On the other hand, if a new sales tax were to have no net impact on the general price level (the market adjustments described earlier pushing nontaxed product prices lower to about the same extent that taxed product prices rose), consumer tax burdens would be greatly reduced and might well be mildly progressive in their vertical incidence. This may be seen by supposing that a 10 percent sales tax were imposed on half of total consumption expenditures, raising prices there by 10 percent but, as the market responded, gradually reducing prices in the nontaxed sector by enough to keep the general price level from rising. If the ratio of taxed to total consumption were the same in each income group, each group would experience about the same small net consumer burden or benefit (depending on how the weighted group price indexes were computed), and the vertical distribution of consumer tax burdens, if any, would be close to proportionality.

TABLE 3. SALES TAX BURDEN RATIOS BASED ON ANNUAL AND LIFETIME INCOMES

Income Decile	Annual	Lifetime
Lowest	2.2	1.1
Second	1.6	1.1
Ninth	1.0	1.0
Highest	0.7	0.9

Evidence derived from the typical state retail sales tax in this country, however, shows that taxed sales appear to constitute a rising percentage of total consumption as one ascends the income scale. Such being the case and given an unchanged general price level, the tax used in this illustration could be expected to confer net consumer benefits on low-income families and net burdens on high-income households. Its vertical burden pattern would be progressive, but the degree would be very small, on the order of plus or minus 0.05 percent of lifetime incomes at the extremes of distribution. The principal burdens of such a sales tax, this evidence suggests, would not be on consumers but rather on wage and capital income receivers, and the vertical distribution of those burdens could also be expected to be mildly progressive.

While the burdens of a national sales tax might well turn out to be less regressive than most people expect them to be, that possibility is not likely to defuse the regressivity issue. Therefore, it is important to consider the various ways in which excessive sales tax burdens could be eliminated, offset, or converted into a progressive pattern.

How Could Sales Tax Regressivity Best Be Handled?

THE SIMPLEST RESPONSE

The simplest response to the challenge posed by that question would be to design a national sales tax to meet criteria other than vertical equity, to recognize that this probably would produce a regressive pattern of tax burdens, and to offset the excessive portions of these burdens for low-income families by making suitable adjustments in the federal government's income tax rates and transfer expenditure programs. Such a multiple-instrument approach is highly regarded by policy theorists, but it is a risky road to take in practice. In fact, vertical inequity in one instrument may not be counteracted by changes in other instruments. Sales tax critics are sufficiently aware of this problem that they are not likely to be mollified by promises alone. For many of them a new national sales tax would not be acceptable unless it came with its own built-in solutions to the regressivity problem.

THE MOST COMMON RESPONSE

The most commonly adopted antidote to excessive regressivity is a sales tax structure that places few, if any, burdens on necessities and relatively high burdens on luxuries. Plausible as such a solution may seem on the surface, it is in fact capable of achieving only moderate gains in vertical equity at relatively high cost to tax administrators, to businesses who must comply with a complex law, and to consumers who have to live with a seriously tax-distorted set of market prices. Moreover, it could be hard to sell to a populace already alarmed by the inequities created by a badly eroded income tax base. The fundamental economic difficulty is that the separation of consumer goods and services into categories that make a feasible distinction between necessities and luxuries for the application of differing sales tax rates is an equity-defying task. A nutritionist, for example, could define the basic outlines of a well-balanced, minimum-level family diet that clearly would fall into the "necessity" class, and yet differences in tastes are such that little agreement could be reached on specifics since one person's necessity is another's luxury. The basic political difficulty is that any departure from a single, uniform tax rate applied to a broad consumption base open up a Pandora's box of special interest pressures and favors that make for a steady erosion of the tax base. As Henry Aaron notes in his summary of the proceedings of a 1980 Brookings Institution conference on European experience with the value-added tax:

> The central technical lesson of European experience is that multiple rates can be used to eliminate the regressivity of the value-added tax, but that the penalties in administrative complexity, increased compliance cost, and distortions in consumption decisions have been high and probably unjustified.

THE MOST PROMISING RESPONSE

Given these problems with a format that employs differing sales tax rates, the most promising solution to the regressivity problem involves combining a broad-based national sales tax with a special, refundable, vanishing income tax credit designed to relieve low-income families of any excessive sales tax burdens. If 80 percent of a poverty-line income of $10,000, for example, were found typically to be spent on taxable commodities, the annual tax credit would be $80 for each percentage point of value-added tax. The credit should be refundable because many low-income families would not have enough federal income tax liability to absorb it fully, and it should be phased out gradually at higher income levels where sales tax burdens are not excessive. A special tax credit of this sort, which has been used in a number of states since 1965, would convert a national sales tax into a progressive levy for the majority of families in the country and could also eliminate the tendency of sales taxes to overburden large families relative to smaller ones at the same income level. By permitting the application of a single, low tax rate to a broad range of consumer goods and services, the credit also would reduce VAT administrative and compliance costs.

Sales tax credits do, of course, have their own special problems, but experience indicates that these can be dealt with readily. Paying a tax first and claiming credit for it later obviously can create liquidity problems for low-income families, but these pressures could be reduced to acceptable levels by integrating the credit with the federal government's income tax withholding mechanism, social security benefits, and income-tested transfer payments. While not paying a tax in the first place is simpler than paying it and claiming reimbursement, the income tax forms needed for this purpose can be simple in design and readily available to all who need them. It is not to be expected that utilization rates would approach 100 percent, but vigorous use of widespread public information programs should ensure that few honest taxpayers would fail to file for their refunds. Compliance cost could be kept low, though at some loss in tax equity, by basing the credit on income data already required for federal income tax purposes. In fact, a new sales tax credit could be integrated with the earned income credit (added to the federal income tax in 1975) by extending the earned income credit to all taxpayers and basing it on adjusted gross, rather than earned, income. Greater equity would be achieved by using an expanded concept of family income that included most of the kinds of income that low-income families receive. Such equity gains, however, should be balanced against the additional compliance cost these inclusions would impose. Finally, it must be noted that credit claims would increase federal handling and auditing costs by adding to the number of income tax returns filed, but these additional costs should be less than those that would be imposed by a multiple-rate, narrow-based sales tax.

If a sales tax with an income tax credit is regarded as too complicated, an alternative solution to the regressivity problem would be to enact a levy similar to Robert Hall and Alvin Rabushka's flat tax proposal. Their plan imposes a single tax rate on all income but collects the revenue separately from individuals and businesses. The individual compensation tax is based on wages, salaries, and pensions and has a set of inflation-indexed personal allowances but no other personal deductions. The allowances both protect the poor from excessive tax burdens and make the tax rate structure progressive in relation to earned income. The business tax is based on business income computed with no deductions for dividends, interest payments, or the cost of employee fringe benefits, which accordingly are not included in the individual compensation tax. The business tax would allow immediate expensing of all capital asset purchases, not only eliminating all of the complexities of depreciation accounting but also converting the nationwide base of the tax from income to consumption. The plan, therefore, can be regarded as a way of levying a national consumption tax with a built-in solution to the regressivity problem.

There are, then, a number of practical ways in which a national consumption tax could be established without imposing excessive burdens on low-income families. The regressivity problem can be handled, but the degree of progressivity that could be achieved by the means just presented would be regarded by many as inadequate. In a reformed federal tax system that contained a sales tax, significant progressivity would have to be achieved through the use of one or more separate and additional tax instruments. The list of possibilities would include a progressive, broad-based income tax, a progressive personal consumption-expenditure tax, progressive estate and gift taxes, or even a national annual net wealth tax.

Would a National Sales Tax
Increase the Size of the Federal Government?

While the liberals' main criticism of the sales tax has centered on the regressivity of its burdens, the main concern of conservatives has been the danger that a new, productive source of revenue would lead inevitably to higher federal government expenditures than otherwise would be approved. These fears are based on the view that the growth of government spending, unless constrained in some way, is dominated by unending pressures for special interest benefits to be paid for by the less well organized general taxpayer. Two potential constraints that are relevant here are large federal deficits and highly visible tax burdens. A value-added tax could weaken both of these curbs significantly. If enacted as a source of additional revenue it would reduce prospective deficits and impose a set of relatively invisible tax burdens. To be sure, a national retail sales tax would presumably state its burdens separately on all taxable sales slips, and a value-added tax could be structured in the same way, but it is doubtful that many people would keep close track of the totals of all those separate items each week or month. If the sales tax were enacted as a means of reducing income tax rates, its hard-to-compute burdens would be substituted for the regularly reported amounts of withheld income taxes.

Exactly how much additional federal spending a new national sales tax might stimulate is subject to much dispute. What evidence there is from other countries is not reassuring in this respect. In Europe, for example, enactment of the value-added tax, while intended as a substitute for other taxes, was typically followed by rising VAT rates and higher government spending. As Henry Aaron puts it:

> While the value-added tax might be used to reduce other taxes and as part of a program of fiscal retrenchment in the United States, it is important to recognize that the United States would be blazing a trail of fiscal forbearance not traversed by any of the countries [covered in *The Value-Added Tax: Lessons From Europe*].

There is no foolproof way of ensuring that a new national sales tax would not stimulate federal spending. Segregating its revenue in a special fund dedicated to deficit reduction might help for a while, but over the long pull such bookkeeping refinements are not likely to have much influence on expenditure authorizations and appropriations. Placing a cap on sales tax rates would help if future Congresses and administrations found it more difficult to raise the cap than to increase tax rates that had no such limits. Placing a cap in the United States Constitution would provide a stronger constraint but at the cost of reduced federal fiscal flexibility.

Would a National Sales Tax Hurt State and Local Governments?

While some worry about higher federal spending, others are concerned about the pressures that a national sales tax might place on state and local government operations. The sales tax has long been a prerogative of those governments, and they are naturally reluctant to see the field opened to a new and powerful competitor.

How serious that competition might prove to be is not easy to predict. Much depends, for one thing, on what the relevant alternatives are. Higher federal deficits, for example, hurt state and local governments by driving up the interest rates they must pay on new borrowings, although these higher rates also tend to reduce their pension costs. A broader federal income tax base would hurt them if it included municipal bond interest in its scope, if it eliminated the deductibility of certain state and local personal taxes, or if it reduced the tax subsidy to charitable contributions that substitute for various kinds of state and local spending. Higher federal income tax rates would hurt by raising total income tax burdens, but at the same time they would reduce the effective state and local tax rates for all who itemize their deductions on federal income tax returns. Another relevant consideration is how much federal tax reform, which might include some use of a national sales tax, would help state and local governments by improving the performance of the general economy. High employment and low inflation levels do much to strengthen state and local taxing powers.

Economic realities, then, support two general conclusions. First, well-designed federal fiscal and tax reforms, by stimulating noninflationary economic growth, would help rather than harm state and local governments. Second, any federal tax increase, regardless of its particular form, would restrain state and local taxing powers to much the same degree. All tax revenue comes from the same total national income flow, and higher tax collections by one level of government necessarily reduce the proportion of the flow that can be tapped by other levels. Economic realities, however, are not the only important consideration. Political realities suggest that the specific form in which federal tax increases are imposed makes a substantial difference. A federal sales tax might reduce directly—and significantly—the general public's tolerance for state and local sales tax rate increases. Such, at least, is the loud and clear message conveyed by state and local government officials when they indicate, on one hand, strong opposition to any separately stated set of national sales tax rates and, on the other, very ukewarm support for a federal VAT, even though its rates would remain largely hidden from public view. If these concerns remained undiminished even after broad public discussion of the countervailing factors considered here, enactment of a national sales tax might have to be accompanied by increased federal aid to state and local governments. That would reduce, of course, the net amount of federal revenue derived from the new sales tax.

All these potential drawbacks of a national sales tax must be weighed carefully, but there is another side to the issue. On that side are found the good economic effects that might result from the addition of such a levy to the federal tax structure.

What Economic Benefits
Might a National Sales Tax Generate?

One of the main attractions of a sales tax is its ability to raise revenue with relatively little distortion of market mechanisms—i.e., the ways in which an economy organizes its resources to bring the highest possible levels of present and future satisfaction to consumers. No practicable tax can be completely neutral in these respects, but a broad-based, single-rate retail sales or value-added tax would rank relatively high on a neutrality scale.

NEUTRALITY ON CAPITAL INCOME

Nowhere are these comparative advantages of a sales tax more conspicuous than in the tax treatment of capital incomes, a topic that presents policy makers with one of the most impenetrable thickets of problems in the fiscal world. Business, property, and investment incomes are all more difficult to measure accurately than wages and salaries, especially when general price inflation makes nominal dollar values a biased indicator of real gains and losses. Lurking behind these complexities of implementation are the ever-present risks that capital income taxation will unduly discourage saving and investment and reduce the rate of economic growth below acceptable levels. Progress through this thicket requires persistence, a reliable compass that points to the best attainable set of rules for taxing capital incomes, and a determination to avoid taking easy pathways, all of which lead to a morass of special favors for some kinds of savings and investments and constraints on others. Once trapped in that swamp, loaded down with investment tax credits, accelerated depreciation allowances, capital gains exclusions, bond interest exemptions, limited loss deductions, safe-harbor leasing, and many other special tax rules, the economy drifts aimlessly, wasting productive resources in inferior uses and sidetracking energies into the fabrication of tax-avoidance schemes. Worse still, the more energetic the efforts to escape from these difficulties, the deeper the system seems to sink into them.

The sales tax solves all of these problems simply by avoiding them. By taxing consumption and exempting saving and investment, the sales tax takes a side road around both thicket and swamp. Investments in particular assets, industries, or sectors of the economy are neither taxed nor subsidized, and all saving is freed from tax burdens regardless of its purpose. The economic benefits include freeing business and personal investment decisions from tax influences, both positive and negative, a process that allows private markets to allocate resources to their most profitable uses. Such tax neutrality is not universally applauded, but many see it as distinctly preferable to the morass of special rules and regulations that were added to the federal income tax laws in the 1970s and early 1980s.

NEUTRALITY ON PRIVATE SAVING

Another benefit attributed to the sales tax is its avoidance of any distortion of household choices between consuming now and saving now in order to consume later. The nature of this distortion is easily indicated. Consider a worker earning $100 and deciding whether to consume now or to save and consume a year later. If the rate of return on saving is 10 percent and there are no taxes, the gain from waiting a year, per dollar saved now, is $1.10. If a 25 percent tax is applied to all income, the worker's maximum current consumption is $75, compared to a maximum future consumption of $80.62 (equal to the $75 saved plus the net-of-tax interest earned on it). The gain from postponing consumption for a year is therefore reduced to $1.075 per dollar saved. If, on the other hand, a comparable sales tax is imposed, the worker's maximum current consumption remains at $75, but the maximum future consumption rises to $82.50, so that the rate of return resulting from postponing consumption is restored to its nontaxed level of $1.10.

This example illustrates another important difference between income and sales taxes. Tax rates for the two kinds of levy are not directly comparable because income tax rates ordinarily apply to a base that includes the tax whereas sales tax rates apply to a base that does not include the tax. In the present example the tax-inclusive income tax rate of 25 percent is equivalent to a 33.33 tax-exclusive sales tax rate. Unless care is taken, therefore, it is easy to overstate sales tax rates when comparing them to income tax rates.

The sales tax, then, is both more neutral and more favorable to private saving and investment than is the income tax. Set against these efficiency gains, however, are some important equity losses. Advocates of the income tax as the nation's basic ability-to-pay levy stress the fiscal goals, such as tax burden progressivity, that can be achieved only by going through the capital income taxation thicket. For them the underbrush is not impenetrable, and any detour around it is seen simply as a cop-out. By not tackling the impossible, they argue, policy makers will often miss the opportunity to accomplish things that prove to be merely difficult.

Indeed, income tax reform is one of the major alternatives to enactment of a national sales tax. But, the longer that reform is delayed and the less it accomplishes in the end, the stronger the case for a federal sales tax will become.

SIMPLICITY AND EFFICIENCY

Other important advantages of a national sales tax can also be found in the related areas of tax simplicity and fiscal efficiency, but these, too, are difficult to evaluate abstractly. It does seem clear that a well-designed retail sales or value-added tax would be less complex than a well-designed individual or corporation income tax, for the reasons already given, and, hence, could be operated at lower compliance and administrative costs. Adding a new tax to the U.S. tax system, however, would entail significant start-up costs, and if the new tax did not completely replace either or both of the two federal income taxes, their administrative and compliance costs would continue, perhaps at only slightly reduced levels. In order to accomplish much in this area one would have to go all the way and substitute, say, Hall and Rabushka's "low, simple, and flat" tax for the federal individual and corporation income taxes, but achieving a result accepted as a "fair" tax might be difficult. For less radical reforms, such as adding a sales tax to the federal revenue system, the most important point to note is that operating cost is largely independent of the tax rate imposed, with the result that cost as a percentage of revenue tends to fall as revenue rises. This means that it would not be worthwhile to add a low-rate VAT to the federal system, and raising the tax rate above a minimum level would not increase operating cost significantly. There is a limit, however, as high tax rates do intensify temptations for evasion, and beyond some hard-to-identify level these pressures could raise administrative cost unduly and cause much time and effort to be wasted on nonproductive activities.

ECONOMIC CHANGES

Other economic changes that enactment of a national sales tax might bring about would depend on how its revenue was used. There are numerous possibilities, but only the most important one, which is a substitution of sales for income tax revenue, will be considered here. All of the following potential changes are worth noting, and some deserve further study, but in the aggregate their total net benefits to the country are not likely to be great.

Labor Supply—Substituting a national sales tax for a part of the personal income tax would strengthen incentives to work by lowering income tax rates and would weaken them by raising tax rates on consumers. High savers might work harder under the sales tax, but there is little evidence to indicate that the effects would be large. Substituting the sales tax for part of the corporation income tax would shift tax burdens from capital to wage income and would thus combine disincentives to work with incentives to save and invest.

Exports and Imports—Some of the earliest support for a value-added tax in this country was founded on the argument that it would help the balance of international payments by stimulating exports and discouraging imports. In part this support derived from a misunderstanding of the intended effects of the tax. In particular, these advocates saw the VAT's border tax adjustments as subsidies to exports and as taxes on imports rather than as a means of offsetting the domestic price-increasing effects of the tax. A more sophisticated case for balance of payments gains was made by those who viewed the VAT as a substitute for a corporation income tax whose burdens were shifted forward fully to consumers through higher prices. Such a tax exchange, according to this argument, would have little net impact on the general price level, but the border tax adjustments permitted under international rules for the operation of a VAT would, in a world of fixed exchange rates, stimulate U.S. exports and depress imports. The foundations for this prediction were never strong because the effects of the corporation income tax on consumer prices are highly uncertain and controversial, and they were undermined further by the world's move away from fixed exchange rates.

Nevertheless, the whole discussion does highlight the importance of the price-increasing effects of a value-added tax. If these are less than the full amount of the tax and if the accompanying border tax adjustments reflect that full amount, the resulting shifts in the relative competitive positions of U.S. exporters and importers would tend to strengthen the dollar on foreign exchange markets. A stronger dollar, in turn, would offset both the cost improvements initially enjoyed by U.S. exporters and the cost increases suffered by importers.

International Capital Flows—If the shift from income to consumption taxation did increase saving, investment, and economic growth in the United States, some reallocation of direct business investment by both U.S. and foreign firms would be expected. Such an improved business climate would strengthen the dollar on foreign exchange markets, and that change would discourage U.S. exports and stimulate imports. Competitive forces in domestic markets would intensify, business risks would increase, and the general environment thereby might become a less attractive one for business investment. Again the main point is that in a world of flexible exchange rates the effects of a sales tax on international trade and capital flows, even if initially important, are not likely to remain so for long.

Innovation and Invention—The importance of these activities to economic progress has long been explicitly recognized in the structure given to the federal income tax. Research and development expenditures can be deducted in full in the year incurred, and a special incremental tax credit for them was introduced in 1981. Small corporations are subject to lower tax rates than are large ones and can elect to be taxed as partnerships, subject to Subchapter S rules, if that treatment would lower their tax burdens. Successful innovators receive a large portion of their rewards in the form of favorably taxed long-term capital gains rather than as ordinary income. Opportunities to deduct business losses immediately, while deferring tax on accruing capital gains, tend to strengthen risk-taking incentives. Given such a pattern of income tax favors, a national sales tax is not likely to be a major stimulus to innovation and invention.

Economic Stabilization—Adding a sales tax to the federal revenue system would weaken the built-in cyclical stabilizing powers of the system but also would expand the government's discretionary policy options. The weakening would occur because income tax revenue falls more rapidly during recessions, and rises more rapidly during economic booms, than would sales tax revenue. In general, then, the restructured federal tax system would automatically dampen the amplitude of business cycles less than one relying mainly on income taxes. The size of these differential effects would depend on, among other things, the scope of the new sales tax base, particularly its treatment of cycle-sensitive consumer-durable expenditures and cycle-insensitive necessities.

Used skillfully, a national sales tax could be a powerful discretionary stabilizing instrument. Temporary changes in sales tax rates would have stronger effects on aggregate consumer spending than would temporary changes in income tax rates with equivalent revenue gains and losses for the government. The main operational problems are the perverse antistabilizing effects created by early expectations of a sales tax rate change and by any significant gap between announcement and enactment of the change. In an inflation-threatening boom, for example, anticipation of a sales tax increase would stimulate an immediate spending spree, and expectations of tax reductions during a developing recession would intensify the downswing. Use of temporary sales tax rate changes for stabilization purposes, then, would require a careful handling of public expectancy, with a minimum of anticipatory excitement arising before the enactment of the changes and a maximum of certainty prevailing with respect to their termination. These requirements could be realized only if such rate changes were applied infrequently and for only as long as needed to steady the economy. In the absence of these conditions, rate juggling could not be effective as a stabilizer, and the government's credibility could not be maintained.

Would a Value-added Tax
Be Better Than a Retail Sales Tax?

The choice between the value-added and retail sales variants of a federal sales tax rests not on their comparative economic effects, which are virtually identical, but on their relative administrative and compliance costs and the ease with which they could be integrated into our intergovernmental revenue systems.

The retail sales tax could offer greater gains in intergovernmental fiscal efficiency but probably faces stronger political opposition. The fiscal gains would be realized only if the federal retail sales tax base were adopted by all, or most, of the states using the tax. Such piggyback arrangements, with each level of government applying its own tax rate to a uniform base, would greatly simplify the separate listing of the tax amounts on retail purchases; would replace the haphazard and relatively ineffective operation of state use taxes with an efficient, even-handed system of federal collection of taxes on interstate sales for all destination states; and would create opportunities for significant savings in operating cost through centralized administration. Political opposition to sharing a retail sales tax could be minimized, on the one hand, by the federal government's adoption of a broader base than that used by most states, so that few states would lose revenue by conforming their own bases to the federal tax and, on the other, by offering the prospect of credible gains in administrative and compliance costs. Nevertheless, many state and local officials would be concerned about a move that not only would be a direct invasion of their own taxing territory but also would place relatively visible additional tax burdens on their consumer-constituents.

A federal value-added tax whose burdens were not itemized on sales to final consumers would lessen these state and local fears but at the cost of intensifying concerns about the expenditure-stimulating effects of the new tax. Separate listing, in contrast, would raise the compliance cost for retailers who would need to itemize two or more different lists of taxable sales, thus subjecting them to the same difficulties that they would face under an uncoordinated federal-state system of retail sales taxes.

Coexistence between a federal value-added tax and an independent set of state retail sales taxes, each operating in its own special sphere, need not create any serious intergovernmental problems. The information requirements of a federal VAT would be comparatively closely related to the federal income tax, and most businesses could readily integrate their records to comply with the two types of levy. A federal VAT would not provide any major incentive for state and local governments to shift their sales taxes to the value-added variant or to adopt VATs closely related to the federal tax. Because border tax adjustments would be more troublesome administratively for states than for the federal government, state VATs would have to be origin-based levies. Any shift from the retail sales to the value-added variant for state sales taxes, therefore, would represent an important change in taxable capacity from a system favoring market states that are net importers to one favoring producing states that are net exporters. Of course, producing states might justify a VAT on a benefits-received basis, and, as long as geographically mobile businesses looked beyond the VAT burdens to the incremental benefits financed by the tax, there would be no fiscal distortion of business location decisions. If that benefit-tax connection were not highly visible, however, origin-based state VATs would not be locationally neutral unless all states adopted the levy and used the same tax rate. Such a uniform rate system would be equivalent to a federal VAT with part of the revenue shared with the states. Its chief drawbacks are that it would require complex additional computations for all interstate businesses to allocate their total value added to all contributing states and that it would lack the fiscal freedoms enjoyed by states under a piggyback federal-state retail sales tax system that allowed states to set their own tax rates.

What Is the Bottom Line?

Like any of the tax proposals competing for public acceptance, the value-added tax has its own special strengths and weaknesses, most of which are shared with the retail sales tax. Its strengths are its high degree of neutrality toward different kinds of business and consumer choices, its relatively favorable treatment of saving and investment, and its low administrative and compliance costs. It also may deserve a higher horizontal-equity rating than either an individual income or a personal consumption-expenditure tax. This is true because, in practice, collection of taxes can be more effectively accomplished at or near the source than under the self-assessment systems needed for income and consumption-expenditure taxes. The chief weaknesses of sales taxes are found in the vertical-equity area. They can, in the ways previously examined, be structured to achieve a fairly high degree of burden progressivity over the lower ranges of family income, but they cannot achieve a similar result at higher income levels. For that purpose a different tax instrument is required.

A national sales tax, therefore, could be used best as part of an integrated, ability-based federal tax system. One possibility would be a two-tier system, such as that proposed for the United Kingdom in 1978 by the Meade committee's report on *The Structure and Reform of Direct Taxation*. That would combine a federal VAT with a progressive consumption-expenditure tax that allowed sufficiently high personal exemptions to restrict its burdens to the highest income groups. Alternatively, a consumption-type flat rate tax plan, such as the one proposed by Hall and Rabushka, could be modified by adding higher tax rates at the top of its range and be combined with strengthened federal gift and estate taxes. There are many avenues leading to effective federal tax reform, and a national sales tax is one that deserves serious consideration.

Michael J. Graetz

7

The Estate Tax—
Whither or Wither?

For several decades, total revenue raised by estate and gift taxes has roughly equaled that raised by excise taxes on alcohol. Yet no distinguished editor ever has asked me to write on alcohol excise taxes. The law firms of America do not have divisions devoted to excise tax planning. The public does not hear of the suffering of widows and orphans (or even of farmers and small business owners) because of alcohol taxes. Philosophers and economists do not routinely debate the merits of such taxes. Perhaps most significantly, increases in such excise taxes do not arouse fears that this country is about to eliminate the concept of private property and embrace socialism or even communism. The estate tax, however, evokes just such responses.

In 1983, estate taxes accounted for less than 1 percent of total Internal Revenue Service (IRS) collections of $627.2 billion, while the individual income tax alone raised $523.5 billion. Only the 5.1 percent of all gross estates that exceeded $275,000

MICHAEL J. GRAETZ *is a professor at the Yale University Law School. He has been a consultant on tax issues to the U.S. Department of the Treasury and has written numerous articles on taxation for prestigious journals. He is the author of* Federal Income Tax: Principles and Policies. *Much of the material in this chapter was presented earlier in "To Praise the Estate Tax, Not to Bury It," 93* Yale Law Journal, *259 (1983). Dr. Graetz wishes to thank Hal Gann and Barbara McDowell for research and editorial assistance.*

were required to file estate tax returns that year, and, after exclusions, deductions, and credits, just 2.8 percent of all estates were actually taxable. The total estate tax on those $32.6 billion worth of estates was $5.2 billion—just under 16 percent.

The Structure of Transfer Taxation

Since 1916, the United States has taxed the right to transfer property at death. Inter vivos transfers were taxed from 1924 until 1926 and again, beginning in 1932, in order to prevent taxpayers from avoiding death taxes by simply making lifetime gifts to their families. For more than forty years, each transfer tax had its own exemptions and rates. It was significantly cheaper to transfer wealth during life than at death.

RECENT TRENDS IN TRANSFER TAXATION

In 1976 Congress adopted a series of revisions intended to make estate and gift taxes apply on a more regular and uniform basis. Congress enacted a series of provisions unifying estate and gift taxes into a single wealth transfer tax with one cumulative rate schedule and one exemption level; this legislation also expanded the marital deduction and established a new tax on certain "generation-skipping" transfers. The intent of Congress was to produce a more structurally coherent tax—to move toward a genuinely progressive estate and gift tax, typically imposed once each generation and without huge disparities due to decedents' patterns of lifetime giving. The 1976 legislation significantly improved many, though not all, of the structural problems of estate and gift taxes.

These changes were expected to lose revenue in the short run, principally as a result of the phased-in increase in the size of tax-exempt estates from $60,000 (or $90,000 if the lifetime gift tax exclusion were used fully) to $175,625 and the expansion of the marital deductions for smaller estates. These changes were to have no effect on total tax revenue over the long run, however, because they were to be offset by additional revenue from the new tax on generation-skipping trusts and by new carry-over basis rules applicable to appreciated property transferred at death. In fact, the enactment of the carry-over basis was an explicit trade-off for the support of the estate tax revisions by key Democrats on the House Ways and Means Committee.

Having moved toward a basically sound and well-structured wealth transfer tax system, Congress reversed direction a few years later. In 1980, Congress repealed the carry-over basis rules and returned to the unfair and economically distorting step-up of basis to fair market value at death. The tax writing committees did not even consider replacing the carry-over basis rule with an income or additional estate tax on appreciated assets transferred at death. Then, in 1981, Congress enacted additional increases in the wealth transfer tax credit to produce an immediate tax-exempt level of $275,625; further credit increases were to be phased in ultimately to produce an exemption for all estates with a net worth of $600,000 or less. At the same time, Congress extended an unlimited marital deduction to all estates regardless of size, reduced the top rate of estate tax (applicable to estates with net worth of $10 million or more) from 70 to 50 percent, and increased from $3,000 to $10,000 the amount that can be transferred annually to any donee free of gift tax. These changes will ultimately reduce the death tax base by about 70 percent and reduce the long-term revenue from taxation of bequests to, at most, 33 percent of what would have been collected if the 1976 structure had remained unchanged.

The Role of Transfer Taxation

SOURCE OF REVENUE

The estate tax was originally enacted to raise revenue to help finance World War I. Today, revenue yield will not justify the tax; an increase of one percentage point in federal income tax rates would raise more revenue than does the present estate and gift tax. Furthermore, the estate tax has limited potential as a source of federal revenue. Although the estate tax accounted for nearly 11 percent of federal revenue at its zenith in 1936, estate and gift taxes have never produced more than 2.5 percent of total revenue since the end of World War II. Even if the most recent trends were reversed by returning to the pre-1976 tax-exempt level of $60,000, estate and gift taxes would only double their current total and again produce only about 2 percent of total revenue. If these taxes were increased still further to produce a postwar high of 2.5 percent of total revenue, they would generate only an additional $10 billion, an amount that would make only a small dent in the federal deficit as currently projected.

The limitation on potential estate tax revenue is an inherent one, not merely a product of political obstacles. Decedents annually transfer a total of about $120 billion in net assets. An average effective tax rate of 20 percent would produce total revenue of around $24 billion, approximately four times the current level. With any substantial exemption, plus exclusions for certain amounts of property passing to surviving spouses or charities, a higher average effective rate seems unrealistic. The inherent limitation on bequests as a source of revenue cannot be overcome by even a dramatic structural revision of estate and gift taxes, such as converting to an inheritance or accessions tax, taxing gifts and bequests as income to the recipient, or as consumption of the donor in a consumption-tax world. A tax on transfers of wealth at death, therefore, will never serve as a major source of federal revenue.

CONTRIBUTION TO PROGRESSIVITY

A far better reason to maintain the estate tax lies in its contribution to the progressivity of the tax system. Other than the dramatic increases in total tax revenue, the most striking change in federal revenue sources over the past fifteen years has been the diminishing relative significance of progressive tax sources. If employment taxes are viewed, as they often are, as a system of purchasing retirement and disability insurance from the government, their huge rise reflects a dramatic increase in taxes based on "benefit" rather than "ability to pay." In addition, employment taxes impose ceilings on taxable labor income so that some of the wages of highly salaried individuals are exempt from tax. Combined with recent reductions in tax on individual and corporate incomes, capital gains, and estates, employment tax increases threaten the progressivity of federal taxation. Moreover, proposals for significant, long-term changes in federal taxation—a modified flat rate income tax and a consumption tax—that currently seem to enjoy the great-

est favor in academic and certain political circles may pose
further threats to progressivity.

Through much of this fifteen-year period, the estate tax has
had a significant progressive effect. In 1970 the average ratio of
tax to adjusted gross income on individual income tax returns
was 13.7 percent. Those taxpayers who were taxed at an average rate of at least 14 percent paid a total tax of $43 billion. If
they had been taxed at the average rate, they would have paid
only $30.5 billion. The total revenue raised through individual
income taxes in excess of the average rate was, therefore, $12.5
billion. By comparison, estate and gift tax collections—all of
them necessarily from wealthy donors and decedents—were
just under $3.7 billion in fiscal 1970. Thus, despite their low
revenue yield, estate and gift taxes contributed nearly 25 percent of the total progressivity of the individual tax structure.
This occurred even though the estate tax imposed a smaller
levy on inheritances than would have been imposed if bequests
had been taxed as ordinary income.

This picture changed dramatically by 1982, however, when
the estate tax accounted for only about 11 percent of total progressivity. The increases in the estate tax marital deduction and
tax exemption enacted in 1981 will cause the estate and gift tax
to decline even further as a source of progressivity. Law professor Harry Gutman has estimated that, if these changes were
fully effective in 1981, "the contribution to progressivity [of the
estate tax] would be reduced to approximately 4 percent."
Whatever progressivity remains in the federal tax system will be
supplied almost exclusively by the income tax.

TAXATION OF CONCENTRATED WEALTH

A popular and dangerous myth maintains that the estate
tax's only role is to break up large concentrations of wealth.
There is some historical evidence for this notion, which was
repeated often in the congressional debate over the 1981 act.
The line of thought implies that no estate tax should be imposed on "smaller or moderate-sized estates." In 1981, "smaller
and moderate-sized estates" meant those of the wealthiest 1 to 6
percent of the population. The narrowing of the estate tax base
that accompanies political acceptance of this myth necessarily

defeats the contribution of this tax to other goals, especially the federal tax system's progressivity.

In fact, the estate tax has done little to dilute the greatest concentrations of wealth. The portion of total wealth held by the richest 1 percent of the population has remained remarkably stable. This group possessed roughly 25 percent of the national wealth in every year from 1958 to 1972. A recent study advances a tentative estimate that its holdings declined from about 25 to 20 percent of total wealth between 1972 and 1976. Even assuming that such a decline actually occurred, however, nothing suggests any significant causal role for the estate tax.

It has been suggested also that the estate tax assures that wealth accumulated through income-tax-preferred sources is taxed at least once. Certain sources of income from capital have been long accorded preferential treatment under the income tax. Although the aggregate contribution of the individual income tax to federal revenue has been relatively stable, recent revisions of the income tax base have tended further to exclude income from capital. Among the most significant of these were the 1978 expansion of the capital gains exclusion, the 1980 repeal of the carry-over basis at death rules, the 1981 reductions in the top rate of tax on dividends and interest income from 70 to 50 percent, and increases in depreciation allowances and tax-free retirement accounts. The income tax base, therefore, may not reflect a taxpayer's true economic income or ability to pay for government services. When the taxpayer dies, however, the need to encourage certain types of investment ends. It then seems fair to recapture some of the wealth that the taxpayer accumulated during life because income from capital was leniently taxed.

Revitalizing Transfer Taxation

REAFFIRMING PROGRESSIVITY

The most important reason to revitalize the estate tax is to reaffirm a commitment to progressivity. There are a number of problems in relying exclusively on a progressive income tax to ensure that this nation's tax burden is distributed in accordance with ability to pay. For one thing, realized rates of return apparently tend to fall as wealth increases. Thus, any tax system that relies solely on a realization-based income tax to attain progressivity will not tax sufficiently the underlying wealth that generated the income. In addition, high income tax rates create marginal disincentives to productivity and may stimulate legal and illegal noncompliance. Many claimants for income tax relief have more appealing cases—in both economic and equity terms—than the beneficiaries of decedents subject to the estate tax. Since they are less likely to affect incentives to earn and invest, higher estate taxes seem preferable to higher income taxes. Furthermore, increasing progressivity through estate taxation serves another social value—reducing the disparity of opportunity between descendants of the wealthy and descendants of the poor. The claim that estate taxes inhibit capital formation is simply not convincing. The estate tax is such a small revenue source that its effects on saving and investment are no doubt dwarfed by those of other taxes and of fiscal and monetary policies. Perhaps for this reason, the impact of the estate tax on aggregate saving has not received much explicit theoretical or empirical examination. Modern economic literature does, however, contain observations by Richard Musgrave, Lester Thurow, and Gerard Brannon that death taxes on capital, such as estate taxes, are likely to have smaller disincentive effects on saving than lifetime income taxes. Ultimate resolution of this issue awaits discovery of individuals' true planning horizons.

Taxpayers accumulate wealth for a variety of reasons, including personal financial security, prestige and power in the community, as well as a desire to maximize the comfort of, or their control over, their heirs. Whatever the economic or sociological explanations, a survey of estate planners by George Cooper, "A Voluntary Tax? New Perspectives on Sophisticated Estate Tax Avoidance," revealed that:

> there is certainly a significant group of clients who are ambivalent about transfer tax saving or, at least, accord it a low priority. Saving estate taxes apparently does not generate the same high level of enthusiasm as saving income taxes, for the obvious reason that the benefits to the client from estate tax avoidance are much more indirect and intangible. (*Columbia Law Review*, 1977)

The implication, of course, is that a deficit-ridden government will create fewer disincentives to investment by raising estate taxes than by raising income taxes.

GOALS OF TRANSFER TAXATION

Any tax reform effort must seek to enhance and reconcile the often competing goals of fairness, economic efficiency, and administrability. Reform should ensure that those with equal wealth pay equal taxes and that those with different amounts of wealth pay appropriately different taxes. It should not induce people to make different economic decisions than they would in its absence. Generally, the tax should be simple enough to be understood by those taxpayers to whom it applies, should minimize the benefits of complex tax planning, and should be enforceable at reasonable cost to both taxpayers and government.

The more specific goal of estate and gift tax reform must be the elimination of large differences in tax liability based on the nature, form, or time of the transfer. The tax should, therefore, strive for as much neutrality as feasible in its effect on investment and allocation decisions. There remain questions regarding the period and the perspective to be used when evaluating equality of treatment under the estate and gift tax. Should equality be measured as often as annually or as occasionally as once in a generation? Should equality be measured from the perspective of donors of wealth or from the perspective of donees? The current unified gift and estate tax, of course, generally focuses on the taxpaying ability of donors, evaluated on a lifetime basis. It may well prove necessary to reexamine these assumptions when seeking to revitalize the estate and gift tax.

Credits and Exemptions

In 1975, the $60,000 estate tax exemption (in effect since 1942) meant that only the wealthiest 6.5 percent of decedents paid estate taxes. If the $60,000 exemption had remained unchanged, the tax would have applied to about the wealthiest 10 percent of decedents in 1982, but the 1976 act's increase in the exemption level to $175,000 meant that the estate tax applied only to the wealthiest 3 percent in 1981. However, the owners of farms and small businesses convinced Congress that 3 percent was still too large and that no tax should be imposed on estates of as much as $600,000 when the unified credit is fully phased-in in 1987.

If the unlimited marital deduction does not change the level of marital bequests, only 0.30 percent of decedents will incur estate tax liabilities in 1987. If all decedents use the unlimited marital deduction to eliminate the tax on the first spouse's death, only 0.14 percent of decedents will incur an estate tax. Taxing only the largest 0.14 percent of all estates would have allowed some estates with $3 million in assets to escape tax in 1983.

The 1981 legislation also increased from $3,000 to $10,000 the amount that a donor may give tax-free each year to each of an unlimited number of donees, not including payments for tuition and medical expenses. Married couples can transfer $20,000 per donee. This annual exclusion, originally enacted to exempt gifts (i.e., birthdays, weddings, Christmas) too small to justify the compliance and enforcement costs, has become a standard technique to transfer large sums of money to one's heirs. For example, a married couple with two children and two grandchildren could avoid paying any tax on the transfer of $2 million of wealth if they supplemented their $1.2 million of unified credit with $800,000 of gift tax exclusion over a ten-year period. Such avoidance might be minimized by reducing the amount of annual exclusion and by exempting from tax all transfers for support or consumption, tuition, and medical expenses. Another choice, suggested by the American Law Institute in 1968, would be to impose a cumulative limit on the donor's gift tax exclusion.

The Unlimited Marital Deduction

The 1981 legislation also permits a decedent to transfer an unlimited sum tax-free to his or her surviving spouse. The law had previously allowed a deduction of no more than the greater of $250,000 or 50 percent of the value of the adjusted gross estate. The purpose of the original provision was to ensure that the estate was not so depleted by taxes that the surviving spouse's standard of living was dramatically and forcibly reduced. It is clear that an unlimited marital deduction is not necessary to achieve this purpose. Indeed, the combination of the $600,000 unified credit and the unlimited deduction will, by 1987, permit a married couple with $1.2 million to receive the same tax-free treatment as a single decedent with no estate.

When making the marital deduction unlimited, Congress apparently concluded that spouses, as single economic units, should be able to share their assets without incurring taxes. This view, however, seems inconsistent with the practice of allowing each spouse a separate $600,000 unified credit for transfers outside the unit. Furthermore, the couple is allowed to treat all gifts as if each spouse contributed half, even after their $1.2 million of unified credit is exhausted. The effect is to tax such couples at lower marginal rates than single individuals. For example, a single woman will pay $588,000 of tax in 1987 on a gift of $2 million. A married couple will be able to give away $2 million at a cost of just $306,000. Of the couple's $282,000 tax savings, only $192,800 is attributable to their "extra" unified credit. The other $89,200 is simply the benefit of paying the transfer tax at a lower marginal rate than the single woman does. The marital deduction may, therefore, permit taxpayers to violate the principle that all transferred wealth should be taxed at least once per generation. Given the determination of estate planners, it might also encourage remarriages "in contemplation of death" between members of different generations.

Equity to the single taxpayer seems to require that the couple receive just one unified credit and that all gifts be taxed as if made by the marital unit. But this stipulation creates a large "marriage penalty" for spouses who each own substantial assets. As in the income tax, this dilemma requires a compromise that causes some inequity both to single persons and to couples. For example, married couples could get a single unified credit (between $600,000 and $1,200,000) and a rate schedule of their own (between the effective rates on split gifts and the current rates for single taxpayers). This solution might be more equitable, although slightly more complex, than the current system. For example, new adjustments would be necessary to ensure parity between residents of community-property and common-law states. This system might well reduce distortions overall, since some gifts to spouses would go elsewhere in the absence of tax benefits.

Unified Transfer Tax Rates

In 1976, Congress created a single rate schedule and a unified credit for the estate and gift taxes. The purpose was to make the transfer taxes apply uniformly to inter vivos gifts and bequests, and thereby increase the efficiency of transfer taxation. Considerable disparity remains, however, because one rate schedule is applied to a tax-exclusive gift tax base and a tax-inclusive estate tax base. That means that the estate tax base includes the tax paid as well as the amount of the bequest, but the gift tax base does not. The unification law, therefore, ignores the fact that a tax-inclusive rate of 40 percent, for example, is equivalent to a tax-exclusive rate of 67 percent; 50 percent, to 100 percent; and 75 percent, to 300 percent.

If the gift tax is a backstop for the estate tax, protecting the estate from lifetime diminution, effective tax rates on transfers by gift should equal effective rates on transfers by will. Transfer taxes should be a neutral factor in taxpayers' timing decisions. The current system, however, still significantly favors lifetime gifts over bequests. Vertical equity dictates that taxpayers with more wealth should pay more transfer taxes, but many wealthy taxpayers remain able to give away significant amounts of capital during their lives, while less wealthy taxpayers can less easily forgo the income and security from their savings. Moreover, the current advantages of lifetime giving require complex and arbitrary rules to decide when a gift is completed and whether it is taxed as a gift or as a bequest.

The current answer to unified effective rates provides that the estate is "grossed-up" for estate tax purposes by adding the amount of gift taxes paid on gifts within three years of death. This provision eliminates most of the incentive for death bed transfers, but it has no effect on gifts made more than three years before death.

Some people argue that keeping gift tax rates lower than estate tax rates encourages transfers of wealth into younger hands, from which dynamic, innovative, and risky investments are more likely. However, the importance to economic vitality of transfers from rich old people to rich young people has never been convincingly shown. Unified effective transfer tax rates may increase the disincentives to dispose of assets, but, as shown later, there may be positive incentives for lifetime gifts even if the effective rates are unified.

PROPOSALS FOR IMPROVEMENT

There are many possible improvements for the present provision. In 1969 the U.S. Department of the Treasury proposed to gross-up gifts by dividing the value of all gifts by one minus the estate tax rate. But, as law professor Theodore Sims demonstrated, this method of achieving a tax-inclusive base asks the taxpayer to perform complex calculations of gift tax rates and brackets. An alternative recommended by Sims is for the Treasury to do the calculations for the taxpayer and publish two graduated rate schedules, one for gifts and one for estates. The schedules would have different brackets and different *nominal* rates but would, in fact, impose identical *effective* rates. The problem here is a political one—taxpayers may not understand that two rate schedules that look extremely different are, in fact, identical. The Treasury adopted this approach in its 1984 tax reform proposals. The proposed gift tax rates, which were designed to be the effective equivalent of present estate tax rates, range from 58.73 percent on the first $94,500 of gifts (in excess of the $600,000 unified credit) to 100 percent on gifts over $1,667,000. It is questionable whether a rate schedule that appears so confiscatory will be able to win congressional approval.

An alternative proposal, offered by law professor Joseph Isenbergh, would gross-up the estate by the amount of *all* gift taxes previously paid by the decedent rather than by only those paid within three years of death. This plan could eventually collect almost the same amount of tax on gifts as on bequests. However, the taxpayer who can afford to make lifetime gifts would reap the benefits of interest-free tax deferral between the date of gift and date of death. Isenbergh suggests that this problem could be resolved by grossing-up the estate by the compounded future value at the date of death of gift taxes previously paid. A potential risk of this proposal is that there may not be sufficient assets in the estate to pay the grossed-up estate tax.

Gifts with Strings

The differential tax treatment of gifts and bequests has produced a set of complex and arbitrary rules to determine whether a gift actually has been completed. Their intent is to make lifetime transfers difficult to complete so that those that are essentially testamentary in nature will be taxed as bequests rather than as gifts. The effect of these rules is sometimes to tax transfers *more* severely if made during life than at death.

THE FORM OF TRANSFER

For example, the gross estate is increased by the value of all property transferred during life (except bona fide sales for adequate consideration) over which the decedent retained a life interest of possession, enjoyment, or income. The theory is that preferential gift tax rates should not be extended to a donor who enjoys income from, or possession of, the "transferred" property until death.

This rule is often a trap for the unwary or ill-advised, because it can be easily circumvented by devices such as the purchase of a private annuity by the donor from the donee. This transfer would not be pulled back into the donor's estate because that provision does not apply to transfers for which the donor is deemed to receive adequate consideration. Such arbitrary results have led many to call for the repeal of the present rules, which would be unnecessary under a truly unified transfer tax system. Removal of the rate disparity that encourages lifetime gifts instead of bequests, they claim, will not influence transfer timing decisions. Transfer taxes then would hinge not on the form but the substance of transactions. Taxpayers with equal wealth would be taxed equally. The law would be simpler, and fewer disputes would arise.

THE TIME TO TAX

Others have recognized that rules regarding when a transfer is completed still will be necessary after full unification in order to determine the time at which taxes should be imposed. But, the current "hard-to-complete" rules for lifetime transfers could be replaced with "easy-to-complete" rules. The Treasury moved in this direction in its 1984 reform proposals by, for example, treating as irrelevant a retained power to control the beneficial enjoyment of the transferred property if the power could not be used to distribute income or principal to the donor.

Instead of pulling these revocable interests and reversions back into the taxable estate, Isenbergh would tax such transfers at the date of gift. Because the donor's right to revoke or alter the interest influences the value of the current gift, Isenbergh would value the transfer as if it were irrevocable and unconditional.

APPRECIATION AND VALUATION BENEFITS

The problem with repealing the present rules, even under a truly unified transfer tax, is that rate discrepancies are not the *only* tax benefits of lifetime giving. There also may be appreciation and valuation benefits. The gift tax permits taxpayers to choose the most opportune moment to value their wealth. They can "freeze" their estates at their fair market values on the date of gift and transfer all future appreciation to their heirs free of tax. Fair market value has been defined by the IRS and the courts as the price at which the property would change hands between a willing buyer and a willing seller, neither being under any compulsion to buy or to sell and both having reasonable knowledge of relevant facts. But, problems arise because taxpayers often have more than a "reasonable knowledge" of relevant facts.

TAX-AVOIDANCE TECHNIQUES

Private Annuities—How do taxpayers exploit their knowledge about value? One technique is to buy a private annuity from one's beneficiary. The Internal Revenue Code values life annuities based on national mortality statistics. A person who expects to die before the statistical life expectancy can make a tax-free gift by purchasing an annuity from a family member. The amount of the gift is the difference between the fair market value of the annuity based on mortality statistics and the amount the annuitant actually received. The rate unification proposals do not affect this technique, because purchasing an annuity for its fair market value is not a gift as long as "value" is determined by reference to a hypothetical buyer and seller with only "reasonable knowledge of relevant facts."

Shifting Appreciated Value and Risks of Loss—Another disguised gift technique is the "checkerboard oil deal." A father owns a tract of potential oil land that has a relatively modest fair market value because the existence of oil is uncertain and required exploration costs are substantial. The father divides his tract like a checkerboard and gives all but a narrow strip in each square to his children, paying gift tax on the fair market value of the land transferred. He then expends a lot of money exploring for oil, drilling from his own narrow strips of land. If he locates oil, the value of his children's land will skyrocket; the children may then concentrate their drilling to reap high yields at low risk. The children's gains will be taxed at lower rates, many years later, or both. The IRS might attempt to attack the father's drilling cost as disguised gifts, but he can argue that most of these expenses were necessary to exploit his *own* land. Other common techniques for shifting the risk of loss without paying transfer tax include parents' guaranteeing their children's loans from banks, loaning their children money for risky ventures, and acting as general partners while giving their children limited partnership interests in speculative ventures. None of these techniques relies upon preferred gift tax rates.

Recapitalizations—A more common appreciation and valuation technique is a recapitalization of a closely held partnership or corporation, usually by issuing preferred stock. For example, an owner of a small business can exchange common stock for voting preferred stock and nonvoting common stock in a tax-free recapitalization. All of the voting preferred stock is kept, and all of the nonvoting common stock is given to the owner's children. Because the voting preferred stock is worth as much as the entire corporation at the date of recapitalization and because the owner is the only voting shareholder, the fair market value of the common stock to hypothetical buyers and sellers is exceptionally low. But the common stock is hardly worthless to the children. The owner will continue to control the company and contribute energy and expertise, while future appreciation in the value of the business will pass to the common stockholders free of transfer tax. Similar dual stock structures are quite common for new family business ventures. Merely unifying effective estate and gift tax rates will not stop these common avoidance techniques.

Responses—Law professor Alvin Warren would eliminate many of these problems under a fully unified transfer tax by valuing all transfers at the date of death, even if made during the donor's life. The gift tax would serve merely as a tentative prepayment of the estate tax that ultimately would be imposed. Any gift tax previously paid would be compounded to the date of death and credited against the estate tax liability. The donee of a lifetime gift, then, would not have more after-tax wealth on the date of the donor's death than if the gift had been delayed until that time. An alternative proposed by Warren—to calculate date-of-death values by applying a compound interest rate to date-of-gift values—would fully unify the estate and gift taxes, even under a graduated rate schedule, but it would not address these "personal" valuation estate planning techniques.

A somewhat similar approach to this recapitalization problem has been proposed by George Cooper. He would value the stock and impose the tax at the time that the transferor dies or the stock is sold. This approach is also suggested in the 1984 Treasury proposals for valuing lifetime gifts of fractional interests in property if the donor retains a fractional interest.

Valuation Discounts

Another technique to avoid estate taxes utilizes valuation discounts. When a gift or bequest includes stock in a closely held corporation, courts have sometimes allowed generous discounts from the appraised value of the corporation's assets before applying the transfer tax rate. The hypothetical buyer and seller standard has been interpreted to call for discounts to reflect the limited marketability of the stock regardless of whether or not the transferee actually intends to sell the stock.

Blockage discounts of as much as 20 percent are allowed if the estate contains a large block of stock that would depress the market if sold at one time. Courts routinely ignore the fact that the actual transferee will not be selling the stock or that the stock might be sold over a long period of time without depressing the market.

Minority interest discounts of 15 to 20 percent are often allowed if a buyer would hold a noncontrolling interest in a family corporation. Thus, courts may ignore that the transferee may be a member of the family or already may own a substantial interest in the corporation. No premium has been required where the transfer consists of a controlling block of shares.

Selling expenses of up to 10 percent are also routinely allowed if the stock has no established market or could not be sold without an underwriting. Substantial discounts are allowed if the corporation's assets are difficult to market, carry a low basis, or possess other potential tax liabilities. Also, restrictions on the sale of stock in closely held corporations are often used to justify discounts. In each of these cases, the transferee's clear intent to retain rather than sell the stock or assets is disregarded for valuation purposes.

Cooper has found that a court may pile two or three discounts on top of one another and that appraised values are often reduced by 50 percent or more for estate tax purposes. Since these valuation techniques affect the tax *base* and not the tax *rate*, unified rate schedules will not solve the problem of valuation discounts. One response to this difficulty is stricter enforcement of current law. The matter, however, is complicated because value is assessed from the perspective of "a hypothetical buyer and seller" instead of the actual transferee. However, the desirability of a more subjective standard may be outweighed by the administrative costs imposed on the IRS and the courts. Some of these problems might be reduced by the Treasury's 1984 proposal to value shares of stock and other fractional interests owned by the donor or decedent on the same basis, regardless of whether such interests are transferred by gift or at death.

Illiquidity Relief

The vast majority of estate tax returns declare more cash than estate tax liability and, on average, have more than twice the liquid assets necessary to pay the tax. Nevertheless, some estates will suffer liquidity problems. Congress may decide, for example, that the estate of a small business owner should not be forced to sell a specified portion (say, 25 percent) of its stock to pay estate taxes. But, in general, liquidity relief should not subsidize illiquid estates. The goal should be to tax liquid and illiquid estates equally, without forcing illiquid estates to raise cash by selling assets immediately.

THE CURRENT STATUS

The Internal Revenue Code gives the IRS discretion to defer estate tax liabilities for up to ten years, with interest, for "reasonable cause," which includes showing that liquid funds are unavailable at the due date and cannot be raised without financial loss. Although this is a sensible provision to relieve unusual liquidity problems, it was not enough for farmers and small businesses who secured additional concessions in 1976. If farmland or real property used in a closely held business comprises 50 percent of the gross estate, the executor may elect to value that property at its current use, instead of its fair market value. This policy provides an estate tax reduction if heirs run the farm instead of selling it to pay estate taxes, and it allows a valuation discount of as much as $750,000. This tax benefit is recaptured *without interest* if the property is disposed of or ceases to be used for a qualifying purpose within ten years of the transferor's death.

If this provision is viewed solely as a solution to a liquidity problem, it is difficult to understand why any limit on the recapture period is appropriate or why the recaptured estate tax benefit should not be compounded at a market interest rate. If Congress wished to enable heirs to select the time to sell the family farm, it could defer any estate tax attributable to the difference in values—or even a greater amount—with market interest, as long as the heirs continued to use the land for farming. When the farm is sold at the higher value, the deferred estate tax and interest could be collected. If the business is sold for less than its estate tax value, a proportionate reduction in tax might be provided.

The law contains other valuable tax deferral opportunities for estates containing farms and small businesses. If a farm or small business comprises more than 35 percent of the gross estate, the executor can elect an interest-free deferral of estate tax on the farm property for five years, followed by installment payment of the tax over a ten-year period. The $153,000 of tax on the first $1 million of property value is subject to only 4 percent interest during the installment period. Harry Gutman observes that the 4 percent interest rate alone is worth $93,636, if the market interest rate is 15 percent. This reduction of more than 60 percent of the estate tax otherwise payable leads him to ask whether a business is worth subsidizing if it can not even generate enough cash to pay off a market rate loan.

Moreover, the law fails to condition this subsidy on whether or not the estate is, in fact, illiquid. An estate comprised of $800,000 of stock in the family business and $1 million in cash is subsidized even though it could pay its tax nearly twice over; an estate with $1.8 million of rental property and $200,000 in cash must sell the property to raise the other $360,400 necessary to pay its tax. Such horizontal inequity is not unlikely; perhaps 80 percent of estates that contain farms or small businesses have at least 33 percent more net liquid assets than necessary to cover estate taxes and administration expenses.

PROPOSALS FOR IMPROVEMENT

While serious for certain estates, liquidity problems are far from common. Relief should be provided only where illiquid assets constitute a substantial percentage of the estate. But relief should not be so great as to induce investments in illiquid assets. In many instances, careful business and estate planning can mitigate potential liquidity problems—purchasing insurance, for example. The estate tax subsidy to illiquidity should not render such planning uneconomical. Instead of subsidizing farms and small businesses, the estate tax should provide generous extended payment rules for all estates if a market interest rate is charged. Why should a subset of the wealthiest 3 percent of the population receive a lower rate of interest on deferred estate tax than is generally available on other deferred tax payments?

The Treasury's 1984 proposals would increase the equity and efficiency of the estate tax by basing the availability of illiquidity relief on the ratio of liquid assets to estate tax liability instead of on the type of assets held by the estate. The new provision would allow an automatic one-year extension, after which the estate tax would be immediately payable to the extent of 75 percent of the estate's cash and liquid assets. Most estates would be able to pay their entire tax at this time. Any remaining tax liability could be deferred for up to fifteen years; the estate would pay only interest for the first five years and make installment payments on principal and interest for the last ten. A market rate of interest would be charged for all deferrals. Any number of equivalent proposals could be devised. As long as a market rate of interest is charged, deferral would create a tax benefit only for estates that suffer a substantial decline in value, e.g., those that go bankrupt.

Unrealized Gains at Death

The Internal Revenue Code allows unrealized appreciation of property to escape both income and estate taxation by providing for a tax-free step-up of basis to fair market value at the date of death. When the 1981 changes are fully phased in, the amount of appreciated property transferable at death free of both income and estate taxes will have increased tenfold since 1976—from $60,000 to $600,000. No more than $3 billion of the more than $20 billion of unrealized appreciation annually passing through estates (at 1979 levels) will then be subject to estate tax. The remainder will escape both income and estate taxation. Of this $20 billion of appreciation 60 percent is owned by less than 6 percent of all decedents, and the ratio of unrealized appreciation to gross estates increases as the size of the gross estate increases.

A tax on unrealized gains at death would be decidedly progressive, would directly tax income from capital that is excluded from the income tax base, and could raise several billion dollars of additional tax revenue. This proposal would necessarily involve some trade-off in administrability, since it would increase the complexity of death taxes and the time and cost of administering an estate. In return, equity and efficiency would increase. Under current law, taxpayers incur capital gains taxes if they sell appreciated property before death, but they avoid both income and estate taxes if they hold such property until death. An heir who receives appreciated property gets a fair market value basis; the donee of a lifetime gift, the donor's basis. A tax on unrealized gains at death would treat inter vivos and testamentary transfers alike and would reduce the incentive to hold appreciated investments until death, the "lock-in effect."

CARRY-OVER BASIS RULE

The most common proposals for taxing unrealized gains at death are the "carry-over basis rule" and the "unrealized appreciation tax." A carry-over basis rule, such as that adopted in 1976 and repealed in 1980, would treat the property as if it had been transferred during life; the transferor would pay no transfer tax, and the transferee would take the transferor's basis in the property. Any carry-over basis rule, however, carries the political baggage of its 1980 repeal and would be complex to administer. The executor would have to compute the estate tax attributable to each asset's appreciation since, to prevent double taxation, the basis of every asset not bequeathed to a spouse or to charity would have to be adjusted by the amount of estate tax paid. Carry-over basis would require basis records to be maintained for several generations, and the opportunities for deferral might even increase the lock-in effect. Finally, despite possible economic efficiencies, carry-over basis would make it extremely difficult to distribute estate assets in kind; the value of each asset to a transferee would depend upon the asset's historical basis, the transferee's marginal tax rate, and the probability that the transferee will want to sell the asset.

UNREALIZED APPRECIATION TAX

These problems could be avoided by taxing estates on unrealized appreciation. An unrealized appreciation tax would treat the property as if it had been sold just before death; estates would be reduced by the tax paid on the "realized" gains, and transferees would take a fair market value basis in any property distributed to them by the estate. The tax might be imposed at capital gains or other special tax rates, and illiquid estates could defer the liability for an extended period by paying a market rate of interest on the deferral. An exemption should be provided for gains on personal and household effects, and compliance costs might be limited by exempting all estates currently exempted from the estate tax.

Life Insurance—Life insurance, perhaps the single most important weapon in the estate planner's arsenal, should not be exempt from the tax. Otherwise, inefficiency would increase as taxpayers shifted even more of their savings into this tax-preferred asset solely for tax reasons. The difference between proceeds and premiums paid should be taxed; even if there were vast political opposition to taxing the "pure insurance" element of the contract, the interest element of the proceeds could be taxed at death if not taxed as earned.

Exclusions—Charitable gifts might be excluded from the tax to encourage bequests to charity. Given current estate tax rules, there should be no marital exclusion. However, the unlimited marital deduction, which treats the couple as a single taxable unit, makes current law's tax-free step-up of basis particularly inappropriate for property left to the surviving spouse. Indeed, such basic step-ups might be disallowed whether or not appreciation is taxed at death. By transferring all appreciated assets to the spouse who will die first, couples currently pay no income, estate, or gift taxes on capital appreciation until the second spouse dies. In the early 1970s, the American Bankers Association developed a proposal for an additional estate tax on appreciation that it regarded as an administratively feasible solution if the step-up of basis to fair market value were restricted. This proposal merits renewed attention.

Generation-skipping Transfers

In 1976, Congress enacted a tax on generation-skipping transfers (the GST tax). This tax is aimed at situations where, for example, donors establish a testamentary trust to provide income to their children for their lives with the remainder to the grandchildren. Without the GST tax, none of the trust would be included in the children's estates since they had only a life interest—a violation of the assumption that wealth should be taxed at least once per generation. The GST tax treats the children as "deemed transferors" and adds the trust corpus to their taxable estates. The GST tax approximates the transfer tax results had the decedent given the assets to the children outright. All generation-skipping trusts or "trust equivalents" that a member of the "skipped" generation has power over or an interest in are subject to the tax. A $250,000 per "deemed transferor" exclusion is allowed for transfers to the grantor's grandchildren.

There is considerable agreement that some sort of GST tax is needed—although the American Bar Association, for example, supports simple repeal—but the 1976 rules are universally regarded as so complex that they create inequity and administrative problems. Moreover, by taxing trusts and "trust equivalents" that the decedent's children have power over or an interest in, but not taxing outright gifts to grandchildren, the GST tax creates inefficiencies and inequities. Wealthy taxpayers more often can afford to make outright gifts that skip generations. Although periodic wealth taxation requires a tax on generation-skipping transfers, vast political obstacles to such a tax create problems. Voters, for example, simply would not understand why direct transfers to grandchildren must be taxed more heavily than direct transfers to children.

THE TREASURY'S PROPOSAL

Nevertheless, two major GST tax proposals have emerged that would tax outright gifts that skip one or more generations. The Treasury's proposal would exempt $1 million per donor and tax all other GSTs (on a tax-inclusive basis) at 80 percent of the maximum estate tax rate. This approach is substantially more equitable and efficient than current law, but some problems remain. The tax rate on GSTs would leave some nonneutrality in the system. Because the value of carefully planning and structuring transfers will rise with the size of the transfer, as well as the transferor's wealth, some vertical inequity still would remain. Moreover, the $1 million per donor exemption would eliminate all appreciation on that sum from tax. Finally, the proposal would tax a transfer that skips two generations no differently than a transfer that skips one, resulting in inequity and inefficiency because wealthy taxpayers could set up trusts for their great-grandchildren.

THE AMERICAN LAW INSTITUTE PROPOSAL

The American Law Institute (ALI) would avoid most of these problems by treating a generation-skipping trust as an "owned trust" if a portion of it is available to a person (deemed the "owner") and cannot be diverted during life without consent. All transfers from owned trusts would be taxed as transfers by the owner, at the owner's marginal transfer tax rate. The tax actually would be paid, however, by the trust. Any other generation-skipping trust would be a "nonowned trust." Any "taxable distribution," a transfer to a person two or more generations below the donor, made by nonowned trusts would be taxed to the trust at the maximum marginal transfer tax rate. Transfers to charity or for medical or tuition expenses would be exempt, and all donors would get a $417,000 credit to allocate to their nonowned trusts. A nonowned trust would be deemed to terminate and pay estate tax at the maximum marginal rate at the end of each generation of beneficiaries or every thirty-five years. A surtax would be imposed upon any outright transfer or trust for donees who are two or more generations below the donor. The surtax would be computed as if the transfer flowed through a nonowned trust. ALI's proposal seems more equitable and efficient than the Treasury's but also substantially more complex. However, either proposal appears to represent a significant improvement over the existing system.

Whither or Wither?

There are good reasons to strengthen the estate and gift tax system and dozens of proposals for doing so. But, as observed earlier, there are practical barriers to this goal. First is the inherent limitation on the revenue potential of an estate tax. There simply is not enough wealth transferred annually to permit a wealth transfer tax to become a significant source of federal revenue. Given the immense current and projected federal deficits, only substantial revenue sources seem likely to dominate the political agenda in the near term. Thus, tax increases grounded predominantly on distributional fairness seem to have little chance of success.

The second practical barrier is that taxation of bequests is extremely unpopular politically. It is often said that opponents of tax increases hide behind selected widows. Even with the unlimited marital deduction, when estate taxation is considered, both widows and orphans are readily at hand. The fact that most heirs of wealthy decedents are themselves rich adults has little or no political significance. The effect of the American people's abhorrence of estate taxation, whether grounded in notions of entitlement or in grand optimism, should not be underestimated. It is not only the wealthy who oppose estate taxes. A 1982 California initiative to repeal the state's inheritance tax garnered a 64 percent positive vote. This was a greater majority than those that voted in favor of a nuclear freeze or against gun registration on a subsequent initiative ballot. Perhaps the explanation of the phenomenon lies in the optimism of the American people. In California, at least, 64 percent of the people must believe that they will be in the wealthiest 5 to 10 percent when they die.

A perhaps more important political obstacle to estate taxation lies in the objections of owners of small businesses and farms. Coherent and progressive estate tax revision seems unlikely unless the political obstacles posed by these lobbies are neutralized. This ultimately may require more special exceptions and benefits for these politically powerful groups, such as the special valuation and deferred payment provisions discussed earlier. Prospects of rescuing the transfer tax system might well be increased greatly by exempting all farms and small businesses from estate tax.

The combination of these political obstacles to the estate tax's rejuvenation and the tax's inherent limitations as a significant revenue source leads to the conclusion that the estate tax seems far more likely to wither than to thrive. As suggested, this prediction feeds a fear of the demise of progressive taxation in the United States. In the long term, rescuing progressivity may require enactment of a periodic low-rate wealth tax similar to those of many European nations. Such a tax offers significant revenue potential and substantial economic advantages over high marginal tax rates on the income from capital. Developing the case for a wealth tax, however, is a subject for another day.

If this undesired prediction is fulfilled and the years ahead complete the demise of the estate tax, the federal tax system will have lost more than an important and useful mechanism for achieving progressivity; it also will have lost a source of great humor. No longer will the laughter of students or colleagues be heard when stories are related of the advantages of tax-saving gifts knowingly made in contemplation of death; of antics such as those of Mrs. Stowe, who won her contemplation-of-death case because at age eighty, no doubt on the advice of her lawyer, she proved her life-related motives by dancing the night away at the St. Regis Hotel; or such thoughtful estate planning advice as that recently heard in the office of a well-known New York practitioner. In this instance, a client had asked anxiously what he might do to minimize the estate taxes of his ninety-year-old widowed mother who had a large fortune composed of cash and extremely valuable art. The lawyer thought for a great long while, no doubt running through his bag of estate planning tricks, when all of a sudden, with a gleam in his eye, he looked up and said calmly, "Marry her."

It would be a real shame if a tax that produces such creative advice were to disappear.

Emil M. Sunley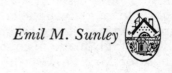

8

Alternatives for Tax Restructuring and Increased Revenue

Introduction

As Richard Goode suggests in chapter 1, two conditions combined to make federal tax policy one of the premier issues before the Ninety-ninth Congress: tax revenue is no longer sufficient to support federal expenditures, and, consequently, the budget is running a record deficit. At the same time, taxpayers, practitioners, and academics are increasingly dissatisfied with the income tax, the primary revenue tool in the existing tax system.

The deficit is a product of several factors. In part, inflation and a two-decade proliferation of tax preferences have chiseled away at the income tax base. Additionally, in 1981, Congress enacted a substantial tax cut without reducing federal spending. As a result, Congress faces projected federal deficits of over $200 billion a year.

Previous Congresses have attempted to check the widening

EMIL M. SUNLEY *is a director of tax analysis in the National Affairs Office of Deloitte Haskins & Sells. Previously, he served as deputy assistant secretary of the Treasury for tax policy and also as associate director of the Office of Tax Analysis. Dr. Sunley has written numerous articles, and his recent publications include "The Analytics of Safe Harbor Leasing" and "Treasury's Views on Tax Treatment of Future Costs: A Critique," both of which appeared in* Tax Notes.

gap. The Tax Equity and Fiscal Responsibility Act of 1982 (TEFRA) restricted many of the business tax cuts enacted in 1981. The Deficit Reduction Act of 1984 (DEFRA) offered a modest "down payment" by, among other things, repealing even more of the 1981 provisions. Nevertheless, the federal deficit is projected to continue to account for an unprecedented share—between 4.5 and 5 percent—of gross national product (GNP).

Economists generally agree that protracted deficits of this magnitude are economically harmful. Though the deficit need not be eliminated in the next several years, it should be reduced. But this budget gap should not be closed solely through reductions in spending. To do so would require intolerably deep cuts in national defense and social security. These programs, together with net interest payments, comprised more than 58 percent of the federal budget in fiscal 1983.

That additional tax revenue is needed is clear. The more important issue is whether the federal government can—or should—use the existing tax structure to raise the needed revenue or should adopt a major new revenue source.

Dissatisfaction with the individual income tax, the major source of federal revenue, is widespread. Taxpayers increasingly perceive the tax as unfair and complex. With its badly perforated base and high marginal tax rates, the tax has become a pervasive factor in daily economic decisions. The tax's impact is often an elemental factor in decisions regarding the form in which employees take their income, the type of investment investors make, or the goods and services consumers purchase. Consequently, the income tax distorts the allocation of resources in the economy toward those activities that the tax code favors and away from those activities not specially treated. To squeeze more revenue from the income tax by raising marginal tax rates would magnify the distortions and inequities of the tax.

Several tax alternatives are under consideration. Some, such as a tax on "consumed" income, offer a replacement for the current income tax. Others, including variations of a broadbased, low-rate tax on income, would restructure the existing federal income tax. Still other alternatives, such as a valueadded tax or a national retail sales tax, are offered as supplements to the existing structure and probably would not be discussed except for the need to close or narrow the gap between federal spending and revenue.

Income versus Consumption

Until recently, income and wealth generally have been viewed as the most appropriate tax base. The current fiscal situation and state of the income tax, however, have increased interest in consumption as an alternate tax base. Though the debate over income versus consumption is somewhat arcane, it is critical to the question of whether the United States should replace its income tax with a broad-based consumption tax or, alternatively, should supplement existing revenue with a value-added–type consumption tax.

Proponents of the consumption base argue that the income base is inherently biased against saving. An income base includes both the amount of savings and the return on those savings. This double taxation of saved income encourages present consumption at the expense of saving or future consumption.

Replacing the income tax with a consumption tax at least would improve allocative efficiency in the economy. Savings would not be double taxed, and, in contrast to the current income tax, all savings would be treated alike. In addition, taxing consumption instead of income would increase the net return on savings. There is some evidence that such an increase may raise the total amount of savings in the economy.

Critics of the consumption base argue that, despite these enhanced efficiencies, income is simply a better measure of the "ability to pay" taxes than is consumption and, thus, a "fairer" tax base. Under a consumption tax, for example, taxes are highest when spending needs are greatest. Persons with moderate means but extraordinary expenses will pay high taxes. Moreover, it is argued, saving is a personal decision about the use of income that does not diminish the saver's capacity to bear taxation.

The importance of these arguments for or against a consumption tax, however, may be exaggerated in the debate over what constitutes an appropriate tax base. The practical choice is not between a "pure" consumption tax and a "pure" income tax. More likely, the choice is between a consumption base that excludes major portions of consumption, such as housing and food, and an income base that excludes major portions of income, such as unrealized gains and losses. As much as an imperfect consumption tax may, for example, improve efficiency in the economy, an imperfect income tax could be structured to do nearly the same. Thus, the choice between the income or consumption base may rest on other criteria such as revenue-raising potential, political perception, and administrative feasibility.

Income Tax Reform

BROAD BASE AND LOW RATES

Those who believe that income remains the appropriate tax base are considering several comprehensive reforms of the income tax. The theme of these reforms is that complexity and economic distortion imposed by the income tax should be minimized. Generally, this can be accomplished by broadening the tax base and lowering the marginal tax rates.

Broadening the tax base by eliminating or reducing the array of special exclusions, deductions, and credits would necessarily simplify the income tax. Taxpayers no longer would need to contend with all the potential means of reducing their tax liability. Other forms of base broadening, however, such as extending the income tax to all in-kind income or certain employee benefits, would increase complexity.

In any case, extending the income tax to a more comprehensive income base would permit the lowering of tax rates for any given revenue yield. In terms of economic efficiency, this combination is a move in the right direction. A tax base with fewer tax preferences would reduce distortions that occur under the existing income tax. To the extent that some forms of income would remain sheltered from taxation, lower tax rates would reduce the tax incentive for channeling income to the sheltered form and, therefore, would reduce the intensity of the distortion.

THREE ISSUES

In addition to the evident complexities and distortions of the existing income tax, any reform of the income tax must attempt to resolve three important issues—capital recovery, double taxation of dividends, and the impact of inflation. These problems do not exist under a broad-based consumption tax and, thus, their resolution may enter into the debate over which tax base—income or consumption—is preferable.

Capital Recovery—The appropriate allowance for wear and tear of capital equipment has been a controversial issue since the imposition of the income tax. In recent years depreciation allowed for tax purposes has been accelerated in an effort to promote investment. A tax credit is granted for investments in certain properties. Like other preference items, however, accelerated depreciation and the investment tax credit interfere with efficient allocation of resources. For an income tax to be neutral among types of depreciable property, tax depreciation should be limited to the actual decline in the economic value of the property, and no investment tax credit should be allowed. To achieve this neutrality in practice would be difficult, but the distortions of the current income tax could be reduced significantly.

Double Taxation—The second issue is the double taxation of dividends. On tax policy grounds it is difficult to justify a separate tax on corporate income where distributed corporate income is taxed both at the corporate and shareholder levels. Such a tax biases the choices between investment in the corporate and noncorporate sectors, debt and equity financing, and retaining or distributing earnings. Abolition of the corporation income tax, however, is not the right answer. If the individual income tax is retained, the absence of a corporation income tax would make the corporate form the preeminent tax shelter. Income would be accumulated tax-free within the corporation.

The right answer lies in some form of integration of the corporation and individual income taxes. Most of the major European countries treat part of the corporate tax as withholding at the source. Shareholders "gross-up" their dividends by the amount of "withheld" tax and take a credit for this tax against their regular tax liability. Double taxation also could be relieved by providing a deduction at the corporate level for dividends paid to shareholders.

Alternatively, the corporate-shareholder relationship could be treated like a partnership. All corporate earnings, whether distributed or not, would be imputed to shareholders and taxed at individual marginal tax rates. The corporation income tax would remain in place and serve as a true withholding tax, creditable against shareholder tax liability. However, no nation has adopted the partnership approach to integration, and significant technical problems with such an approach would have to be solved.

Inflation—The reality of inflation must be recognized and addressed by the income tax law. Inflation can distort an income tax base that is measured in historical dollars. With rising nominal incomes it can push taxpayers into higher marginal tax brackets. The high rates of inflation experienced in the 1970s increased interest in indexing the income tax.

The indexing issue has two parts—the definition of income and the proper tax treatment of income once defined. Analytically, they are separable. The nominal dollar amounts in the Internal Revenue Code could be adjusted without adjusting the measurement of income, or vice-versa.

Beginning in 1985 the major fixed-dollar amounts for the individual income tax were adjusted annually for inflation. Congress has not provided explicit inflation adjustments for the measurement of income. However, inflation is one of the major justifications for accelerating tax depreciation that is based on historical cost and for excluding a portion of long-term capital gains. Last in/first out inventory accounting also provides inflation relief for most expanding companies.

PROPOSALS FOR REFORM

There are currently several specific proposals for income tax reform. They all follow the theme of base broadening and rate reduction, and, generally, they are designed to raise the same total revenue as current law.

The Flat-10 Tax—Representative Mark Siljander of Michigan is promoting a flat tax plan. His "flat-10" tax would eliminate the standard deduction and most special exclusions, deductions, and credits. It would, however, retain certain preferences such as mortgage interest, state and local taxes, and charitable contributions. The significant distinction of Siljander's flat tax is that the flat tax rate and the absence of a standard deduction would sharply redistribute the income tax burden. Those taxpayers in the higher income classes would pay less tax relative to current law; those in the lower classes would pay more.

The "Fair" and "Fast" Tax—Similar to the Siljander proposal, though less comprehensive, the Bradley-Gephardt "fair tax" and the Kemp-Kasten "fast tax" would broaden the income tax base by eliminating many of the existing exclusions, deductions, and credits. In contrast to Siljander's flat tax, however, these proposals would retain a graduated rate structure, a standard deduction, and roughly the same distribution of the tax burden as existing tax law.

The "Modified Flat Tax"—In his 1984 State of the Union Message, President Reagan asked the U.S. Department of the Treasury to perform its own exploration of a range of reform alternatives, from income tax options to replacements. In conclusion to its study, the Treasury submitted its recommendation for a "modified flat tax" on income. The Treasury's plan is similar to, though more comprehensive than, the Bradley-Gephardt and Kemp-Kasten proposals. Like those proposals, the Treasury's plan consolidates the rate schedule of the individual income tax and lowers its rates; instead of 1984's fourteen rates that range from 11 to 50 percent, the Treasury's plan has three rates of 15 percent, 25 percent, and 35 percent. The corporation income tax rate is reduced from a top rate of 46 percent to a flat rate of 33 percent.

Also like the Bradley-Gephardt and Kemp-Kasten proposals, the Treasury's plan claims revenue neutrality. Though total taxes would not increase, the plan would shift the tax burden toward corporations and away from individuals. On an average, individual income taxes would decrease about 8 percent, while corporation income tax payments should increase an average of about 30 percent. The plan only slightly changes the distribution of the tax burden among individuals by concentrating the individual tax reductions in the lower end of the income scale.

While all of these proposals advocate base broadening and rate reduction, the Treasury's proposal is most responsive to other elements of income tax reform—capital recovery, inflation, and taxation of dividends. The plan includes several innovative features not incorporated in any of the other three congressional plans. Under the Treasury's plan, depreciation, capital gains, and inventories are all indexed for inflation. As another adjustment for inflation only a portion of interest expense is deductible and only a portion of interest income is taxable. Additionally, corporations would be granted a partial deduction for dividends paid.

None of these reform proposals is likely to be considered as an "all-or-nothing" proposition. The case is strong for moving to a tax with a broader base and lower marginal rates. But, the move from where we are to where we might like to be requires the repeal of many tax preferences, each of which has strong advocates. The Treasury's proposal particularly eliminates some of the most entrenched tax preferences, such as the deduction of consumer interest and state and local taxes. In challenging each of these tax preferences, crucial questions must be addressed. Is the original purpose of the tax preference still valid? Is the tax system the most efficient mechanism for delivering the government subsidy? Should the tax preference be replaced by a direct spending program? These are hard questions. Even if the subsidy is deemed valid, tax expenditures cannot be easily converted to regular budget expenditures, given the existing pressure to reduce federal spending.

Particularly in the context of revenue shortages, an incremental reform of the income tax may, therefore, be more palatable. The Treasury's proposal, for example, could serve as a menu from which to choose such incremental changes. Such an approach might also be preferable from the standpoint of transition problems. It should be recognized, though, that the coherence and consistency of the Treasury's plan would be lost if only some of it were adopted.

REVENUE POTENTIAL

As noted, proposals for reforming the income tax are generally presented in revenue-neutral terms. To raise additional revenue, it would be possible to broaden the tax base as suggested by the Treasury's plan, for example, but not reduce tax rates as much as it proposes. Higher marginal tax rates, however, could undermine the Treasury's proposal for taxing capital gains as ordinary income. This proposal, which would simplify income tax planning, may not be workable in a world with high marginal tax rates since taxpayers could choose to delay realization of gains.

Alternatively, the Treasury's plan incorporates many changes that, by themselves, could produce additional revenue. For example, even without making major structural changes to the corporation income tax, substantial revenue could be raised. Its four major structural changes—the reduced corporate tax rates, the deduction for dividends paid, the changes in depreciation and loss of the investment tax credit, and indexing—are relatively revenue neutral. Over the five-year period from 1986 through 1990, enactment of these provisions would reduce federal revenue by less than 2 percent of expected corporate receipts. However, other corporate changes—primarily the elimination of specific industry preferences—could potentially generate as much as $174 billion in increased corporate revenue over five years. Under the Treasury's plan, this increased revenue is used to finance reductions in individual income taxes. To the extent that some of the individual cuts are forgone, part of the $174 billion in other corporation income tax changes would yield a net increase in federal revenue. Of course, any revenue-generating compromise such as this loses many of its reform elements.

There are also income tax alternatives to base broadening that could produce the needed revenue. For example, a corporation and individual income tax surcharge of 10 percent levied on the existing income base could yield as much as $45 billion in federal revenue in fiscal 1986. The distortions inherent in a narrow income base would remain, however, and the higher tax rates would exacerbate the impact of these distortions. Nevertheless, a surcharge might be justified on the grounds that the federal deficit requires immediate redress. The revenue could buy Congress the time to take a long-term look at fundamental tax reform.

Progressive Consumption Tax

If the arguments for favoring a consumption base are compelling, this mood for tax reform provides an opportunity to replace the income tax with a personal tax on consumed income. The tax base would consist of "consumed" income—income and borrowings for the year reduced by annual additions to savings and repayment of debt. As under an income tax, the tax could be levied at a flat rate. Most consumed income proposals, however, impose a progressive rate schedule.

Over a taxpayer's lifetime, this consumption base would be equivalent to a lifetime income base if gifts and bequests were treated as consumption. A donor would not be allowed a deduction for amounts gifted or bequeathed. Total lifetime income, whether consumed directly or gifted or bequeathed, would thereby be subject to tax. On the other hand, gifts and bequests could be treated as savings by the donor and taxed, instead, to the recipient who ultimately consumes them by purchasing goods and services. This latter treatment, however, would permit wealthy taxpayers to transfer accumulated savings tax-free to subsequent generations. It would reduce the revenue-raising potential of the tax system and its intragenerational equity.

THE PROBLEMS WITH A CONSUMPTION TAX

Difficulties with imposing a tax on consumed income in lieu of the income tax focus on three points—complexity, international implications, and transitional problems.

Complexity—A consumed income tax would be both conceptually and practically more complex than the existing income tax for the average individual. It may be true mathematically that consumption can be financed either through income or borrowings and, therefore, that the consumption base must include annual loan proceeds. Intuitively, however, taxpayers may find it difficult to understand that loan proceeds should be taxable to them. Furthermore, tax liabilities under such a system would be highest when the portion of income that is consumed is highest—during poverty, young adulthood, and retirement. This runs counter to a well-ingrained sense of fairness as it has been defined under progressive income taxation.

In practice, a tax on consumed income would extend the complexities of tax estimating and withholding to taxpayers who are now free from such burdens. Taxpayers who borrow could be required to withhold tax on a loan. Similarly, a system for refunding taxes that have been overwithheld because of repayments of loans probably would be required.

International Implications—The second problem of a consumption tax relates to integration with the tax systems of other countries. If such a tax were enacted, the United States would be the only country with a tax on consumed income. Would the tax imposed in the United States on a foreign-controlled subsidiary be creditable against the home country's tax liability? How would foreign taxes paid by a U.S. company be treated for U.S. tax purposes? The practical and political difficulties of renegotiating existing tax treaties would be substantial.

Transition—Perhaps most significantly, replacing the existing income tax with the fundamentally different consumption tax would require a long and complex transition period. Consumption financed out of already taxed income could not be rightly retaxed under the new system. Yet exempting all such consumption would severely reduce the revenue yield of the new tax or, at least, necessitate the use of unusually high tax rates.

POTENTIAL REVENUE

Coupled with these implementation and transition problems is the fact that the consumption base is inherently smaller than a comprehensive income base. In contrast to treatment under an income tax, taxation of savings is deferred until the savings are ultimately consumed, either by the original savers or their donees or heirs, depending on the treatment of gifts and bequests. In addition, under consumption tax there is no need for a separate tax on corporations. The corporation income tax and its revenue would not, at least directly, be replaced by another tax.

Collectively, these features significantly diminish the attractiveness of a personal tax on consumed income as a solution to the combined problems of the income tax and the federal deficit. Clearly a personal consumption tax could be implemented to supplement the existing tax system, leaving intact a modified income tax. However, the administrative and compliance burdens of such an effort would seem to outweigh the benefits of supplementary revenue. A direct tax on consumption, such as a value-added tax or a retail sales tax, or other excise taxes would be simpler supplementary taxes.

Direct Consumption Tax

Instead of imposing a personal tax on consumed income, a tax could be placed directly on consumption. Traditionally such taxes have been collected from the sellers of the goods or services. A direct consumption tax generally takes one of two forms—a retail sales tax (RST), such as the sales taxes used by most states, or a value-added tax (VAT), such as those used extensively in Europe and some developing countries. A direct consumption tax could replace the existing income tax, but it is most often considered as a supplement to existing federal revenue sources.

Though they differ in form, in substance a sales tax and a value-added tax are the same. A sales tax is imposed only at the retail level, like sales taxes levied by the states. In contrast, a VAT is imposed at each stage of the production and distribution process on the value added at that stage. A business firm that collects a VAT on its sales is allowed a refund or, more typically, a tax credit against its VAT liabilities that is equal to the amount of the VAT paid on its purchases.

EXEMPTIONS

Because the ultimate tax base under both taxes is current consumption, it is important that expenditures that represent investment—as opposed to consumption—are exempted from the tax. Under a sales tax this problem is "solved" by differentiating between sales to a consumer, which are taxable, and sales to another business for reuse or resale in that business, which are nontaxable. As most of the states have discovered, this is moderately practical but short of ideal. The seller often does not know whether or not a sale should be taxable, so some consumption is double taxed and some not taxed at all. Under a value-added tax, the same problem is tackled through the credit mechanism. Every transaction, including the sale of investment goods, is taxed, but, if the buyer shows that the purchase was used in the business, then the firm receives a credit against its own current VAT liability for the tax paid on the purchase.

As under the income tax, a more comprehensive tax base is preferable to a more selective one. The broader the tax base, the greater is the economic efficiency of the tax. The revenue potential of the tax for a given tax rate is also greater. Experience with the European VAT and the U.S. state sales taxes, however, suggests that many consumption items would be preferentially treated under a national VAT or RST.

DIFFICULTIES

Because low-income families and individuals tend to spend more of their income on consumption than do high-income families and individuals, sales taxes and VATs are regressive relative to income. This shortcoming could be dealt with by making the income tax more progressive or providing either a lower rate on, or an exemption for, certain "necessities." Most European countries with VATs exempt food, medical and hospital care, education, postal services, and exports. Every exemption, however, complicates administration and compliance and reduces the tax base.

A VAT or RST would be inflationary. Experience in other countries suggests that there is some reason to expect the increase in prices under a VAT or RST to be greater than the tax itself because of adjustments in wage contracts, social security payments, and other items indexed to the consumer price index. The price effect, however, is a one-time occurrence that proponents view as a price of adopting a broad-based consumption tax.

Opponents of a VAT or RST argue that either would infringe on a tax base that is traditionally the domain of the states. Supporters, however, counter with the response that, currently, both federal and state governments tax income, liquor, cigarettes, telephones, estates, and gifts without apparent conflict.

REVENUE POTENTIAL

Both an RST and a VAT would provide a very stable revenue base. Each percentage point of tax could raise as much as $15 to $20 billion, depending on the comprehensiveness of the tax base. In fact, some oppose these taxes on the very grounds of their revenue potential. They fear that if the federal government acquired yet another tax, it would surely use and spend its revenue accordingly.

Energy and Other Excises

Interest in energy taxation was aroused initially during the 1973–74 oil embargo when policy makers focused on the formation of a national energy policy and the possibility of articulating that policy through the tax system. The current federal deficit has renewed that interest. Though energy tax revenue alone certainly could not close the deficit gap, the production and consumption of energy nevertheless offer a potential source of supplementary tax revenue.

In addition to raising revenue, any imposition of new or enhanced energy taxes would need to be consciously integrated with energy policy objectives. Any energy tax would necessarily affect the energy economy. Depending on the type of tax and the definition of the base, a tax on energy would change how much and what type of energy is consumed, as well as who consumes it.

The basic economic case for taxing energy is that its consumption involves real social costs that are not fully reflected in market prices. Called externalities, these costs include, for example, damage to the environment caused by energy production and usage and the cost of overreliance on unstable sources of imported oil.

Energy taxes also achieve secondary policy objectives. The crude oil windfall profits tax, for example, transfers to the government some of the windfall gains that accrued to oil producers upon the decontrol of previously regulated prices. The existing motor fuels tax, a type of "user charge," provides revenue to fund federal highway programs that primarily benefit those who pay the tax.

The greatest problem with any energy tax is that the burden of the tax tends to be concentrated on particular consumers, regions of the country, or particular industries. A fee on oil imports, for example, would have a greater impact on New England, where reliance on home heating oil is greater; an increase in the motor fuels tax, on the other hand, would hit harder in the West, where the automobile is more important. In addition, as with other taxes, the more narrow the tax base, the more distortive the impact of the tax. Such inefficiencies tend to make narrow-based energy taxes less desirable than broad-based taxes.

Four types of energy tax options are generally suggested as means of generating revenue—an oil import fee, an excise tax on all oil, a broader excise tax on all energy, and an enhanced motor fuels tax. Table 1 shows the revenue potential of these four taxes at specific, low rates. The tax revenue, of course, would vary with changes in the tax rates or the comprehensiveness of the base.

OIL IMPORT FEE

A tax on imported oil could be used to decrease the U.S. reliance on imported oil. An import fee would increase the price of oil, increase producer profits, and encourage domestic production of oil as well as the development of alternative energy sources. The shift in relative prices among energy sources caused by taxing imported oil would have an uneven impact across households, industries, and regions. Households and companies with oil-intensive capital investments would

TABLE 1.   REVENUE IMPACT OF FOUR ENERGY TAXES IN FISCAL YEAR 1985

	($ billions)
Oil import fee at two dollars per barrel	4.2
Excise tax on domestic and imported oil	8.4
Ad valorem tax on major fuels at rate of two cents	5.5
One cent increase in motor fuels excise tax	0.8

Source: Center for National Policy, *Budget and Policy Choices 1983: Taxes, Defense, Entitlements* (Washington, D.C.: Center for National Policy, 1983), p. 22.

Note: Estimates are net figures after accounting for reduced income tax receipts.

experience capital losses. Oil companies rich in domestic reserves would be in a relatively better position. Generally, the tax would hurt oil-intensive industries relative to those industries that rely on other forms of energy. It would have a particularly adverse impact on those oil-using firms that are competitive in international markets. They would now be competing with foreign companies who face a lower world price of oil. Regions and households that are heavily dependent on oil as a source of energy would be similarly burdened. Finally, an oil import fee, like any energy consumption tax, would be disproportionately burdensome for low-income persons, who tend to allocate a greater portion of their incomes to purchasing fuel oil and gasoline.

OIL EXCISE TAX

An excise tax on both domestic and foreign oil would raise more revenue than an import fee of the same rate. Generally, the effects of an excise tax on oil would be similar to those experienced under an import fee. In contrast, however, an excise tax would not enhance oil producer profits and would not generate the domestic supply response created by an import fee. Instead, consumption would shift strictly toward the development and use of alternative, nonoil energy resources.

BROAD-BASED EXCISE TAX ON ENERGY

If, instead, the broader policy goal is to reduce energy consumption generally, a tax could be imposed on all fuels. Given this policy objective, this broad-based approach is preferable inasmuch as it would cause less distortion in the economy and create less regional and interindustry disparity. The major difficulty associated with such a tax is technical in nature. How should the tax rates for the various fuels, and thus, the change in relative prices among those fuels, be determined? A tax could be levied at a fixed rate based on the British Thermal Unit (BTU) content of the fuel. While it seems an appealing idea, BTU content is not the only factor that determines a resource's value in the economy. If the goal is to slow the rate of consumption of more valuable fuels, excises based on BTUs would not be appropriate.

Alternatively, the tax could be an *ad valorem* tax, levied at a
fixed rate on the price of the fuel. This type of tax gives rise to
the question of where in the chain of production the tax should
be imposed. Conceptually, the tax probably should be imposed
on the value of the resource in the ground. A practical compromise, however, might be to fix the tax at the wellhead or
minemouth, where the tax base would include the cost of extraction.

For a given tax rate, a broad-based energy tax would produce
the most tax revenue of all the alternatives discussed. It would
also be the most efficient of the tax proposals and minimize the
distortions among energy sources. But economic efficiency
could be enhanced even more if, instead of taxing all energy, all
consumption were taxed under a value-added or sales tax.

MOTOR FUELS TAX

The revenue from the existing motor fuels tax is used exclusively to support the programs of the federal Highway Trust
Fund. The tax rate could be increased, however, and the additional revenue allocated to the general fund. Because the tax is
so narrowly based, it would have very targeted effects, hitting
western consumers, low-income persons, and the commercial
transportation industry the hardest. The potential revenue
from this source is about $1 billion for each one-cent increase in
the tax.

Conclusion

There are no easy choices. Alternatives for reducing the
deficit involve trade-offs among the competing goals of equity,
efficiency, and simplicity. Some of the fundamental issues involved in choosing among the alternatives include how much
tax revenue should be raised; whether a new federal tax should
be adopted; whether income or consumption is a better measure of ability to pay; to what extent the income tax can be
made simpler and its economic distortions reduced by pruning
special deductions, credits, and exclusions; and what degree of
progressivity should be maintained.

Bibliography

AARON, HENRY J., *The Value Added Tax: Lessons from Europe*. Washington, D.C.: The Brookings Institution, 1981.

——, AND HARVEY GALPER, *Assessing Tax Reform*. Washington, D.C.: The Brookings Institution, 1985.

ADVISORY COMMISSION ON INTERGOVERNMENTAL RELATIONS, *Changing Public Attitudes on Government and Taxes*. Washington, D.C., 1984.

AUERBACH, ALAN J., *The Taxation of Capital Income*. Cambridge, Massachusetts: Harvard University Press, 1983.

BOSWORTH, BARRY B., *Tax Incidence and Economic Growth*. Washington, D.C.: The Brookings Institution, 1984.

BRADFORD, DAVID F., AND U.S. TREASURY DEPARTMENT TAX POLICY STAFF, *Blueprints for Basic Tax Reform*, Second Edition, Revised. Arlington, Virginia: Tax Analysts, 1984.

FRIEND, IRWIN, ALBERT ANDO, AND MARSHALL E. BLUME, *The Structure and Reform of the U.S. Tax System*. Cambridge, Massachusetts: Massachusetts Institute of Technology Press, 1985.

GOODE, RICHARD, *The Individual Income Tax*, Revised Edition. Washington, D.C.: The Brookings Institution, 1976.

HALL, ROBERT E., AND ALVIN RABUSHKA, *The Flat Tax*. Stanford, California: Hoover Institution Press, 1985.

HALLBACH, EDWARD C., ED., *Death, Taxes, and Family Property*, American Assembly. St. Paul, Minnesota: West Publishing Company, 1977.

KING, MERVIN A., AND DON FULLERTON, *The Taxation of Income from Capital: A Comparative Study of the United States, the United Kingdom, Sweden, and Germany*, National Bureau of Economic Research. Chicago: University of Chicago Press, 1984.

LUCKE, ROBERT, *Revising the Corporate Income Tax*, Congressional Budget Office. Washington, D.C.: U.S. Government Printing Office, 1985.

MCLURE, CHARLES, JR., *Must Corporate Income Be Taxed Twice?* Washington, D.C.: The Brookings Institution, 1979.

MINARIK, JOSEPH J., *Making Tax Choices*. Washington, D.C.: Urban Institute Press, 1985.

PECHMAN, JOSEPH A., ED., *What Should be Taxed: Income or Expenditure?* Washington, D.C.: The Brookings Institution, 1980.

————, *Federal Tax Policy*, Fourth Edition. Washington, D.C.: The Brookings Institution, 1983.

————, ED., *A Citizen's Guide to the New Tax Reforms*. Totowa, New Jersey: Rowman and Allanheld, 1985.

SURREY, STANLEY S., AND PAUL R. MCDANIEL, *Tax Expenditures*. Cambridge, Massachusetts: Harvard University Press, 1985.

The Structure and Reform of Direct Taxation, Report of a Committee chaired by Professor J.E. Meade, Institute for Fiscal Studies. London: George Allen and Unwin, 1978.

U.S. Treasury Department, Office of the Secretary, *Tax Reform for Fairness, Simplicity, and Economic Growth*, Three Volumes, The Treasury Department Report to the President. Washington, D.C., November 1984.

Index

FINAL REPORT
of the
SIXTY-NINTH AMERICAN ASSEMBLY

At the close of their discussions the participants in the Sixty-ninth American Assembly, on *Reforming and Simplifying the Federal Tax System*, at Arden House, Harriman, New York, April 11-14, 1985, reviewed as a group the following statement. This statement represents general agreement; however, no one was asked to sign it. Furthermore, it should not be assumed that every participant subscribes to every recommendation.

THE PROMISE OF TAX REFORM

The federal tax system is widely regarded as unfair, excessively complicated, and inefficient. The general perception is that the system favors wealthy taxpayers and large business firms at the expense of the average taxpayer. Too often people pay widely different taxes even though they have the same income. The public is demanding tax reform to improve the distribution of tax burdens, simplify the tax structure, and eliminate tax distortions in the economy.

A number of tax reform proposals are now being advanced to achieve these objectives. Although they differ in essential details, all would broaden the tax base and use the revenue to reduce tax rates for individuals and corporations. Most plans would increase personal exemptions and the standard deduction to relieve families and individuals with incomes below the poverty line from paying tax. Otherwise, the distribution of tax burdens of individuals would remain roughly the same as it is under present law. A major feature of the proposals is a reduction in the wide differences in taxes paid by people in essentially the same economic circumstances. Some plans address the proper role of taxation of corporations in relation to the taxation of individuals.

The tax system has been used to achieve numerous social and economic objectives, many of which are laudable. But the proliferation of deductions, exclusions, and tax credits has gone too far. A simple tax system with lower tax rates would improve equity and economic efficiency. Nevertheless, the far-reaching changes now being contemplated would have major consequences for important groups in our society and for the economy as a whole. Tax reform legislation must be carefully crafted to avoid unnecessary economic disruptions and individual hardships.

WHAT SHOULD BE TAXED

Some people believe that many problems now encountered under the income tax can be avoided by substituting a progressive tax on consumption expenditures for the tax on income. An expenditure tax would not distort individual decisions to consume or to save and would be free of many problems now encountered in measuring income from capital.

Because it exempts saving, an expenditure tax is roughly equivalent to a tax on labor income and might not be regarded as equitable by the public. The expenditure tax would increase the tax burdens of young families and the elderly and reduce the taxes of families headed by those in their middle years who save more. Moreover, the problems of transition from an income tax to an expenditure tax would be extremely difficult. Special rules would have to be adopted to avoid taxing those who consume out of previously taxed income.

For these reasons, <u>we recommend that the federal government continue to rely on income taxation as the basic revenue source</u>. However, income is difficult to measure accurately, and a number of critical problems of implementing an income tax not addressed properly under existing laws must be resolved. These include adjustment of the tax base for inflation, measurement of depreciation, treatment of capital gains and losses, and taxation of corporate profits at both the individual and corporate levels. We address these questions later in this statement.

An alternative method of taxing consumption would be to adopt a value-added tax, which is often proposed as a supplement to the income tax. The value-added tax is equivalent to a sales tax, except that the sales tax is levied only at the retail level while the value-added tax is collected as goods move through the system of production and distribution. The advantages of the value-added tax are that it can raise large amounts of revenue and that, in its pure form, it is neutral toward different kinds of business and consumer choices.

The major objection to the value-added tax is its regressivity; that is, it takes a larger percentage of income from those with lower incomes than from those with higher incomes. The regressivity of the tax can be addressed by exempting necessities, such as food and medicine, or by providing a refundable credit against income tax for those at the lower end of the income scale. Suitable exemptions could substantially reduce regressivity, and such a credit could make a value-added tax progressive up to a moderately high income level, but regressive beyond that. However, exemptions and credits would greatly complicate the tax and raise the cost of administration and compliance. The value-added tax could also result in at least a one-time increase in prices and might exacerbate the problem of containing inflation, although this effect could be mitigated if cost-of-living adjustments in wage and other contracts were required to be based on price indexes that excluded the effect of the value-added tax. We conclude that the value-added tax should be considered only as a last resort if it is necessary to raise a substantial amount of additional revenue.

Estate and gift taxes account for less than 1 percent of internal revenue collections. They are, nevertheless, an important component of a progressive tax system and should be retained and strengthened to the extent that this can be done without creating undue hardships for such groups as farmers and family-owned businesses. The taxation of gifts and bequests would be critical if a consumption expenditure tax were adopted. Otherwise, the exemption of saving from tax could lead to an increasing concentration of wealth. The estate and gift taxes now being levied should be improved or restructured, even though they cannot be expected to yield large amounts of revenue.

TAXATION OF BUSINESS AND INVESTMENT INCOME

The present tax system provides generous depreciation allowances and investment tax credits for most capital investments. These provisions encourage investment, but in their present form they have made tax burdens highly uneven among industries—in some cases, this "burden" becomes a subsidy—and substantial distortions are introduced into the economy. Tax shelters have grown rapidly to take advantage of these provisions.

We recommend replacement of the present depreciation rules and the investment credit by a system of "real" economic depreciation. Such a system would provide depreciation deductions adjusted for inflation, so that a business could recover its investment tax-free in dollars of current purchasing power. This would achieve neutrality in the treatment of assets across industries and eliminate other distortions. Many participants felt that, in order to promote economic growth and international competitiveness, it would be unwise to eliminate all special incentives for investment in plant and equipment. It was agreed that, if an investment incentive is retained, it should be designed to minimize discrimination among industries.

There was general agreement that the inflation component of capital gains should not be taxed. The method would be to adjust the cost of assets for inflation between the time they were purchased and the time they were sold. Although such adjustments would add complications for taxpayers (mainly in keeping track of the exact dates when small investments are made, for example, in mutual funds and stock purchase plans), it is important to avoid overtaxing investment income during periods of inflation.

Most participants agreed that capital gains should be treated as ordinary income if they are adjusted for inflation and if the top marginal rate is substantially reduced as a result of base broadening. Others felt that lower rates should be applied to capital gains than to ordinary income in order to promote investment and risk taking. Promoting risk taking could also be accomplished by raising the limit now imposed on the deductibility of capital losses or by eliminating such limit after taking into account unrealized gains on assets with readily determinable values. Unrealized gains on property transferred by gift or upon death should be taxed.

Another income source that is affected by inflation is interest. Part of any interest payment is a reimbursement by the borrower to the lender for the erosion of the capital value of the loan as a result of inflation. To adjust for inflation, the inflation component of interest received by lenders should not be taxed, and the deduction for the inflation component of interest expenses should be denied. Such adjustments are complex and difficult to make for all assets, and approximate methods have been proposed as a substitute. More refined methods are necessary for financial institutions and larger corporations than for other taxpayers.

Indexing of interest even on an approximate basis is desirable on both equity and economic grounds. However, the denial of even a portion of the interest deduction on home mortgages is widely regarded as politically unacceptable. Nonetheless, we believe that the allowance of a full deduction for home mortgage interest, coupled with curtailment of the deduction for other interest as a result of indexation, would introduce unnecessary complications and encourage many people to take advantage of the mortgage interest deduction to finance the purchase of other assets. Because of these complications, some felt that indexing of interest should be avoided as long as the inflation rate remains at moderate levels.

The present tax system encourages debt over equity financing because dividends are taxed at both the corporate and individual levels, whereas interest is taxed only at the individual level. Most of the participants supported some modification of the present provisions in order to reduce or eliminate the so-called double taxation of dividends. One possibility is to allow a deduction for all or part of dividends paid by corporations. Another is to give individual taxpayers a credit for the taxes paid at the corporate level. The dividend deduction reduces the corporate tax for tax-exempt and foreign shareholders as well as for U. S. shareholders, while the dividend credit provides relief only to taxable shareholders. Other participants considered such measures too costly of revenue and would prefer a nondiscriminatory incentive for new investment.

Correction of the deficiencies in the taxation of business and investment income would improve the allocation of economic resources and increase economic efficiency. Interest rates may decline as a result of indexation because lenders would be encouraged to lend more and borrowers would be discouraged from borrowing. However, the proposed reforms may have serious short-term distortive effects. Adequate transition rules would need to be adopted to avoid serious harm to the economy.

THE INDIVIDUAL INCOME TAX

A properly designed personal income tax would include all income in the tax base and provide deductions for expenditures that clearly reduce ability to pay. The present federal income tax violates this rule in numerous respects. We believe that most of the exclusions, deductions, and credits in the tax law should be eliminated, so that the tax return can be simplified and tax rates can be significantly reduced. The net effect of these changes, together with the rate structure adopted, should, however, maintain approximately the same degree of progressivity in effective tax burdens as under current law.

The tax preferences now in the law are not confined to any particular income group. Where feasible, all forms of income should be included in the tax base. Adequate personal exemptions, standard deductions (now called zero bracket amounts), and earned income credits should be the mechanisms by which the poor are relieved from tax liabilities. From 1969 until 1978, Congress followed the principle that minimum taxable levels should be at least as high as officially estimated poverty levels. This principle should be reintroduced as quickly as possible, and the resulting exemptions and zero bracket amounts should be automatically adjusted for inflation, as under present law. The earned income tax credit, which reduces the tax burdens of low-income families with children, should also be automatically adjusted for inflation.

Today, unemployment compensation benefits are included in taxable income only for those with other income of at least $18,000 if married and $12,000 if single. Half of social security benefits are included for those with other income of at least $32,000 if married and $25,000 if single. We believe that equal treatment of those with the same income would be better served if income limitations on the taxation of unemployment and social security benefits were gradually removed. Rates and exemptions should be adjusted to avoid an increase in the tax burden of low-income groups.

Individual retirement accounts (IRAs) were originally designed to permit employees not eligible for a private pension plan to set aside their own savings for retirement. In 1981, all employees were allowed to deduct contributions to an IRA, even if covered by a private plan.

Most people have simply transferred assets from other accounts to IRAs without increasing their saving. We believe that IRA contributions should be allowed only to the extent that the employer has not made a current provision for the employee up to the limit allowed by law.

Fringe benefits, in general, should be treated like cash wages for tax purposes. Many participants believed that employer contributions to nondiscriminatory health insurance and group term life insurance plans, however, should be excluded up to a reasonable minimum on social policy grounds.

Beneficial treatment of the private pension system, in general, should be retained but confined to its purpose of sponsoring retirement saving. Borrowing by participants should be precluded and other improvements made to prevent abuse.

The tax exemption for interest on bonds issued by state and local governments to pay for public services and facilities should be retained. However, the tax exemption for interest on bonds issued to finance investments for nongovernmental purposes should be removed. There is no reason why the federal government should subsidize such investments. Further consideration should be given to provisions of optional issuance of taxable state and local bonds or a federal tax credit to the holders of taxable bonds to minimize windfall gains to high-bracket taxpayers.

Personal deductions are too generous. We believe that interest on consumer credit should not be deducted and a limit should be placed on the deduction for mortgage interest. Some felt a deduction should be permitted for all interest up to the amount of property income reported on the tax return plus $10,000 or $15,000. Others would allow a deduction only for principal-residence interest on a mortgage amount up to, say, $150,000 plus an amount equal to the taxpayer's property income. Again, liberal transition provisions would be needed to avoid hardships.

A deduction for charitable contributions should be retained, but the deduction should be limited to substantial gifts and donations, say, above 1 or 2 percent of income. If unrealized gains on transfers by gift or at death are taxed as recommended, the deduction for gifts of appreciated property to charity should be limited to the inflation-adjusted cost of the property to the donor rather than the total value of the property, but not otherwise. The charitable deduction for nonitemizers should be eliminated. Some members of the group felt that the deduction should be retained in its present form on the grounds that it encourages gifts to charity by people in all income classes. Others proposed that the deduction should be converted to a tax credit.

The deduction for state and local taxes loses a great deal of revenue and indirectly subsidizes local public services. Most of the participants supported reduction or elimination of state and local tax deductions on the grounds that the federal government should not encourage or discourage these activities through tax deductions. Some felt that a deduction should be maintained for at least state and local income taxes. In theory, the more efficient approach would be to provide grants to state and local governments for outlays that are of national concern through categorical grants or revenue sharing. In practice, there is little likelihood that direct federal grants to states and localities will soon take the place of the indirect aid now provided by the deduction of state and local taxes. Deductions should be phased out gradually over a period of years, however, to avoid severe disruptive effects on states with social obligations funded by higher tax rates.

Outlays for unusual medical expenses and large casualty losses reduce ability to pay. The present deductions for medical expenses in excess of 5 percent of income and for casualty losses in excess of 10 percent should be retained.

DEFICIT REDUCTION AND TAX REFORM

Unless action is taken by Congress and the president, the federal budget will run large and unacceptable deficits for years to come. Deficits of this magnitude raise interest rates, increase the exchange rate of the dollar, and impair the competitiveness of U. S. industry in world markets. Eventually, the large deficits are likely to crowd out private investment and reduce the rate of economic growth. A major economic priority for Congress should be to take action to significantly reduce the deficits.

Both tax reform and deficit reduction are important objectives in their own right. We should not hold deficit reduction hostage to tax reform should the latter be delayed; neither should we hold tax reform hostage to the deficit. We believe our recommendations have merit—with or without deficits.

The administration and Congress have a rare opportunity to make tax reform a reality. The public has made it clear that they are unhappy with the current tax system, and a number of proposals have been put forward that would make the great majority of taxpayers better off. It would be a mistake to underestimate the political strength of those who wish to use the tax system to accomplish a variety of special purposes—or the value of some of their individual causes. But based on our own deliberations, it appears both feasible and desirable to eliminate most, if not all, of these special provisions. The end result would be a simpler, fairer, and more efficient tax system with lower rates.

HENRY AARON
Senior Fellow
Economic Studies Program
The Brookings Institution
Washington, D.C.

DAVID D. ARNOLD
Program Officer
The Ford Foundation
New York, New York

ALAN J. AUERBACH
Professor
Department of Economics
University of Pennsylvania
Philadelphia, Pennsylvania

J. GREGORY BALLENTINE
deSeve Economics
Washington, D.C.

** CAROL M. BERGREN
Harriman Scholar
Graduate School of Business
Columbia University
New York, New York

MARK BLOOMFIELD
Executive Director
American Council for Capital
 Formation
Washington, D.C.

** LOREN A. BOSTON
Harriman Scholar
Graduate School of Business
Columbia University
New York, New York

GEORGE F. BREAK
Professor
Department of Economics
University of California at Berkeley
Berkeley, California

DAVID H. BROCKWAY
Chief of Staff
Joint Committee on Taxation
United States Congress
Washington, D.C.

E. CARY BROWN
Professor
Department of Economics
Massachusetts Institute of Technology
Cambridge, Massachusetts

JOHN C. BURTON
Dean & Arthur Young Professor
Graduate School of Business
Columbia University
New York, New York

SUSAN M. BYRNE
President
Westwood Management
New York, New York

ARNOLD CANTOR
Assistant Director
Department of Research
AFL-CIO
Washington, D.C.

ROBERT W. CHASTANT
Director of Revenue
Department of Finance
State of Delaware
Wilmington, Delaware

BRUCE F. DAVIE
Chief Tax Economist
House Committee on Ways & Means
United States Congress
Washington, D.C.

GINA DESPRES
Counsel
Tax & International Affairs to
 Senator Bradley
Washington, D.C.

JOHN FAVA
Assistant Budget Director
Office of Management & Budget
City of New York
New York, New York

MAXINE FORMAN
Director of Policy Analysis
Women's Equity Action League
Washington, D.C.

WILLIAM H. FORST
Commissioner
Department of Taxation
Commonwealth of Virginia
Richmond, Virginia

KAREN FORTIN
Associate Professor & Director
M S in Taxation Program
University of Miami
Miami, Florida

GAIL D. FOSLER
Chief Economist
Senate Budget Committee
United States Congress
Washington, D.C.

** Rapporteur

IRWIN FRIEND
Director
Rodney L. White Center for
Financial Research
The Wharton School
University of Pennsylvania
Philadephia, Pennsylvania

HARVEY GALPER
Professor
School of Law
Georgetown University
Washington, D.C.

JOSEPH GOFFMAN
Staff Attorney
Congress Watch
Washington, D.C.

RICHARD GOODE
Guest Scholar
The Brookings Institution
Washington, D.C.

RICHARD A. GORDON
Arthur Anderson & Company
Washington, D.C.

MICHAEL J. GRAETZ
Professor
School of Law
Yale University
New Haven, Connecticut

JOHN J. GUNTHER
Executive Director
U.S. Conference of Mayors
Washington, D.C.

ROBERT D. GUY
Vice President & General Tax Counsel
The Coca-Cola Company
Atlanta, Georgia

J. ELLIOTT HIBBS
Director
Arizona Department of Revenue
Phoenix, Arizona

WALTER K. JOELSON
Chief Economist
General Electric Company
Fairfield, Connecticut

FRANKLIN A. LINDSAY
Chairman (Retired)
Itek Corporation
Lincoln, Massachusetts

ROSEMARY D. MARCUSS
Assistant Director
Tax Analysis
Congressional Budget Office
Washington, D.C.

DAVID MUNRO
General Director
Macro & International Economics
General Motors Corporation
New York, New York

* JOHN S. NOLAN.
Attorney-at-Law
Miller & Chevalier
Washington, D.C.

† NORMAN J. ORNSTEIN
Resident Scholar
American Enterprise Institute
Washington, D.C.

† RONALD A. PEARLMAN
Assistant Secretary
United States Department of Treasury
Washington, D.C.

JOSEPH A. PECHMAN
Senior Fellow
Economic Studies Program
The Brookings Institution
Washington, D.C.

JOSEPH M. PLUMMER
Editorial Writer
Pittsburgh Post-Gazette
Pittsburgh, Pennsylvania

PERRY QUICK
Consultant
Quick, Finan & Associates
Washington, D.C.

WILLARD C. RAPPLEYE, JR.
Editor
Financier
New York, New York

ALBERT REES
President
Alfred P. Sloan Foundation
New York, New York

* ISABEL V. SAWHILL
Senior Fellow
The Urban Institute
Washington, D.C.

* FRANK W. SCHIFF
Vice President & Chief Economist
Committee for Economic Development
Washington, D.C.

FRANCIS H. SCHOTT
Senior Vice President & Chief
Economist
The Equitable Life Assurance Society
of the United States
New York, New York

* Discussion Leader
† Delivered Formal Address

JOSEPH A. SCIULLO
Assistant Controller
Allegheny Ludlum Steel Corporation
Pittsburgh, Pennsylvania

JOHN SHANNON
Executive Director
Advisory Commission on
  Intergovernmental Relations
Washington, D.C.

** DAVID SIMON
Harriman Scholar
Graduate School of Business
Columbia University
New York, New York

JAMES SITRICK
Chairman, Executive Committee
Coudert Brothers
New York, New York

EUGENE STEUERLE
Deputy Director (Domestic Taxation)
Office of Tax Analysis
United States Department of Treasury
Washington, D.C.

JOSEPH E. STIGLITZ
Professor
Department of Economics
Princeton University
Princeton, New Jersey

DON J. SUMMA
Senior Partner
Arthur Young & Company
Rumson, New Jersey

** Rapporteur
† Delivered Formal Address

EMIL M. SUNLEY
Director of Tax Analysis
Deloitte Haskins & Sells
Washington, D.C.

JAMES M. VERDIER
Lecturer in Public Policy
Kennedy School of Government
Harvard University
Cambridge, Massachusetts

AGATHA VORSANGER
Regional Counsel
North Atlantic Region of the Internal
  Revenue Service
New York, New York

† CHARLS E. WALKER
Chairman
Charls E. Walker Associates, Inc.
Washington, D.C.

ALVIN C. WARREN, JR.
Professor
School of Law
Harvard University
Cambridge, Massachusetts

BENJAMIN WEBERMAN
Economics Editor
Forbes.
New York, New York

KENNETH WERTZ
Economist
Joint Committee on Taxation
United States Congress
Washington, D.C.

AMERICAN ASSEMBLY BOOKS

ABOUT THE AMERICAN ASSEMBLY

The American Assembly was established by Dwight D. Eisenhower at Columbia University in 1950. It holds nonpartisan meetings and publishes authoritative books to illuminate issues of United States policy.

An affiliate of Columbia, with offices in the Sherman Fairchild Center, the Assembly is a national, educational institution incorporated in the State of New York.

The Assembly seeks to provide information, stimulate discussion, and evoke independent conclusions on matters of vital public interest.

American Assembly Sessions

At least two national programs are initiated each year. Authorities are retained to write background papers presenting essential data and defining the main issues of each subject.

A group of men and women representing a broad range of experience, competence, and American leadership meet for several days to discuss the Assembly topic and consider alternatives for national policy.

All Assemblies follow the same procedure. The background papers are sent to participants in advance of the Assembly. The Assembly meets in small groups for four or five lengthy periods. All groups use the same agenda. At the close of these informal sessions participants adopt in plenary session a final report of findings and recommendations.

Regional, state, and local Assemblies are held following the national session at Arden House. Assemblies have also been held in England, Switzerland, Malaysia, Canada, the Caribbean, South America, Central America, the Philippines, and Japan. Over one hundred forty institutions have cosponsored one or more Assemblies.

Arden House

Home of The American Assembly and scene of the national sessions is Arden House, which was given to Columbia University in 1950 by W. Averell Harriman. E. Roland Harriman joined his brother in contributing toward adaptation of the property for conference purposes. The buildings and surrounding land, known as the Harriman Campus of Columbia University, are fifty miles north of New York City.

Arden House is a distinguished conference center. It is self-supporting and operates throughout the year for use by organizations with educational objectives. The American Assembly is a tenant of this Columbia University facility only during Assembly sessions.